Scarecrow Studies in Young Adult Literature
Series Editor: Patty Campbell

Scarecrow Studies in Young Adult Literature is intended to continue the body of critical writing established in Twayne's Young Adult Authors Series and to expand it beyond single-author studies to explorations of genres, multicultural writing, and controversial issues in young adult (YA) reading. Many of the contributing authors of the series are among the leading scholars and critics of adolescent literature, and some are YA novelists themselves.

The series is shaped by its editor, Patty Campbell, who is a renowned authority in the field, with a thirty-year background as critic, lecturer, librarian, and teacher of YA literature. Patty Campbell was the 2001 winner of the ALAN Award, given by the Assembly on Adolescent Literature of the National Council of Teachers of English for distinguished contribution to YA literature. In 1989 she was the winner of the American Library Association's Grolier Award for distinguished service to young adults and reading.

1. *What's So Scary about R. L. Stine?* by Patrick Jones, 1998.
2. *Ann Rinaldi: Historian and Storyteller*, by Jeanne M. McGlinn, 2000.
3. *Norma Fox Mazer: A Writer's World*, by Arthea J. S. Reed, 2000.
4. *Exploding the Myths: The Truth about Teens and Reading*, by Marc Aronson, 2001.
5. *The Agony and the Eggplant: Daniel Pinkwater's Heroic Struggles in the Name of YA Literature*, by Walter Hogan, 2001.
6. *Caroline Cooney: Faith and Fiction*, by Pamela Sissi Carroll, 2001.
7. *Declarations of Independence: Empowered Girls in Young Adult Literature, 1990–2001*, by Joanne Brown and Nancy St. Clair, 2002.
8. *Lost Masterworks of Young Adult Literature*, by Connie S. Zitlow, 2002.
9. *Beyond the Pale: New Essays for a New Era*, by Marc Aronson, 2003.
10. *Orson Scott Card: Writer of the Terrible Choice*, by Edith S. Tyson, 2003.
11. *Jacqueline Woodson: "The Real Thing,"* by Lois Thomas Stover, 2003.

12. *Virginia Euwer Wolff: Capturing the Music of Young Voices*, by Suzanne Elizabeth Reid, 2003.
13. *More Than a Game: Sports Literature for Young Adults*, Chris Crowe, 2004.
14. *Humor in Young Adult Literature: A Time to Laugh*, by Walter Hogan, 2005.
15. *Life Is Tough: Guys, Growing Up, and Young Adult Literature*, by Rachelle Lasky Bilz, 2004.
16. *Sarah Dessen: From Burritos to Box Office*, by Wendy J. Glenn, 2005.
17. *Native American Characters and Themes in Young Adult Literature*, by Paulette F. Molin, 2005.
18. *Gay and Lesbian Literature for Young Adults*, by Michael Cart, 2005.

Humor in Young Adult Literature

A Time to Laugh

❦

*3:1. To every thing there is a season, and a
time to every purpose under the heaven:
3:2. A time to be born, and a time to die; a time to plant,
and a time to pluck up that which is planted;
3:3. A time to kill, and a time to heal;
a time to break down, and a time to build up;
3:4. A time to weep, and a time to laugh;
a time to mourn, and a time to dance;*

(Ecclesiastes 3:1–4)

Humor in Young Adult Literature

A Time to Laugh

Walter Hogan

Scarecrow Studies in Young Adult Literature, No. 14

THE SCARECROW PRESS, INC.
Lanham, Maryland • Toronto • Oxford
2005

SCARECROW PRESS, INC.

Published in the United States of America
by Scarecrow Press, Inc.
A wholly owned subsidary of
The Rowman & Littlefield Publishing Group, Inc.
4501 Forbes Boulevard, Suite 200, Lanham, Maryland 20706
www.scarecrowpress.com

PO Box 317
Oxford
OX2 9RU, UK

British Library Cataloguing in Publication Information Available

Library of Congress Cataloging-in-Publication Data

Hogan, Walter, 1949–
  Humor in young adult literature : a time to laugh / Walter Hogan.
    p. cm. — (Scarecrow studies in young adult literature ; no. 14)
  Includes bibliographical references and index.
  ISBN 0-8108-5072-9 (hardcover : alk. paper)
  1. Humorous stories, American—History and criticism. 2. Young adult fiction,
American—History and criticism. 3. Young adults—Books and reading—United
States. I. Title. II. Series: Scarecrow studies in young adult literature ; 14.

PS374.H86H64 2005
813.009'9283—dc22

2004018903

To my wife, Wendy, with love.

In memory
of my friend and colleague,
Sarah Cogan,
who left us much too soon.

~

Contents

Introduction   xi

Chapter 1   Family   1

Chapter 2   Friends   23

Chapter 3   Bullies   51

Chapter 4   Authorities and Adversaries   67

Chapter 5   What's Wrong with Me?   95

Chapter 6   Could This Be Love?   119

Chapter 7   The Ironic Perspective   147

Chapter 8   Coming of Age: Who Am I, and What Am I Going to Do about It?   179

Bibliography   205

Index   215

About the Author   223

Introduction

Young adult (YA) literature is often associated with teen angst, heartache, and serious life lessons. However, alongside the problem novels, tearjerker romances, and hard-knocks sagas, there are many excellent books tackling the challenges of adolescence with wit and humor.

The humor of YA literature is diverse. Series by Eoin Colfer, Deb Gliori, and Lemony Snicket will delight those who enjoy silly puns, grossness, and nonstop action. Karen Cushman's historical fiction, and regional novels such as Ric Lynden Hardman's *Sunshine Rider* and Robert Newton Peck's *Horse Thief* are filled with quaint dialects and colorful oaths. Jean Ferris, Gail Carson Levine, Diana Wynne Jones, and Terry Pratchett are among the authors who have given us superb comic fantasies.

Daniel Pinkwater and Louise Rennison make us laugh out loud, while Sarah Dessen and Carolyn Mackler offer understated humorous perspectives. Meg Cabot, Catherine Clark, and Gordon Korman write sparkling, light situation comedies, while Joan Bauer and Ron Koertge present realistic coming-of-age novels with witty, self-deprecating narrators. Humor is employed in YA novels with male, female, and nonhuman protagonists. There are funny novels for both young and older adolescents, and for fans of every genre. Multiethnic comedies are becoming more prevalent, and some excellent humorous treatments of same-sex attraction have recently been published.

Nevertheless, there is no previous book devoted to an exploration of humor in young adult literature. Michael Cart's fine book on humor in children's books, *What's So Funny?*, does not address fiction for adolescents.[1] The use of humor is occasionally addressed in the periodical literature. However, extended discussions of humorous YA literature are scarce, and it has been suggested that "funny YA novel" may be an oxymoron.[2]

Most of the authors who have produced major bodies of humorous YA literature have not as yet been the subject of a book-length study. Richard Peck,[3] Daniel Pinkwater,[4] and William Sleator[5] are among the few exceptions. There are bio-critical studies of Diana Wynne Jones[6] and Phyllis Reynolds Naylor,[7] both of whom often employ humor in their fiction, but neither of those critical studies discusses the use of humor at any length. Joan Bauer, Anne Fine, Ron Koertge, Gordon Korman, and Jerry Spinelli are among the considerable number of veteran YA authors acclaimed for producing high-quality comedies over two or more decades, who have not yet been treated in a book-length bio-critical study. One of the aims of this book is to celebrate the accomplishments of those authors. Writers of humorous YA literature are not necessarily underappreciated. Many have won literary awards, and the excellence of their respective works has been recognized in journal articles and in reference works, if not often in critical monographs. But perhaps being known as humorist is more a liability than an asset, since comedy is all too often regarded as an inferior genre.

A standard encyclopedia of American literature notes, "There is a common misperception that comedy is less important than tragedy . . . even though the human condition and the nature of existence are central concerns of the humorist."[8] In her discussion of the awarding of the first Los Angeles Times Book Prize for YA literature to Joan Bauer's humorous novel, *Rules of the Road*, Patty Campbell described a successful effort by members of the awards committee to overcome just that misperception:

> In the end, we realized that the fact that *Rules of the Road* is entertaining doesn't mean that it isn't serious literature. The power and sweetness of laughing with—not at—the pain of the human struggle to grow up had been demonstrated to us.[9]

The wisdom of that observation is confirmed in the works critiqued in this book. The discussion here will show how the works of leading YA authors such as Joan Bauer are strengthened, not trivialized, by their humorous content.

By bringing together the foremost humorous YA authors, a comparison of their various strengths, similarities, and differences can be made. In addition, works by authors who have produced a smaller output of high-quality humorous YA literature will be examined. Among these are new authors who have recently arrived on the scene, as well as veterans primarily known for serious fiction or fiction written for an audience other than young adults. The approach of this book will be topical, to facilitate a comparison of distinctive treatments by different authors of adolescent life events such as sibling rivalry or first dates.

The chapter plan roughly follows the stages of adolescent development. Typically, one grows up within a family, then becomes involved with an expanding circle of peers, including friends and bullies. One encounters authority figures such as teachers, coaches, and employers, develops romantic attachments, and evolves away from childhood toward adulthood. Chapters 1–4, 6, and 8 follow those stages of adolescence. Chapters 5 and 7 cut against the grain. Chapter 5 explores works that emphasize self-image concerns experienced by adolescents of varying ages, and chapter 7 examines some special genres of humorous fiction. The final chapter discusses coming-of-age novels in particular, and also recapitulates overall themes of this book, since the gradual process of growing from childhood to adulthood is implicit in all adolescent settings.

The organization of most chapters around life stages and social settings of adolescence allows insights into the ways that comedy can be generated from typical situations encountered by teens. Even though much of the humor in YA literature overlaps that found in fiction for younger readers and for adults, the special circumstances of adolescence create a distinctive setting for YA comedy. Some comic situations, such as the mocking of pompous authority figures, are especially resonant in the YA context. Other situations, involving puberty, coming of age, and various "firsts," are unique to adolescence and give rise to much of the best YA comedy.

The organization of this book at the intersection of two concepts—young adult literature and humor—mandated the exclusion of some very funny books that aren't quite YA, as well as some fine YA books that aren't sufficiently humorous. Works are grouped according to the most common social settings of adolescence, such as family, friends, and romance. This multidimensional organization of the material, plus the notorious folly of any attempt to dissect humor, has made an assessment of the literature challenging.

> It is . . . difficult to define humor or to describe the way it functions in cultural and social contexts. This is understandable since there is little agreement on what makes things funny.[10]

Or as Patty Campbell put it, "Analyzing the rare gift of comedy is in the end as futile as dissecting a mouse to find the squeak."[11] I have tried to avoid such dissection by selecting illustrative passages, then allowing the authors and their characters to "squeak for themselves."

The scope of this book was determined first by deciding what is considered to be young adult literature, and next, what can be regarded as humorous examples of that literature. Decisions also had to be made whether to include nonfiction, short fiction, and older titles. Young adult literature is most commonly defined as works written for and marketed to adolescents, aged approximately twelve to eighteen. In realistic YA literature, the presence of a teen protagonist is not sufficient. The story must be told from an adolescent perspective, with a genuine adolescent voice, rather than from the viewpoint of an adult recalling his youth. Since the vast majority of YA authors are adults, the creation of a convincing teen protagonist (and narrator, since most YA literature is told in the first person) is an impressive feat from the outset.

Fantasy, supernatural, and science fiction novels with YA appeal often feature adult, child, or nonhuman protagonists. Such works are judged to be YA based upon the issues presented and their treatment, since speculative fiction tends to be read across all age groups. For example, works by Diana Wynne Jones, Terry Pratchett, and J. K. Rowling have been marketed to every audience, sometimes with different pricing and packaging for children, YAs, adults, and special genre fans, respectively. As a general rule, fantasy and science fiction titles that have been marketed to young adults by publishers, and treated as YA literature by the review media and by libraries are discussed here. The decision was made to limit the coverage to works of fiction. There is some humorous YA nonfiction, including excellent autobiographies by YA fiction authors Chris Crutcher, Jack Gantos, Walter Dean Myers, William Sleator, Jerry Spinelli, and Paul Zindel.[12] However, autobiographies have been excluded along with all other nonfiction. Coverage is restricted to works published in English and distributed in the United States, allowing for the inclusion of many works by British, Canadian, and Australian writers. The main focus is on novels, although some short stories published in edited collections are also discussed.

The vast majority—around 85 percent—of the works discussed here were published in the 1990s or later. Exceptions were made only for notable titles that are still frequently read, and preferably still in print. Early works of some prominent authors whose careers extend back through several decades (e.g., Richard Peck) are cited. High-quality fiction has been preferred, as determined by critical consensus on the merits of the title, as well as the literary reputation of the author. While awards were not a criteria for inclusion, many medal and honor books are discussed. Formula series are omitted.

Coverage was also restricted to books in which humor is a major element. Most works of fiction include at least a bit of humor, and many downbeat YA novels contain some terrific and very quotable humorous passages. But pulling good examples of humor from the entire universe of YA literature did not seem a practical undertaking. Moreover, it would lead to a narrower kind of book: one devoted to the analysis of a literary technique, rather than the celebration of a lively genre.

A two-step process was employed in deciding whether humor was a major element in any given book. First, a variety of sources was consulted to find novels and short stories that have been described as humorous by readers and reviewers. Those sources included book reviews, reference works, the YALSA-BK discussion list,[13] and the websites of numerous public libraries. Promising books were read and evaluated for suitability. As the author of a book on Daniel Pinkwater and a VOYA reviewer, I was already familiar with the fiction of well-known, humorous YA authors such as Joan Bauer, Jean Ferris, Ron Koertge, Gordon

Korman, and Richard Peck. As my interest in Daniel Pinkwater might suggest, I've long been a fan of satirical fantasy and science fiction, and so I was well acquainted with the fiction of Bruce Coville, Diana Wynne Jones, David Lubar, Terry Pratchett, and William Sleator. However, at the beginning of this project it soon became clear that many other writers have produced humorous and entertaining YA literature.

There exists considerable disagreement as to what is funny and what is not. Some readers will not be amused by vulgarity, or by politically incorrect humor, no matter how well it is executed. Some prefer their humor dry, while others enjoy a hearty belly laugh. Fortunately, there is such a rich variety of comic, witty, and satirical YA literature that every reader should be able to find books to his taste.

Finally, it's important to remember that humor is but one of the elements of a well-told story. No matter how funny an author of fiction may be, if he shows off his wit in ways that fail to play a natural role in advancing his narrative, he is not writing good fiction. A string of jokes told by flat characters, loosely connected by plot "glue" does not a novel make, and a few laugh-out-loud scenes will not save an otherwise lifeless story. In the following discussions, humorous passages are presented as much as possible in context, to illustrate the contribution a sense of humor can make to a work of fiction.

Notes

1. Michael Cart, *What's So Funny? : Wit and Humor in American Children's Literature* (New York: HarperCollins, 1995). Another work on humor in books for preteens is Patricia L. Roberts, *Taking Humor Seriously in Children's Literature: Literature-Based Mini-Units and Humorous Books for Children Ages 5–12* (Lanham, Md.: Scarecrow Press, 1997).

2. Patty Campbell, "The Sand in the Oyster: Funny Girls," *Horn Book* 75:3 (May 1999): 359. Series editor Patty Campbell told this author that the observation may have originated with Gordon Korman.

3. Donald R. Gallo, *Presenting Richard Peck* (Boston: Twayne, 1989).

4. Walter Hogan, *The Agony and the Eggplant: Daniel Pinkwater's Heroic Struggles in the Name of YA Literature* (Lanham, Md.: Scarecrow Press, 2001).

5. James E. Davis, *Presenting William Sleator* (New York: Twayne, 1992).

6. *Diana Wynne Jones: An Exciting and Exacting Wisdom*, ed. Teya Rosenberg et al. (New York: Peter Lang, 2002).

7. Lois T. Stover, *Presenting Phyllis Reynolds Naylor* (New York: Twayne, 1997).

8. "Humor in the United States" in *HarperCollins Reader's Encyclopedia of American Literature*, edited by George Perkins et al. (New York: Harper Resource, 2002), 478.

9. Campbell, "The Sand in the Oyster: Funny Girls," 360.

10. "Humor in the United States," 478.

11. Campbell, "The Sand in the Oyster: Funny Girls," 363.

12. William Sleator, *Oddballs* (New York: Dutton, 1993); Jack Gantos, *A Hole in My Life* (New York: Farrar, Straus & Giroux 2002); Chris Crutcher, *King of the Mild Frontier: An Ill-advised Autobiography* (New York: Greenwillow, 2003); Walter Dean Myers, *Bad Boy: A Memoir* (New York: HarperCollins, 2001); Jerry Spinelli, *Knots in My Yo-yo String* (New York: Knopf, 1998); Paul Zindel, *The Pigman and Me* (New York: HarperCollins, 1992).

13. YALSA is the Young Adult Library Services Association of the American Library Association. YALSA-BK is one of several useful open lists run by this division of ALA.

CHAPTER ONE

~

Family

Separation from parents and family is a major theme of adolescence. So, it may seem strange to begin with an extended consideration of the parental home, a place many adolescents are eager to escape. However, the interaction of teenagers with parents and families is a vital element in much of young adult literature.

Parents and Stepparents

In his "Characteristics of Good Fiction for Young Adults," Donald Gallo includes just one reference to family life, noting that parents play only a minor role in most young adult books.[1] Gallo was probably seeking here to distinguish YA literature from children's literature, and from that angle his point makes intuitive sense. Yet, while the physical proximity of parents may diminish as an adolescent matures, parents and family have a strong and enduring influence upon teenagers in young adult literature, as in the real world which that literature reflects.[2]

Certainly both the emphasis and the perspective on family life in YA novels is very different from that in stories written for children. Even as they grow into preadolescence and become immersed in peer groups, for most preteens and early teens the parental home is still first and foremost a place of comfort and safety. However, the older adolescent's yearning for space and freedom in which to develop a separate identity cannot be entirely reconciled with the security of home, the intimate proximity of siblings, and the authority of parents. A child's coming of age is often preceded by an extended tug-of-war within the family, a process that has been well-chronicled in young adult literature.

Parents often find it difficult to determine just when and where adolescent misbehavior crosses the line. Lisa Rowe Fraustino's *Ash* is a mordantly funny novel about an eighteen-year-old boy who is eventually discovered to be mentally ill, but who manages to create unbelievable havoc in his family during the months before he is finally diagnosed and institutionalized. Many other novels have portrayed teenagers running amok, to the consternation of their families. Perhaps the funniest is C. D. Payne's *Youth in Revolt: The Journals of Nick Twisp*, an outrageous farce in which fifteen-year-old Nick leaves a trail of destruction up and down the state of California as he commits a string of spectacular felonies in his heedless pursuit of the beautiful Sheeni Saunders.

Society has undergone profound changes, and the "nuclear family" is no longer the norm. Reflecting that development, much of the best-known contemporary fiction for young readers involves nontraditional family situations. J. K. Rowling's Harry Potter and the Baudelaires of Lemony Snickett's A Series of Unfortunate Events are orphans, and Alice McKinley of Phyllis Reynolds Naylor's popular series has lost her mother to a fatal illness. Many of Joan Bauer's young protagonists are missing at least one of their parents.[3]

Families in which one parent has died prematurely may be overrepresented in YA literature. In contemporary American life, the absence of a parent because of separation or divorce from the other parent is far more common. There are literally thousands of YA novels in which the protagonist's parents are divorced. To cite an example made famous by Hollywood: Anne Fine's *Alias Madame Doubtfire*, the source of the film *Mrs. Doubtfire*, features a divorced father who is prepared to go to comically extreme lengths to spend more time with his children. Or, returning to Joan Bauer and Ron Koertge, two of the foremost authors of humorous YA literature, we note that nearly all of Joan Bauer's heroines have but a single functioning parent,[4] and most of Ron Koertge's protagonists also live in one-parent households.[5] In those few instances when the second parent of a Bauer or Koertge protagonist is still amongst the living, he or she has often cheerfully abandoned the daily cares of active parenthood. Among the top authors of humorous YA literature, Gordon Korman may be one of the few whose protagonists usually live with both parents.[6]

Todd Strasser offers the ultimate spin on divorced parents of teenagers in his provocatively entitled *Girl Gives Birth to Own Prom Date*. Chase Hammond and Nicole Maris are high school seniors and lifelong neighborhood friends. At the very end of the novel, after many twists and turns, Chase, who lives with his divorced father, and Nicole, who lives with her divorced mother, fall in love with each other, to the surprise of both. They come home, happy and exhausted from the senior prom (which they had not attended as a couple), unsure how to break the news to their parents. They find that Mr. Hammond is at Nicole's house.

"Kids," Dad says, "there's something we want to tell you."
"It shouldn't come as a surprise," Mrs. Maris adds.
"Mom, what're you talking about?" Nicole gasps.
Dad and Mrs. Maris give each other this warm, happy, cuddly look.
"Nicole," Dad says, "your mom and I have decided to live together."
"So now you really will be like brother and sister," her mom says.
Nicole and I just stare at each other.
Huh?[7]

The mismatched agendas of teens and their divorced parents finds no more perfect expression than in that concluding scene of Strasser's marvellous comedy of errors.

In *Girl Gives Birth to Own Prom Date*, both protagonists (Chase and Nicole narrate alternate chapters) are already quite familiar with the romantic partners of their respective single parents. In other YA novels, sons and daughters engage in matchmaking by attempting to pair a single parent with a chosen partner. Phyllis Reynolds Naylor's *Alice* novels feature Alice McKinley's comically overzealous efforts to transform her attractive teacher, Miss Summers, into her stepmother. More commonly, children and adolescents are presented with a stranger with whom the parent has developed a relationship. Numerous YA novels and stories have effectively used humor to deal with the stressful situations resulting from a parent's new love interest.

Another of Todd Strasser's novels, *How I Changed My Life*, includes a humorous and touching scene of rapprochement between a teen and his stepmother. Amiable, good-looking Kyle Winthrop had been a star of the football team until he injured his knee at the beginning of his senior year. Kyle's life had revolved around sports, watching TV, and hanging out with the other jocks, while ignoring his stepmother and infant half brother. One morning, as the three of them are sitting at breakfast together, Kyle's stepmother runs off crying in frustration upon dropping a glass carafe full of coffee, her nerves shot following a sleepless night with the teething baby. It suddenly occurs to Kyle that he could clean up the mess, and then he even proceeds to fumble about in his first attempt to change a diaper. His stepmother is stunned, and as she shows Kyle how to fold and fasten the diaper, she manages a smile that tells us that she and Kyle have finally found some common ground.[8]

In Kate Gilmore's funny, charming romance, *Enter Three Witches*, there is an ongoing drama as to the outcome of a parent's new romance. Bren West's father, Bob, has separated from his wife, Miranda, because he's the sort of prosaic, earthbound fellow who finds it unnerving to live with a practicing witch.[9] But Alia, his new love interest, most improbably also turns out to be a witch. Spellbound by Alia, Bob doesn't realize he's traded one witch for another until Bren clues him in and Miranda engages Alia in a public duel of sorcery. A reluctant acceptance of uncanny female powers by the novel's male characters is conveyed with warmth and humor.

In one of the first great YA satirical novels, Sue Townsend's *The Secret Diary of Adrian Mole Aged 13¾*, young Adrian chronicles the extramarital affairs of both of his parents. Adrian's ignorance about sex often contributes to the dark hilarity of the situation, as when he innocently describes his mother and the man from next door "working together" in the basement and replying to him that they are unable to open the door just yet.[10] The Adrian Mole Diaries introduced many clever humorous techniques later used in other YA novels presented as a teen's private diary. Compare this entry from Adrian Mole's diary—

6 P.M. Pandora! My lost love!
   Now I will never stroke your treacle hair! (Although my blue felt-tip is still at your disposal.)
   8 P.M. Pandora! Pandora! Pandora!
   10 P.M. Why? Why? Why? (*Adrian Mole*, 24)

—with this entry, from the diary of one Georgia Nicolson a generation later:

> 1:00 A.M. Hot and stuffy. Big full moon. Sitting on the window-sill. (Me, not the moon.)
> 1:05 A.M. I hate him.
> 1:06 A.M. Oh I love him, I love him.[11]

There are other parallels between these two best-selling fictional British diaries. Both Adrian and Georgia devote a great number of journal entries to concerns about their "spots" (pimples) and other bodily imperfections. Adrian's earnest measurements of the length of his penis are curiously similar to Georgia's obsessive musings about the size of her nose and her breasts (or "nunga-nungas" as she calls them).

Both Adrian and Georgia are extremely funny critics of their parents' social and sex lives. One of Adrian's diary entries:

> My father said he had had Doreen Slater for tea. By the state of the house I should think he'd had her for breakfast, dinner and tea! I have never seen the woman, but from the evidence she left behind I know she has got bright red hair, wears orange lipstick and sleeps on the left side of the bed. (*Adrian Mole*, 64)

When Georgia's father returns from New Zealand:

> 6:00 P.M. Mum and Dad practically ATE each other. Erlack! How can they do that? In public.
> 12:30 A.M. All the so-called grown-ups got drunk and started "letting their hair down." Well, those of them that had any.
> 1:00 A.M. Dad was swiveling his hips around and clapping his hands together like a seal. Also he kept yelling, "Hey you! Get off of my cloud!!" like a geriatric Mick Jagger . . . Mum was all red and flushed— she was TWISTING with Mr. Next Door and they both fell over into a heap. (*On the Bright Side*, 218–20)

A number of YA novels have employed humor to describe a prospective stepparent gradually winning the affection and admiration of a teen through patience and fortitude. In Anne Fine's *My War with Goggle-Eyes*, Kitty tells of her protracted resistance to her mother's new companion. Gerald is over fifty, conservative, and set in his ways. He quickly charms Kitty's younger sister Judith, but Kitty behaves horribly, opposing and rejecting Gerald with every imaginable tactic. Steady Gerald takes it all in stride, and when he has a fight with Kitty's mother and disappears from their lives, it is Kitty who effects a reconciliation.

Some months later, a girl in Kitty's class, Helen, comes to school in a terrible mood. Guessing the cause of Helen's distress, and knowing of Kitty's ordeal, their clever teacher Mrs. Lupey asks Kitty to have a private chat with her classmate. Mrs. Lupey, who assigns all her students a number each year, tells Kitty, "We're all counting on you, Number Twenty-two!" The entire novel is built around Kitty's narration to the tearful Helen as they sit together in a closet. Kitty winds up the long story of her war with Gerald by saying, "I just find him soothing and amiable and steady—easy to have around . . . if he and Mum got married I wouldn't mind." Helen, ponders a bit, then replies, "Of course, Toad-shoes is different. He's not like Goggle-eyes at all. He's awful."[12]

Fourteen-year-old Anna Newland, the introverted title character of Patrice Kindl's extraordinary *Woman in the Wall*, is afraid of the forceful Mr. Albright, who is planning to marry her mother. Like her father, who disappeared into the stacks of the Library of Congress one day and was never heard from again, Anna has what her mother calls a "retiring disposition."[13] However, Mr. Albright turns out to be a reasonable man, and we feel, along with Anna, that things will be "all bright" for her as well, now that she has emerged, in her gaudy luna moth costume, from the thick walls of her old house. (Perhaps a mother who has allowed her daughter to hide in the walls through most of her childhood can benefit from such a decisive husband.)

Rachel Cohn's *Gingerbread* is another novel in which a stepfather turns out to be a better parent than the narrator's biological father. Caffeine and sugar-addled "love child" Cyd Charisse is a hyperkinetic, boy-crazy teen with zero impulse control. The "Little Hellion" as she is called, fails to appreciate the stable and loving home her mother and stepfather have made in San Francisco, until they send her across the country to become acquainted with her feckless biological father in New York. *Gingerbread* is a very funny, high-energy narrative laced with hip contemporary jargon and featuring a lively urban protagonist who will remind some readers of Francesca Lia Block's Weetzie Bat. Cohn's later novel, *The Steps*, as the title suggests, is entirely devoted to the theme of stepfamilies negotiating new relationships.

Peter Beagle's *Tamsin*, a ghost story that is also a convincing and humorous coming-of-age novel, features an admirable stepfather, Evan McHugh, who patiently endures months of rudeness and sulking from his new stepdaughter Jenny, giving her plenty of time and space to adjust, until she is at last able to accept her new life. Jenny's mother finally ventures to question her about her feelings toward Evan.

> Then she asked, all of a sudden, "Baby, are you liking Evan any better? As a stepfather, I mean."
>
> I shrugged. "I've never not liked him," I said, which was perfectly true. The only thing I really disliked about Evan was that I didn't dislike him; because if somebody wrecks and devastates your entire life, he ought to at least have the decency to be a full-out David Copperfield-style, vicious rat bastard, not a skinny Limey farmer who liked to play the guitar.[14]

Of course, there are truly bad stepparents, like those in fairy tales and Dickens novels. Humorous treatment of such unpleasantness requires a black humor sensibility, which David Klass carries off in *You Don't Know Me*. A classic villain reminiscent of David Copperfield's loathsome stepfather, Mr. Murdstone, has moved in with the mother of a fourteen-year-old boy. John's exquisite black-humor narration about "The Man Who Is Not My Father" makes bearable for him, and for us, a bleak story that is redeemed at the end when the abusive man does not become John's stepfather after all, having merited a more pressing engagement with the criminal justice system.

Laurie Halse Anderson's short story "Passport," offers a similar black humorous tone, narrated by high school senior Jared as he shuttles back and forth between the "Land of Mom" and the "Kingdom of Dad." Jared's father callously dumps his wife to pursue a shallow young beauty not much older than his teenage son. Jared wonders how long he can deal with his father's "Baywatch fantasy" partner,[15] and describes a "Stealth attack on the Land of Mom":

> Villagers running through their wheat fields screaming. Cities collapsing, forests ablaze.
> Mom, meet Heather. Heather, this is Mom.

Dad masterminded the plan, a bombing raid under the cover of "dropping off Jared." Heather wore a T-shirt cut real high and shorts that drooped wonderfully low. A tanned relief map of abdominal muscle connected the two scraps of cloth.

Mom wore one of Dad's abandoned robes and slippers that looked like something Abby Tabb Kitty had coughed up. Heather held out her arm to shake hands, and a million silver bracelets jingled.

Mom slammed the door. Heather squeaked. Dad chuckled. They drove off laughing with the top down.

Like I said, a stealth attack.[16]

The passport of the story's title turns out to be a literal passport that Jared has been awaiting to take him somewhere, anywhere, far away from both the Land of Mom and the Kingdom of Dad as soon as he graduates from high school.

Brock Cole's novel, Celine, also presents a situation in which a teen narrator's father has taken up with a much younger woman. Catherine, only twenty-two, has been left for months in charge of sixteen-year-old Celine while her new husband, Celine's father, lectures in Europe. Catherine is a perfectly nice young woman, hardly an "evil" stepmother or a bimbo like Heather in "Passport," but she is far too young and self-absorbed to be the only caretaker of a teenager she barely knows.

Celine isn't bashful about pointing this out. "You're supposed to take an interest in my maturation processes!" Celine shouts at Catherine. "I need supervision. People my age need almost constant supervision. Everyone knows that. We're a mass of raging hormones."[17] After calming down, Celine concludes, "Perhaps Catherine is right and I am losing contact with reality. It doesn't seem much of a loss" (Celine, 151). Celine finds herself in an amazing variety of difficulties—most of which could not have occurred were she getting any parental attention—as she narrates a series of misadventures in her unique, quirky voice.

Despite the prevalence of absent or feuding parents as the source of conflicts and challenges for young protagonists, many of the best humorous YA novels of recent years are set in traditional two-parent households. Of course, an intact, conventional family can provide plenty of humor, as we know from early television sitcoms, such as The Adventures of Ozzie and Harriet, and Father Knows Best.

Some of the "nuclear family" parents portrayed in comical YA novels are excruciatingly dull. In Barbara Wersba's Rita Formica trilogy: *Fat, a Love Story, Love Is the Crooked Thing,* and *Beautiful Losers,* the exceptional blandness of Rita's parents sets off the eccentricity of their daughter and her much older boyfriend, Arnold Bromberg. The culture clash of the highly intellectual, perpetual student Bromberg with Rita's earthy, blue-collar father is delicious.

Jerry Spinelli has made good use of similar family dynamics in several of his comic novels about younger teens. The humor of Maisie Potter's cross-gender wrestling venture in *There's a Girl in My Hammerlock* is heightened by the contrast of her fearless nonconformity with the conventional attitudes of her parents and brother. In Spinelli's *Who Put That Hair in My Toothbrush?* the extreme sibling rivalry between Greg "Grosso" and Megin "Megamouth" Tofer is all the more dramatic for being waged within an otherwise unremarkable suburban family.

Ordinary parents and siblings sometimes contrast effectively with more exotic relatives. Ivy Breedlove of Joan Bauer's *Backwater* finds her long-lost Aunt Josephine, a gutsy hermit, to be a more colorful and interesting character than any of the numerous multigenerational Breedlove attorneys with whom Ivy has been raised. The ordinariness of the Delanceys in Gordon Korman's *Semester in the Life of a Garbage Bag* sets off the quirky grandfather who lives with them and who, on a whim, impersonates a long-dead Canadian poet with such verve that the hoax makes him a media star.

In *Political Timber*, Chris Lynch introduces us to high school senior Gordon Foley, who finds himself being manipulated by his larger-than-life grandfather Fins Foley, a notorious political boss whose powerful personality completely overshadows the rest of the Foley family. Having been through their own ordeals with the old reprobate, Gordie's parents just shake their heads ruefully as Fins, from his prison cell, strong-arms Gordie into running for town mayor as soon as he turns eighteen. Fins is well connected and can call on tough guys to do his dirty work, as Gordie discovers in this priceless scene, shortly after he had been roughed up by the large and muscular high school bully Robert O'Dowd:

> The next morning in homeroom we were sitting there half-conscious when Robert O'Dowd walked in.
>
> First off, O'Dowd was not a member of this homeroom.
>
> Second off, he was marching with a purpose . . . ignoring the laughter.

Third off, he had his underwear yanked all the way out of his pants, pulled up his back, over his head, with the remainder of the waistband hooked under his chin. A hall-of-fame wedgie . . .

O'Dowd clung to whatever dignity he could manage, speaking through his briefs.

"I was told I couldn't take it off until I came in here and you saw," he growled. . . . "So now I told you." Then he left, tearing off the shreds of underwear as he ran.

What do you know, I thought. Fins *does* have goons.[18]

In YA literature, parents in intact families are often portrayed as funny, eccentric characters, and their unexpectedly solid marriages are the focus of many good stories. Hilary McKay's beautiful novel *Saffy's Angel* presents an unforgettable pair of eccentric parents, both dedicated artists whose children thrive amidst total chaos. In Judith Clarke's *The Heroic Life of Al Capsella*, fourteen-year-old Al is constantly embarrassed by his bohemian parents, particularly by his mother's unconventional dress and behavior:

All us kids try hard to pass for normal, wearing the same clothes and hairstyles. . . . The Capsellas are a real liability. . . . Mrs. Capsella does one thing a parent should never do: She stands out. She's like an alien who's dropped in from another planet and doesn't know the customs—and she doesn't even try to learn.[19]

Al ruefully describes many of his mother's peculiarities, but comes to appreciate her nonconformity after enduring a painful visit to the home of his mother's smug, racist, and rigidly uptight parents. The novel ends with Al vowing he'll never use the word "normal" again.[20]

Daniel Pinkwater's *The Education of Robert Nifkin* features the evidently happy marriage of Robert's eccentric parents. Robert tells of their joint enthusiasm for finishing their apartment in "French-whorehouse décor": "The effect was stunning. There was a lot of gilded and pickled wood, pale colors, crystal light fixtures, pastel prints, and fake-ceramic knickknacks" topped by a lamp made from "a hunk of driftwood, reaching upward with many spiky branches, stained a dark olive-brown and standing about five feet high."[21] Mr. Nifkin had a delicate stomach and his wife devotedly prepared him horrible-looking and tasteless meals:

If there is a good side to having been raised on my mother's cooking, it is that I am unlikely to encounter anything worse. School cafeteria food is a step up. Sandwiches from a vending machine in a rest stop on the Indiana Turnpike are a step up. Mass-produced packaged imitation liverwurst in a plastic tube you can squeeze out like toothpaste is a step up. (*The Education of Robert Nifkin*, 28)

Most of these humorous family stories feature strong narration by a distinctive protagonist. In fact, most YA literature is narrated in the first person by a teen, whose adolescent perspective is essential to the character of the tale.[22] So, aside from the obvious lack of adult experience, what particular qualities should we expect from a teenage narrator? A thorough and detailed response to that question might require that we consult a panel of adolescent psychologists, and surely none of us wants to go *there*. Instead, let's consider just one well-known aspect of the teen viewpoint, namely, a tendency to be judgmental about, if not hypercritical of, perceived adult shortcomings. Much of the family humor in YA literature derives from those two attributes of the teenage narrator: his youthful inexperience, and his eagerness to lampoon adult follies.

In the diaries of both Adrian Mole and Georgia Nicolson, mentioned earlier, these two British teens poke fun at nearly everyone they know, especially their own parents. Reading between the lines of these diaries-as-novels, we perceive that both the Moles and the Nicolsons are really rather ordinary, lower-middle-class couples. But Adrian and Georgia ridicule their parents with such relish, with such savage glee, that for us, the Moles and the Nicolsons become buffoonish objects at whose expense much of the hilarity of each of the novels is achieved.

During the course of *The Secret Diary of Adrian Mole, Aged 13¾*, Adrian is an only child. However, Georgia Nicolson has a baby sister about whom she is very funny (of course) but also—perhaps surprisingly given Georgia's general demeanor—quite affectionate. Georgia's unexpected tenderness toward Libby dramatizes the potential of siblings to bring out additional dimensions of an adolescent narrator's character and experience.

The narrator who is an only child appears with greater frequency in YA literature than in the world in which we readers live, even after taking into account the diminishing size of today's families. This may often be due to narrative exigency. That is, since most YA stories focus upon a single teen protagonist, often it is not necessary to mention siblings. They might exist—the story may not preclude their existence—but if so they would be superfluous to the story.

As Dr. Gallo noted, YA novels tend to be no more than 200 pages long, and the plots are usually not complicated.[23] In consequence, there's not much room for nonessential, decorative, background material. Accordingly, if siblings are not specifically relevant to the plot, the author may find it most convenient, and most effective, to leave them out altogether. Likewise, if the more complex dynamics of a two-parent household do not contribute to a protagonist's development, it may be simpler for the author and easier for the reader to deal with just a single parent.

There may also be something inherently appealing about the single parent and the only child as fictional characters. Narrative interest is generated when a single-parent situation is the backdrop for plots dealing with a widowed parent's grief over the loss of a spouse, or a divorced parent's struggle to reenter the dating scene. With but a single, distracted, working parent, a teen is more free to run amok and get into interesting difficulties. A lack of balance in the household, and the absence of a guardian and role model of the opposite sex can expose the vulnerability of a teen protagonist. Susan Heyboer O'Keefe's *My Life and Death, by Alexandra Canarsie* is a particularly nice example of a humorous YA novel with this theme.

The stereotypical only child is often characterized as more sensitive, and less experienced with the rough-and-tumble, give-and-take interactions between children in larger families. The only child is often an outsider and observer, more impressionable and perhaps more reflective; hence possibly a more interesting protagonist and narrator. E. L. Konigsberg's *The Outcasts of 19 Schuyler Place* presents a classic only-child heroine in twelve-year-old Margaret Rose Kane. Margaret's extreme unpopularity with a cabin full of fellow campers, followed by her astonishingly deft interactions with a variety of adults, humorously exaggerate predictable only-child social patterns.

The best writers can spin compelling stories out of any situation. For example, one of the great only-child characters in humorous YA literature is Chris Lynch's Elvin Bishop of *Slot Machine* and *Extreme Elvin*. Elvin's father is dead, and his mother is a witty and appealing single mom. But Lynch also gave us *Iceman*, a terrific sibling story about two brothers, their neurotic parents, and the powerful dynamics between these four people living together under one roof. Good YA literature tends to provide multiple siblings and a complete set of parents when those additional characters are intrinsic to the particular story, but when they are not, we are more likely to find single parents and only-child protagonists.

Parents are important characters in YA literature a whole, and certainly a considerable number of YA novels and stories have presented parents, stepparents, and grandparents with comic effect. There are also many humorous YA novels with missing parents, and the absence of a parental figure often creates interesting dilemmas for the protagonist. In her essay, "Get Rid of the Parents?" author Nancy Werlin noted, "The truth is that parents and parental authority figures are usually of great importance in YA novels, even, and perhaps especially when they are not present in the story at all."[24]

Siblings

Interactions between siblings have also been the basis for a great number of stories in young adult literature. The theme is an ancient one: Cain and Abel, Romulus and Remus, and Handsel and Gretel quickly come to mind. One of the finest YA novels, Cynthia Voigt's *Homecoming*, describes the struggles of the four Tillerman children to find a home together after their mother's breakdown. Julie Johnston's *In Spite of Killer Bees* describes, with humor, the struggles of a trio of parentless sisters.

Anne Fine has written of divorced children with an unmatched blend of sensitivity and humor.[25] Her *Alias Madame Doubtfire* is a touching comedy of the battle between Daniel Hilliard and his former wife, Miranda, over their three children, Lydia, Christopher, and little Natalie. The older children and their father are wonderfully witty conversationalists. Daniel's specialty is the colorful insult, and both Lydia and Christopher enjoy wordplay. Despite its downbeat situation, *Alias Madame Doubtfire* is a joyously life-affirming novel that crackles with wit and humor in the face of adversity. The three children are each strong individuals who often disagree and fight amongst themselves, but together they make a marvellous team as they bravely shuttle between

Daniel's flat and their mother's house, loving both of their parents and struggling to make things work.

Several imaginative and humorous YA works have depicted trios of siblings facing dangers together. Lemony Snicket's Series of Unfortunate Events chronicles the grotesque misfortunes of fourteen-year-old Violet, twelve-year-old Klaus, and baby Sunny Baudelaire. The over-the-top, tongue-in-cheek series of melodramatic tragedies visited upon the Baudelaires begins with the loss of their parents in a fire, and goes downhill from there. Evil Count Olaf, appearing throughout the series, undertakes all sorts of dastardly plans to steal the children's inheritance.

Nancy Farmer's *The Ear, the Eye and the Arm* describes the adventures of General Matsika's three children, Tendai, Rita, and Kuda, after they are kidnapped, made to work in a toxic plastics mine, and dragged or pursued through many other amazing places in an imagined Zimbabwe of the year 2194. The three children, who are very much individuals, remain together and support one another through all of their adventures. Much of the humor derives from the exposure of these privileged and sheltered children to the vibrant but seamy underground of a great metropolis.

In Deb Gliori's *Pure Dead Magic*, twelve-year-old Titus, ten-year-old Pandora, and fourteen-month-old Damp Strega-Borgia depart their Scottish castle on a mission to rescue their father from the evil Don Lucifer di s'Embowelli Borgia. A cheerful romp in the spirit of the Harry Potter and Artemis Fowl series, and with some similarities to Snicket's Series of Unfortunate Events as well, *Pure Dead Magic* is brimming with delicious names and puns, exotic monsters, dastardly villains, and thrilling magic. Like Violet and Klaus Baudelaire, the two older Strega-Borgia children combine their talents to foil each ploy of their grotesquely evil adult opponents. Like Sunny Baudelaire, baby Damp does his best to help his older siblings.

Gary Paulsen's *Harris and Me* presents a funny relationship between a younger brother and his big sister. Fourteen-year-old Glennis Larsen, a hearty farm girl, habitually whacks her nine-year-old brother Harris whenever he uses bad language, which turns out to cover most of his conversation.

"We heard your folks was puke drunks, is that right?"

"Harris!" Glennis was walking on the other side of me and her voice snapped. "That's not polite, to talk that way."

"Well, you can just blow it out your butt, you old cow. You ain't no grown-up to tell me what to do. How the hell am I supposed to know things if I don't go ahead and ask them?"

Glennis was a strapping girl, and she reached across my back and slapped Harris on the side of the head so hard his teeth rattled.[26]

Harris is belted innumerable times by Glennis. But then Harris is trampled by a bad-tempered bull and the Larsens fear he has been killed.

It was Glennis who surprised me . . .

"You come back, Harris. You come back now. We don't want you gone. You come right back and I'll never whup you again so help me God . . ."

Harris's legs moved and he raised his arms and his eyes opened and he looked up at Glennis.

"What the hell happened?"

Her hand came up but true to her word she didn't smack him and in fact her vow lasted a whole day, until late the next afternoon when Harris tripped on the edge of the porch and ripped a strip of blue words that almost peeled paint. (*Harris and Me*, 118–19)

In Lisa Rowe Fraustino's *Ash*, fifteen-year-old Wes Libby keeps a private diary describing the change in his eighteen-year-old brother Ash's behavior after an auto accident. Wes's irregular spelling and grammar, and his Northern Maine regional dialect adds flavor to the simultaneously funny and terrible story of Ash's meltdown. Ash's bizarre blending of sex, drugs, and rock 'n' roll with religious fanaticism unnerves the family until he suddenly departs, and all the news they have of Ash for some months is an occasional postcard, always a photo of a religious license plate.

A number of humorous YA novels have shown a younger sibling causing problems for an older sister or brother. A pair of Paula Danziger's YA novels, *Remember Me to Harold Square* and *This Place Has No Atmosphere* each include funny scenes in which the teen narrator is vexed by a younger sib. In *Remember Me to Harold Square*, Kendra Kaye's parents arrange for her to undertake an extensive scavenger hunt in New York City with Frank, the son of their old friends, the Lees. Kendra and Frank are required to take Kendra's little brother

Oscar along. As Kendra and Frank begin to develop romantic feelings for one another, Oscar's function as a chaperone becomes irksome. The novel is filled with punning wordplay, beginning with the characters' names: Frank Lee is forever haunted by the phrase, "Frankly, I don't give a damn." Oscar Kaye says things like, "I'm Oscar Kaye. That means I'm O.K. and you're not."[27]

In Danziger's *This Place Has No Atmosphere*, young sister Starr's good behavior makes thirteen-year-old Aurora's petulance look even worse. Their socially conscious and politically correct parents have volunteered for a five-year hitch to join a barren pioneering community on the moon. Aurora, who had been thoroughly fixated upon shopping, keeping up with her fashionable friends, and a new boyfriend, is required to leave it all behind. Her parents make an uncomplimentary comparison:

> "Aurora, you've done nothing but complain since we've gotten here. Nothing's good enough for you. Look at how well Starr's adjusting. Why can't you? You're the oldest and should be setting the good example, not Starr."
>
> Starr's the one who caused the trouble. She put her foot over me and said "Let's pretend Aurora's a grape. I'll step on her and we'll get a little wine. Whine, get it?"
>
> So I bit her toe.[28]

In *This Place Has No Atmosphere* Danziger displays a light, sure touch. The silly puns are there, as always with Danziger, but the novel is also quite a successful spoof of those science fiction novels in which brave families steadfastly pioneer into the galaxy. Aurora's complaints over her separation from her beloved shopping malls is a more believable response than the stern heroism of the characters in most space adventure tales.

Most parents cannot resist comparing a well behaved younger child with a disgruntled older sibling. In Anne Fine's *My War with Goggle-Eyes*, young Judith's quick acceptance of Gerald makes Kitty's hostility look worse. Although Judith was not intentionally showing up her older sister, comparisons are inevitably made, creating divisiveness in the family.

A pair of Patrice Kindl's novels present transitory sibling rivalries arising out of unusual circumstances. In *Woman in the Wall*, fourteen-year-old Anna Newland emerges from years of isolation into the middle of a Halloween party. Her appearance has changed since her family last saw her and she is also disguised by a full costume. As it happens,

Anna emerges directly into the arms of an attractive eighteen-year-old, Foster Addams, whom Anna's formidable older sister, Andrea, has been dating. Even after Anna's age and identity are revealed, Andrea is still irked by her little sister's spectacular "coming out."

> "Oh, Frank, it's *Anna!*" Mother sobbed.
> "I *know* that," Mr. Albright snapped irritably. "But who *is* Anna?"
> "Anna is my sister," Andrea said.
> Mr. Albright looked blank, as though he wasn't following the conversation.
> "Hey, cool!" said one of the three strange boys.
> "My *little* sister," Andrea continued, "though that may not be so obvious." She turned to Mother. "Do you think she should be allowed to dress like that when she's only fourteen years old?"
> "I think she looks lovely," Mother said, smiling through her tears.
> "Me too," offered another of the three strange boys.
> "That's not exactly the point, Ma," said Andrea sulkily.[29]

The same author's *Goose Chase* also features a scene of humorous rivalry between sisters, again created by the sudden and unexpected appearance of a missing sister. Kindl's protagonist, Alexandria Aurora Fortunato, after many perilous adventures with dim-witted Prince Edmund of Dorloo, completes a quest accompanied by all her dozen geese so that they are restored to human form as her sisters, so many princesses. One of those sisters, Little Echo, had in her goose form been carried about by the Prince after he had accidentally wounded her. When the geese are transformed, the Prince (now a King) suddenly finds himself embracing a young woman. Alexandria asks the King, "What, my lord, have you done with Little Echo?"

> "I do not know, Mistress Alexandria. One moment I held Little Echo in my arms, a fine plump goose. The next thing I knew, I found myself in intimate contact with that"—he pointed at the hussy, who simpered—"young woman."[30]

Later, Little Echo (now Princess Elaine) asks Alexandria if she may have King Edmund: "I think he is just *wonderful*. You cannot imagine how kind and good he was to me in the dungeons of Castle Breakabeen." Alexandria clenches her teeth, and decides then that she must have Edmund after all. The book ends with Alexandria musing: "Someone needed to keep an eye on the King of Dorloo. And that someone most assuredly was not going to be Little Echo" (*Goose Chase*, 213–14).

The classic full-blown sibling rivalry in humorous YA literature is that of Greg "Grosso" Tofer and Megan "Megamouth" Tofer in Jerry Spinelli's *Who Put That Hair in My Toothbrush?* Despite a slightly dopey title, *Toothbrush* has remained in print for twenty years because it is an outstanding comic novel. Narrated by ninth-grade Greg and seventh-grade Megin in alternate chapters, *Toothbrush* is a well-structured comedy, with the rivalry becoming increasingly heated until even the easygoing, tolerant Tofer parents are at their wits' end.

Some of the funniest scenes in *Toothbrush* feature Greg and Megin's competition for the attention of their little brother, Toddie. One day Megin returns home from her job at Dunkin' Donuts:

> I couldn't wait all day for my father to get home and start Grosso's punishment. I needed satisfaction—now. And I knew just how to get it. Torture. Donut torture.
> Grosso loves donuts. All kinds. He never saw a donut he didn't love. And he was up in his room now, holding Toddie hostage by letting him watch cartoons on his TV set.

Megin then lures Toddie away from Greg's room by preparing a little snack of donuts and tea for him. Although she has a dozen donuts, none are offered to Greg. When he grabs a cream-filled donut, Megin squeezes it, causing the filling to squirt all over his face and up his nose. An all-out food fight ensues.[31]

In all families, from the most happy and intact to the shattered and dysfunctional, humor has a healing power. Authors who have written with wit and humor about the awkward and sometimes painful business of growing through the teenage years with parents, stepparents, and siblings, have given us a great gift. For most teens, and parents of teens, there is a YA book that treats some of his or her family issues with a comic flair that allows one to gain a healthy perspective on a vexing problem. And for all of us, there are hundreds of wonderful YA novels and stories that serve up a delicious seasoning of laughter to accompany the warm entrée of a good family story.

Notes

1. "Characteristics of Good Fiction for Young Adults" from YALSA-BK3881 posted by Dr. Donald Gallo, yalsa-bk@ala.org. (15 July 2002) (emphasis mine):
"1)The main characters are teenagers; 2) the length of the book averages around 200 pages; 3) the point of view is usually first-person, and it is usually that of a teenager; 4) the narrator is most often the protagonist; 5) the story is usually told in the voice of a teenager, not the voice of an adult looking back as a kid (as it is in *A Separate Peace*); 6) the language is typical of contemporary teenagers, and the vocabulary, unlike that of adult classics, is manageable; 7) the setting is usually contemporary but also can be historical, science fiction, or fantasy; 8) the book contains characters and issues to which teenagers can relate; 9) in a majority of the books, parents play a minor role; 10) the plot and literary style are uncomplicated but never simplistic, though the plots of a few books are quite complex (e.g., those of Robert Cormier and M. E. Kerr); 11) the outcome of the story is usually dependent upon the decisions and actions of the main character; 12) the tone and outcome of the novel are usually upbeat, but not always (as in the novels of Robert Cormier); 13) with the exception of complicated plotting, all the traditional literary elements typical of classical literature are present in most contemporary novels for young adults—flashbacks, allusions, irony, metaphorical language—though they are used less frequently and at less sophisticated levels; 14) the authors are not condescending; they seem to respect and value teenagers as individuals; 15) the very best books are satisfying reads for adults as well as for teenagers."
2. Psychologists have certainly noted the continuing importance of parents: "All adolescents will face challenges of one sort or another, some of which may seem insurmountable at the time. It is the role of the family to provide much-needed emotional support and adequate role models for their teenagers. Understanding and caring parents can greatly assist those who face difficulties, thus acting as a barrier against hopelessness, depression and suicide." Patrick C. L. Heaven, *The Social Psychology of Adolescence* (New York: Palgrave, 2001), 146.
3. The fathers in both *Squashed* and *Backwater* are widowers, and the father of Mickey Vernon of *Sticks* is deceased. Hope Yancey of *Hope Was Here* actually has no parents whatever: she's been raised by her Aunt Addie, and her mother comes around to say hi once or twice a year. Hope finally gets a surrogate father in the person of G. T. Stroop, who dies a few months later. Parents have a short life expectancy in Joan Bauer novels!
4. Jenna Boller's alcoholic father in *Rules of the Road* can be considered dysfunctional. Likewise Hope Yancey's mother (see note 3, above).

5. Among Ron Koertge's first seven novels, only two (*The Boy in the Moon* and *Mariposa Blues*) present a household in which the protagonist lives with both his mother and his father.

6. Korman's *No More Dead Dogs* is an exception; Wallace Wallace lives only with his mother.

7. Todd Strasser, *Girl Gives Birth to Own Prom Date* (New York: Simon & Schuster, 1996), 204.

8. Todd Strasser, *How I Changed My Life* (New York: Simon & Schuster, 1995), 182–84.

9. (Rather like Larry Hagman/Major Tony Nelson's relationship with Barbara Eden/Jeannie in the TV show *I Dream of Jeannie*.)

10. Sue Townsend, *The Adrian Mole Diaries* (New York: Grove, 1986).

11. Louise Rennison, *On the Bright Side, I'm Now the Girlfriend of a Sex God: Further Confessions of Georgia Nicolson* (New York: HarperCollins, 2001), 79.

12. Anne Fine, *My War with Goggle-Eyes* (Boston: Joy Street Books, 1989), 163–64.

13. Patrice Kindl, *Woman in the Wall* (Boston: Houghton Mifflin, 1997), 4.

14. Peter S. Beagle, *Tamsin* (New York: ROC, 1999), 77.

15. Laurie Halse Anderson, "Passport," in *Dirty Laundry*, ed. Lisa Rowe Fraustino (New York: Viking, 1998), 128–39.

16. Anderson, "Passport," 132.

17. Brock Cole, *Celine* (New York: Farrar, Straus & Giroux, 1989), 137.

18. Chris Lynch, *Political Timber* (New York: HarperCollins, 1996), 157–58.

19. Judith Clarke, *The Heroic Life of Al Capsella* (New York: Holt, 1988), 5–6.

20. Clarke, *The Heroic Life of Al Capsella*, 152.

21. Daniel Pinkwater, *The Education of Robert Nifkin* (New York: Farrar, Straus & Giroux, 1998), 23.

22. As editor Patty Campbell noted, "A book can be about coming-of-age or have a teen protagonist and still not be a YA novel if it is told from the point of view of an adult remembering. A true YA is told by a kid with all the misunderstandings and through all the limitations that lack of life experience imposes. The classic model is *Catcher in the Rye*." Patty Campbell, from YALSA-BK3822, yalsa-bk@ala.org (12 July 2000).

23. Gallo, numbers 2 and 10 (see note 1, above).

24. Nancy Werlin, "Get Rid of the Parents?" *Booklist* 95:21 (July 1995): 1934–35.

25. In particular, Fine's *Step by Wicked Step* (Boston: Little, Brown, 1996) is entirely composed of stories told by children about the difficulties they have experienced since their parents separated or divorced.

26. Gary Paulsen, *Harris and Me* (San Diego: Harcourt Brace, 1993), 9.

27. Paula Danziger, *Remember Me to Harold Square* (New York: Delacorte, 1987), 31.

28. Paula Danziger, *This Place Has No Atmosphere* (New York: Delacorte, 1986), 88–89.

29. Kindl, *Woman in the Wall*, 179.

30. Patrice Kindl, *Goose Chase* (Boston: Houghton Mifflin, 2001), 203.

31. Jerry Spinelli, *Who Put That Hair in My Toothbrush?* (Boston: Little, Brown, 1984), 37–42.

CHAPTER TWO

~

Friends

For many of us, cooperation and rivalry with siblings preceded the extended social connections we would eventually develop with unrelated children in the neighborhood, playground, and classroom. The range of personalities to be encountered outside of the family circle is rich and varied, exciting and sometimes intimidating. For better and for worse, strangers often don't play by the same rules as family members. Learning how to make friends and how to deal with bullies is an integral part of growing up.

Teenagers face some uniquely challenging circumstances when they encounter potential new companions. Friendships with the opposite sex take on a heightened intensity, older or adult friends may become teachers and mentors, and friendships made in childhood are subjected to new stresses as friends enter puberty. Perhaps because adolescent friendships often have this extra resonance, the theme of friendship in YA literature seems to be better expressed in novels than in short stories. Indeed, some of the best portrayals of youthful friendships developing over time are found in multiple-novel sequels and in quality YA series.

Old Friends Approaching Adolescence Together

Several authors of humorous YA literature have done an especially fine job of chronicling the dynamics of a group of preteen friends entering adolescence together. Series of novels about the same characters are often effective in sustaining reader involvement. In J. K. Rowling's Harry Potter series, each book in the series takes place during the course of a single year, as Harry and his friends progress through their secondary school years at Hogwarts School of Wizardry together. However, most fictional series do not have such a precise time progression. The old Hardy Boys series resulted in dozens of books that all implausibly took place during the brief high school years of Frank and Joe Hardy. More frequently, writers find a middle ground between those two extremes, as in Phyllis Reynolds Naylor's Alice series

Alice McKinley and her friends age as the series progresses, but slowly; they are the subjects of several books for each year of their young lives. Alice progresses from the sixth grade in the first book, *The Agony of Alice*, to ninth grade in the fourteenth, *Simply Alice*. The first of several planned prequels, *Starting with Alice*, is set shortly before the time of the original series opener. Throughout all of the series, Alice has two best friends, Pamela Jones and Elizabeth Johnson.

The three girls have consistent, distinctive characters. As with a TV sitcom, much of the humor of the series derives from watching a quirky, beloved character react to new challenges in his or her inimitable fashion. Alice has lost her mother (a common scenario in YA literature) and has to rely for guidance upon an otherwise male household composed of her father and older brother, Lester. Alice's notable traits are an insistent curiosity and a strong will to control her environment. Her interrogations of her father and brother about the mysteries of puberty and adult social behavior supply humorous interchanges in each series entry. The controlling side of Alice's personality occasionally comes to the fore, as when she plays matchmaker for her father and Miss Summers.

Pamela is the most advanced of the three girls, both physically and in her relationships with the opposite sex. By the time of *Achingly Alice*, Pamela's parents have separated and Pamela is a bit wild and more forward with boys than most of her peers. Elizabeth, who comes from a traditional Catholic family, is quite prim and easily embarrassed. Elizabeth was an only child until her mother had a late baby when Elizabeth was thirteen, and this evidence of her parents' sexuality is one of many factors causing her embarrassment. In *The Grooming of Alice*, Elizabeth is ashamed to be seen in her bathing suit. "Elizabeth went first because she wanted to hide her thighs, I went next because I really didn't care, and Pamela went last because she wanted to show off her bright red bikini with the halter top."[1] Alice's intermediate nature is noted: "You're not stuck on a fast track, like Pamela, or stuck in reverse, like Elizabeth" (*Grooming of Alice*, 20).

In *Agony of Alice* it is Alice herself who suffers frequent embarrassments. Naylor's use of the three friends, who are each at different stages of their social development, provides a good basis for her comical observations of the awkward situations faced by teens. Naylor's style allows the reader to contemplate potentially painful situations with a bit of humorous detachment.

Typically, one of the three girls will be facing some adolescent concern, with the others soon finding out about it and suggesting various solutions. Sometimes even their combined knowledge falls short and humorous misunderstandings ensue. In *Achingly Alice*, Elizabeth has a problem that will require her to undergo her first pelvic exam. The exam and corresponding feminine hygiene issues surrounding it fascinate the girls and when a douche is prescribed for Elizabeth, they gather in the bathroom to read the instructions:

"Hold the bag lower!" yelled Pamela.
"No, hold the nozzle higher!" I shrieked.
In the confusion, Elizabeth disconnected the hose from the bag and water poured all over the floor. We all screamed.
Lester tapped on the door.
"Al, do you suppose I could use the john?"
Elizabeth shrieked again.
"Just a minute!" I told him.
I grabbed the bath mat and mopped up the floor, Elizabeth slipped the douche bag under her shirt, and we all traipsed out of the bathroom, dragging the hose behind us.
"Ladies?" came Lester's voice.
We turned, and he gallantly handed us the nozzle and closed the door.[2]

By presenting the intimate involvement of the three friends in one another's initial fumblings with puberty, and by making gentle fun of their collective hysteria and their numerous embarrassing predicaments, Naylor is able to address "the facts of life" quite frankly within a humorous and entertaining package.

Chris Lynch's *Slot Machine* and its sequel, *Extreme Elvin*, offer a male variation on the theme of three young friends approaching the rigors of adolescence together. Elvin Bishop, thirteen-years-old in the first novel, fourteen and entering high school in the sequel, believes that there's something just right about having exactly two great friends, and both novels begin with Elvin's ruminations on his relationships with this special pair. The bond between these three friends survives enormous stress. Mikie is cool, quiet, and confident. Frankie is a good friend to Elvin and Mikie, but he is overly concerned about his popularity with the "in-crowd," and his concern about social appearances creates a rift between these friends, although their bond and support for one another remains strong.

Elvin is a perceptive and articulate observer, even though his own life experiences are often disastrous. He overreacts to stressful situations and his self esteem suffers because he is overweight, out of shape, and geeky. Parts of *Extreme Elvin* are quite painful to read, despite Lynch's effective use of humor in relating Elvin's follies. It becomes apparent that Elvin's troubles cannot be lightly dismissed as he matures; his obesity and emotional insecurities are issues that will dog him for years to come. Elvin is a witty, entertaining narrator who doesn't hold back in recounting his own awkward and foolish misadventures with rueful humor. In *Slot Machine*, Elvin's letters home from camp are consistently funny, as when he describes his wrestling experiences:

> Remember those carnival people you pointed out never to associate with? Well do you know, they've all turned up in my Sector. Every morning we meet, strip together, pull on tights, then spend the rest of the day rolling around on the floor together.[3]

Throughout *Extreme Elvin*, the protagonist has been suffering from hemorrhoids, and as usual, he resists dealing with the situation forthrightly. The frequent hemorrhoid jokes in this novel, while perhaps a bit tiresome (or too serious to be funny!) for adults, is about right for the novel's natural audience of fourteen-year-old boys. To ease Elvin's suffering, his pal Mikie takes Elvin to the local drugstore. "CVS must have something for, er, people like you."[4] Elvin wanders through the store, pretending not to be looking for hemorrhoid medication. "Let's just look for the Ass aisle," he suggests to Mikie.

"Or you could ask someone."

> I tossed the magazine in disgust. "I will not. Gimme a break here, will you? I'm embarrassed enough that you even know. I'm not asking any stranger for help."
>
> "Then do your funny walk around the store a couple of times and let them figure it out for themselves. They are professionals. They'll get it." (*Extreme Elvin*, 67)

And sure enough, Elvin "must have been doing The Walk," because a bit later:

> A large red-faced obese man in a baseball cap and farmer jeans crept up on me with a sad smile and a familiar ridiculous sidestep.
>
> I was afraid. I stood frozen.
>
> "Aisle one, friend," was all the kind stranger said, before padding away. (67–68)

With directions from the kind stranger, Elvin finally makes it to the section with products displaying the words "'Burning' and 'Itching' written in acid red." Continuing to put off the embarrassing purchase, Elvin loiters in aisle one so long that the store manager finally approaches and asks him if he's looking for condoms. At this, Elvin flees the store. Mikie remarks, "Pretty chicken there, El" (71). Elvin's neuroses have finally led him to the outer boundaries of even Mikie's steadfast friendship and enormous tolerance.

Lynch's Frankie and Mikie fill roles similar to Naylor's Elizabeth and Pam in the Alice series: each set of friends show two distinct alternatives to the path taken by the protagonist. Although Elvin has far more "issues" than Alice, both teens can breathe a sigh of relief that they do not have some of the problems of their more adventurous friends: Frankie's drive to be popular results in a horrific hazing ordeal at summer camp, and Pamela's precocious sexuality puts her at peril with older men, such as her mother's boyfriend in *The Grooming of Alice*. Of course, Elizabeth and Alice are curious as to the exact nature of the boyfriend's advances toward Pamela:

> Elizabeth was still concentrating on Pamela. "You know," she said, "even if you don't want to tell us, Pamela, there *is* a hot-line number you can call."
> "I wasn't molested!" Pamela yelled just as Mrs. Price came in the room with some ice-cream sandwiches.
> She stopped and looked around, and then, when Pamela and I cracked up, she said, "Well, that's good to know, Pamela," and left the three of us howling on the bed. (*Grooming of Alice*, 213)

Unlike Chris Lynch and Phyllis Reynolds Naylor, Ron Koertge presents an entirely new cast of characters in each of his novels for young adults. Sixteen-year-old boys in or just past their junior year of high school are the most frequent subjects of his novels, but Koertge also presents early adolescents (*Mariposa Blues*) and eighteen-year-olds finishing high school and about to depart for college (*Boy in the Moon* and *Stoner and Spaz*). One of the funniest friendships in a Koertge novel is that between white Jesse and his black friend Kyle, in *Tiger, Tiger Burning Bright*. The pair are inseparable. Another boy comments, "These two . . . are like married; I never see one without the other."[5] Kyle comes out with some great one-liners about his African-American heritage. When asked how his mother intends to punish him for an escapade, Kyle quickly replies, "She says I still have to live with white folks for two weeks" (*Tiger, Tiger, Burning Bright*, 171).

Some of the opposite sex friendships in Koertge's novels develop into romance, but they generally begin as true friendships. Thirteen-year-old longtime friends Leslie and Graham do not form a romantic attachment in *Mariposa Blues*, because while Leslie has recently developed an interest in the opposite sex, Graham still finds racehorses much more interesting than girls.

> "Do you think," Leslie asked, "that you'll ever have a girlfriend?"
> "I guess so, sometime. Why?"
> "Because nothing and nobody makes you as happy as this horse."
> "I'll probably just get me a girlfriend who wears steel shoes."[6]

The triad of old friends in Koertge's *Boy in the Moon* includes protagonist Nick Bishop, extremely self-conscious about his skinny body and severe acne; Kevin Abernathy, who has been living with his mother in California; and their studious friend, Frieda. The three have been inseparable companions for years in their hometown of Bradleyville, Missouri.[7] As they begin their senior year of high school together, their friendship is subjected to enormous pressures. Kevin returns from California with a self-conscious new image as a surfer boy. However, Kevin is attentive enough to his friends to realize that Nick and Frieda are on the edge of greater intimacy, although they haven't realized it yet themselves. When the three friends visit a museum in St. Louis, Kevin helpfully leads Nick and Frieda to a large work of art:

> We took the sculpture in. At first it was just two stone figures. Then it was a soldier facing a woman with perfectly round stone breasts.
> "It's called Warrior and Maiden," Kevin informed us. "Isn't it great?"
> Frieda squinted. "It's beautiful, Kevin. Very well done. The rhythm is wonderful. Just look how all your attention is inevitably drawn to his sword."
> "That's not his sword."
> "Oh, my gosh."[8]

Humor helps the three teens through some enormously stressful situations. Nick makes funny, self-deprecating remarks about his severe acne: "I spent most of my money on quack cures for acne. Bought a real beauty at the Missouri State Fair: clears up your face *and* makes convertible tops look like new" (*Boy in the Moon*, 17).

New Friends, New Places

In addition to several novels in which childhood friendships are strained by the coming of adolescence, Ron Koertge has also written some fine humorous YA novels featuring new friendships. A teenage male protagonist, sometimes a hyper-mature caretaker of a troubled or grieving single parent, and a West Coast–Midwest cultural tension are common ingredients of Koertge's YA novels. And yet, each of the novels is independent and unique. All except *The Harmony Arms* are narrated in the first person.[9]

Sharp, funny dialogue, and encounters between strong, sharply contrasting characters are other typical features of Ron Koertge's novels. *The Arizona Kid*, one of the author's best-known and most highly praised works, packs many of Koertge's favorite ingredients. Sixteen-year-old Billy Kennedy is spending his summer vacation with his father's brother. Uncle Wes owns a gift shop in Tucson and is gay. Koertge's forthright and funny handling of that controversial situation is one of the novel's many virtues. In addition to learning about his uncle's alternative lifestyle and becoming friends with a gay man he comes to admire,[10] Billy is also immersed into the world of cowboys and horse racing; he has his first girlfriend and his first sexual experiences. Koertge's smooth storytelling gives an authentic feel to Billy's whirlwind summer.

Billy is hired to work as a stable hand for a trainer who has brought several racehorses to a Tucson racetrack for the summer. There he is partnered with Lew Coley, a big, strong local boy who seems to have every possible advantage over Billy. Lew is experienced with horses, familiar with the racing scene, and comfortable in his cowboy hat and boots. But Billy handles himself well and the two become friends. Lew also has a high-spirited girlfriend, Abby, who is stimulated by a particular turn of Lew's conversation. After meeting Billy, Abby makes a request of Lew:

> "Tell me something pessimistic," she said cheerfully.
> "Better live for today," Lew warned her, "for tomorrow we may die."
> She stamped her foot and gave a little enthusiastic wiggle. "God I love that!"[11]

Later, while away from the girls for a moment during a double date, Lew asks Billy for help. "Did you get good grades in English?" Billy is puzzled by the question, but answers, "Pretty good. Why?" "I'm out of things to tell Abby. You know how she likes to hear me talk about the bitter end. Can you remember anything I can use?" Billy manages to dredge up a couple of lines:

> "There's always *carpe diem*," I said.
> "What's that mean?"
> "Sieze the day."

"Like, don't wait, do it now?"

"Uh-huh."

He repeated it to himself. "Anything else?"

"How about, 'The grave's a fine and private place,/But none, I think, do there embrace.'"

"Yeah, anything with a grave in it." (*The Arizona Kid*, 62)

Later that evening, when the car has stopped at a suitable spot and Billy and his date have left the car for a walk, Billy hears the results of his tutoring: "Well," said Lew from the front, "if you don't want to seize the day, seize this," and Abby laughed one of her big outdoorsy laughs (64). And a bit later: "'But none, I think,'" said Lew hoarsely, "'do there embrace . . .'" and Abby moaned (66).

On a visit to Lew's home, Billy learns where Lew has gotten his ideas about "the bitter end" that Abby finds so endearing. Crouching like a commando, Lew leads Billy into the ordinary-looking house. After introducing Billy to his joint-smoking mother, Lew suddenly puts his finger to his lips and hides behind a door. A moment later, the screen door bursts open and a man with a machine gun dives through and rolls to his feet.

"Hand over your squirrel meat," he shouted, "and all edible pupa."

I was trying not to wet my pants. "Lew! Jesus Christ, Lew!"

Right on cue he stepped out, karate-chopped the guy, and wrenched the weapon free. "That'll be ten bucks," he said calmly.

The head-shaven, face-painted machine gunner turns out to be Lew's father, an attorney and survivalist. He quizzes the boys on paramilitary and post-nuclear survival techniques and calls to them as they leave, "'Don't ever,' shouted Mr. Coley, so loud that I jumped about a foot, 'just walk through an entrance like that. Throw a bone through first. See if the mutants leap on it'" (44–45). By the end of the summer, the unlikely pair have become fast friends, and Billy has become nearly as comfortable as Lew in cowboy hat and boots as the boys groom the racehorses and bounce around in Lew's jeep together.

The world of avant-garde artistic expression in Southern California is the setting for Koertge's *Confess-O-Rama*. Sixteen-year-old Tony Candelaria is a typical Koertge protagonist. He's bright, but he just wants to be a regular kid, not a member of any special crowd. So it's a complete surprise to Tony when he develops an attachment to Jordan Archer, an outrageously unconventional girl who likes to create public artworks that deliver a social message with strong, if not shocking effect.

When Jordan meets Tony's prim mother, she is wearing "jeans, a T-shirt, and—outside of that, over it—something electric. Something that flashed: green on the left, red on the right." Tony's mother hisses, "Tony, she's wearing an electric bra!" "She is? I didn't notice."[12] Through Jordan, Tony meets a rich variety of Southern California "types." The stiffness of Tony and his mother with new acquaintances and the humorous battering-down of their inhibitions by repeated exposure to freer spirits is a theme Koertge also develops in *The Harmony Arms* and *Stoner and Spaz*.

Ron Koertge's use of humor goes far beyond mere entertainment. His characters often begin with a lack of self-confidence, making nervous jokes about their perceived imperfections. As they mature and socialize successfully, they learn to laugh more naturally and not take themselves too seriously. Friends can usually distinguish anxious self-mockery from healthy, occasionally self-deprecating humor. The growth of characters in Koertge's novels can be measured by the increased warmth and inclusiveness of their humorous banter.

Many other authors have written quality YA literature featuring humorous encounters with new friends, often in a school setting. The British school novel has a long and great tradition, stretching back to Victorian novels such as Dickens's *Nicholas Nickleby* and Thomas Hughes's beloved series, *Tom Brown's School Days*.[13] The tradition continues with J. K. Rowling's Harry Potter novels, which both partake of and poke gentle fun at the tradition; and Diana Wynne Jones's brilliant *Year of the Griffin*, which, for some readers, leaves Harry Potter as flat in the dust as George MacDonald Fraser's roguish antihero Flashman did Tom Brown.[14]

Year of the Griffin spoofs the fantasy genre, the nostalgic public school tradition, and also the recent wave of school for wizards novels, which J. K. Rowling and other authors developed by combining fantasy with boarding school traditions. Jones's Magic School of Derkholm is a superb meeting place for new friends. The first-year students include

Elda, a huge Griffin with an exuberant personality; Felim ben Felim, brother of a paranoid Emir who regards absence from the court as conspiracy; Claudia, niece of the Emperor; Ruskin, a Marxist dwarf; Lukin, a crown prince who prefers magic to majesty; and Olga, beautiful daughter of a notorious pirate.

Everything in the story is comically exaggerated. Several of the students have run away from home and would be in grave danger if discovered. Naturally, in the manner of educational academies on any planet, the school soon mails donation requests to all of the parents and guardians, thus alerting the various emirs, dwarf lords, royal parents, and pirates to the whereabouts of the runaways. The students bond together against adversity and manage to foil assassins, dwarf warriors, and pirates with half-learned magic spells. Most of the school's professors are incompetent, so the students have for the most part taught themselves, with comically unpredictable results. All of the clichés of boarding school life are here: mind-numbing lectures, horrible food, midnight escapades—all humorously presented and so wonderfully mixed with fantasy that the novel is at once both a satire and a celebration of the school novel genre.

An equally humorous, but more earthbound boarding school is the setting of Ellen Conford's *Dear Mom, Get Me Out of Here!* Thirteen-year-old Paul Tanner has been dropped off at Burnside Academy by his parents, who are too rushed to notice that the school is very run down. Paul's famous Uncle Jack proudly attended the academy many years ago, but like the Magic School in *Year of the Griffin*, Burnside School is now underfunded and decrepit. The students with whom Paul will be spending the school year are not as fantastic as Diana Wynne Jones's pirates and griffins, nor so strange as the psychic boys sent to the remedial school of David Lubar's *Hidden Talents*. But they are a pretty hilarious bunch. The first classmate Paul meets is a fellow who is trying to fly off the roof of the Academy. After crashing to the ground and barely missing Paul, the young aviator politely introduces himself as Orson Autrey. Paul wonders:

> What do you say to someone who's jumped off a roof wearing a nylon body suit, aviator goggles, and bat wings? Did you have a good flight? Are you acquainted with any other superheroes? or, Exactly how many controlled substances do you abuse?[15]

Naturally, Orson is to be Paul's roommate, and after a moment's reflection Paul decides that he might not be such a bad one. Orson is probably crazy, but his flying experiments might get him killed or kicked out of school, in which case Paul could have a private room. Given Burnside's financial straits, the food is even less appetizing than might be expected of institutional fare. The cafeteria provides plenty of opportunities for jokes, if not for nourishment. On his first evening, Paul declines a social invitation. "I'll just go back to the room and—" "And what?" Orson said. "You don't have to do anything till dinner, and after that you'll be too busy throwing up to meet anybody" (*Dear Mom*, 19). Despite everything, Paul ultimately decides he prefers to finish the school year at Burnside rather than join his parents in Europe. "And if he didn't stay at Burnside, where would he go? To a school in Switzerland? He couldn't speak Swiss" (35).

For a realistic meeting-new-friends-at-school novel for older teens, Catherine Clark's *Wurst Case Scenario* is hard to beat. In this sequel to *Truth or Dairy*, Courtney, a hip, vegetarian, animal rights activist from Colorado, has landed at a small rural Wisconsin college where meat and dairy products are practically sacred. Moreover, her roommate, Mary Jo Johannsen, is a classic large-boned Wisconsin farm girl who rises before dawn, loves bratwurst and cheese, and is completely innocent of the counterculture.

Initially, Courtney feels much more comfortable with Thyme, a girl who rooms down the hall. Thyme doesn't shave her legs or underarms and professes fervent left-wing values. When Courtney tells her about her new job at a coffee and bagel place, Thyme replies, "'Have you checked into their investments?' she asked. 'I think they get their flour from some country that's on an Amnesty International watch list. And aren't they owned by some major oil corporation?'" Courtney tries to mollify her with a food offering. "'I get free bagels, so you know, if you ever want some, just come by during my shift,' I offered. 'I can't. Bagels plague my harmonic system,' she said."[16]

Despite Thyme's excesses, Courtney feels much more comfortable with her than with her own roommate. Coincidentally, Thyme's roommate, Kirsten, gets along quite well with Mary Jo, and it strikes Courtney that she should simply swap places with Kirsten. But when Courtney and Thyme go to the residential office, they are told that "part of college was learning people skills and how to get along with others who were different." Disappointed, the pair depart the housing office:

> So we walk out to the front desk, and who's standing there, waiting to talk to the same counselors? MARY JO AND KIRSTEN!! How rude. I mean, it's one thing for me and Thyme to want to switch. We have *reasons*. (58)

Whether they concern ordinary public schools or private boarding schools, humorous stories about young adults at school tend to feature certain stock characters. There are eccentric fellow-students, like nearly all of those in Lubar's *Hidden Talents*, Conford's *Dear Mom*, and Jones's *Year of the Griffin*. And, of course, crazy and/or appallingly bad teachers and school administrators, character types who appear with such regularity that it is difficult to name a funny school novel that lacks them.

Other recurring themes include inedible cafeteria food, stupid rules begging to be broken, and anxieties over class projects, homework assignments, and exams. The boarding school setting permits additional hijinks, including nighttime adventures and the thrill of being completely away from one's parents. And, even at all-boy and all-girl schools, those thrilling encounters with the opposite sex.

Opposite-Sex Friendships

True friendships between male and female adolescents are noteworthy because they defy the stereotype of hormonally charged teenagers being so single-minded that casual, nonsexual friendships between teenage boys and girls are impossible. When such friendships do exist, they are often fragile because external forces tend to put pressure on the relationship. Same-sex friends of either party may not be at ease with the relationship, either because they don't like the opposite-sex friend, or because they may like him or her too much!

Catherine Clark's three YA novels, *Truth or Dairy*, *Wurst Case Scenario*, and *Frozen Rodeo* each include humorous and realistic situations in which relationships between the protagonist and the young men in her life bewilderingly pass through stages of friendship, romance, and betrayal. In *Truth or Dairy*, a longtime friendship between Courtney's younger brother and her best friend unexpectedly turns to romance. In the second novel, Courtney and her boyfriend, Grant, are trying to maintain a long-distance relationship while Courtney has gone off to college. While planning to confront Grant about a report he had been seen kissing another girl at a party back home, Courtney finds herself kissing a boy she had previously considered strictly a friend. Walter Wittenauer happens to also be Corny, the school mascot who dresses as a giant corn stalk on ceremonial occasions. Later, Courtney reflects, "I kissed a school mascot. *Voluntarily*. I really need to get out of here" (*Wurst Case Scenario*, 257).

Unlike the chance encounters by which one meets coworkers and schoolmates, Randy Powell's *Three Clams and an Oyster* presents a very deliberate selection of an opposite-sex comrade. Narrator Flint McCallister, along with two other high school juniors, need a fourth player for the flag football team they take very seriously. After trying out several guys without success, they finally decide to give a girl a chance. Rachel Summerfield is a fine athlete, and also rather attractive, which the boys recognize as a possible problem. However, the season is about to start and they're running out of options. They agree to rendezvous with Rachel before one of her rugby games. Everything seems to be going well, when Flint suddenly notices that his teammates are unnaturally quiet. Finally realizing that they're freaked out by Rachel's hairy legs, Flint tries to move things along.

> It's absurd to be grossed out by one little . . .
> I clear my throat and clap my hands twice. "Okay, let's get started. Why don't we do some shaving."
> They all look at me.
> "Stretching," I say. "Let's do some stretching."
> Beaterson coughs and looks off to the side. Deshutsis watches a bird.[17]

Rachel is a terrific football player and the tryout goes well. Flint wonders to himself, "How do you ask someone you don't know very well, 'What's with the legs?' It really shouldn't matter" (*Three Clams*, 103). Despite some misgivings, the guys do invite Rachel to join and she becomes a great addition to the team. In the final chapter we find the four of them together in Rachel's car on a long drive to a tournament, having easily won all of their games to date. Some of Rachel's road trip behaviors are a bit of an adjustment for the boys.

> She changes lanes a lot for no reason. She listens to smooth jazz, screeching saxophones, when it's her turn to put in a tape. She has a tendency to run stop signs. She doesn't like to eat while she drives, so whenever we stop for cheeseburgers, we have to sit in her car in the parking lot until she finishes her meal. (211)

At the moment, she's indulging one of her most annoying habits, giving the blow-by-blow details of an obscure movie. Finally, one of the guys reminds her, "No summaries of movie plots."

> "I know, I know," she says. "But this was a great movie. It was Japanese with English subtitles, and it was the scariest movie I've seen since The Exorcist."
> She proceeds to tell us, in shot-by-shot detail, the entire plot of the movie. . . . We want to tell her to stop, but we don't. We have a long drive ahead of us. And we like the sound of her voice.
> Still, enough is enough. I wait for a pause in her narrative, and then I jump in, take the plunge.
> "So, Rachel," I say.
> "Yeah?"
> "What's with the legs?" (216)

Randy Powell specializes in this kind of humorous situation, which derives authenticity from being so peculiar that it's hard to imagine it being a fictional invention.

Friendship between an undersized boy and a brawny girl is a frequent comedy situation, especially in fiction about younger teens. In Richard Peck's great short story, "Priscilla and the Wimps," Monk Klutter fails to appreciate the capabilities of his puny, intended victim's big friend. The formidable Beatrice Leep of Carl Hiaasen's *Hoot*, had little trouble disposing of feared bully Dana Matherson, once she had an investment in the continued survival of Dana's victim, Roy Eberhardt. A number of other YA novels have developed this situation. The setting is usually middle school and the protagonist a lightweight young man. He comes into contact with an imposing female classmate and they don't hit it off at first. Like everyone else, he's initially put off by her intimidating, unfeminine manner. But if she happens to rescue his scrawny body from a bully, he may be grateful enough to take the trouble to see past her tough exterior and sometimes to find a friend.

John, the fourteen-year-old narrator of David Klass's *You Don't Know Me* has a poor impression of strapping classmate Violet Hayes. He thinks of her as "Violent Hayes," and during band practice he imagines her to be playing her saxophone with violence.

> Violent Hayes attempts to play the opening interlude, but the monitor lizard that is pretending to be her saxophone has other ideas. It frees itself from her Mongolian death lock with a swipe of its claws, opens its razor-toothed jaws, and lets loose with a reptilian shriek that I believe has not been heard on this earth since the Jurassic era.[18]

But when John gets to know Violet, he finds her to be a warm, genuine person and a good friend. She talks John into escorting her to a dance, and all goes well until he accidentally bumps into football player Chuck Broadbridge, the dance partner of Gloria, a scheming, manipulative girl who wishes John harm. True to form, Gloria urges her musclebound companion to "teach a lesson" to John and, hormones surging, the big oaf grabs John and begins threatening him.

> But before Chuck Broadbridge can say anything else, I hear a loud KEE-WAK sound, unlike anything I have ever heard before, especially during a Holiday Dance. It sounds like the earsplitting crack of a bamboo trunk snapping in half before hurricane winds. Chuck Broadbridge lets out a scream and begins hopping on one leg. Upon reflection, I believe the sound had nothing to do with splintering bamboo, but was actually generated by the impact of Violent Hayes's high-heeled right foot connecting with Chuck Broadbridge's left shin.
> "She kicked me!" he gasps. "I can't believe it. She kicked me. She could have ended my football career!" (*You Don't Know Me*, 314)

You Don't Know Me ends with a public performance of the composition that inspired John's earlier fantasy of "Violent Hayes" wrestling with her reptilian instrument. This time Violet plays her part well.

Violent Hayes nails the opening saxophone interlude. She is looking particularly fetching tonight in a long blue dress, with a red ribbon in her hair, and I suppose the monitor lizard that pretends to be her saxophone is as charmed as I am. (340)

John may still see the saxophone as a monitor lizard, but he now sees Violet Hayes herself quite differently.

The physical defense of a male by a female is intrinsically funny in its overturn of the stereotypical expectation of male strength and feminine dependency. Usually in these plots the girl is a strapping Amazon, but another humorous variation is the small woman who protects her man, either with a fearless personality, or by physical prowess in a petite package, as with diminutive kickboxing champion Stephanie of Perry Nodelman's *Behaving Bradley*.

The hero of Daniel Pinkwater's *The Education of Robert Nifkin* makes his first high school friend in the person of a tough female classmate. Not wanting to formalize his low social status by hanging out with the other rejects, Robert avoids the school cafeteria and hikes over to his favorite lunch destination, a horrible greasy diner called Mel's. Robert is surprised to see a teenage girl at the counter.

About two stools down from me, at the end of the counter, sat a female. This was unusual. Girls and women don't patronize Mel's much. It's mostly men in steel-toed work shoes. I suppose women don't like the smell of hamburger grease in their hair . . . She was nibbling at a triple-double with cheese. . . . Even I am afraid of a triple. Only polar bears and arctic wolves can digest them. . . . I noticed that her nail polish was chipped, and she had Band-Aids on three knuckles of one hand and two knuckles of the other.

She noticed me at the same time I noticed her. She looked at the Band-Aids.

"I was punching out a girl at Pop's earlier," she said. "The bitch was making moves on my boyfriend, Kenny Papescu."[19]

The girl introduces herself as Linda Pudovkin. She and her boyfriend, Kenny, soon become Robert's best friends, drawn together by their stubborn independence and refusal to superficially label people based on their popularity or their looks.

Other humorous YA novels in which a friend of the opposite sex rescues a character from a bad situation include Joyce Carol Oates's *Big Mouth and Ugly Girl*, in which Ursula Riggs is the only one to defend Matt Donaghy from the accusation that he had seriously threatened to blow up the high school; and E. M. Goldman's *Getting Lincoln's Goat*, in which classmates of both sexes retrieve their reckless friend, Francie, just before she is about to run off with a married man. When informed by her friends that Francie is well under the age of consent, her seducer is as relieved as anyone that his plans had been thwarted. Tim Wynne-Jones's short story, "Ick," describes an imaginative ploy undertaken by an entire class of middle school boys and girls to protect a classmate from the inappropriate attentions of a handsome young male teacher.[20]

One of the best stories of rescue by an opposite-sex teen is Todd Strasser's *A Very Touchy Subject*. The novel centers upon the successful effort by sixteen-year-old Scott Tauscher to do the right thing by his sexy fifteen-year-old neighbor, Paula Finkel, who needs the help of a friend much more than she needs another boyfriend. The novel has a sensational opening, simultaneously funny and disturbing. Scott is sitting with his family at the breakfast table in his family's suburban Long Island home:

> While my parents and sister eat their eggs and toast and generally act oblivious of the world, I sit and stare across the yard at Paula Finkel's bedroom window . . . just about every morning at 8:15 a guy crawls out of Paula Finkel's bedroom window . . . lights a cigarette, and takes a leisurely stroll across our backyard, cuts through the bushes, and disappears.
>
> One other thing: Paula Finkel is fifteen years old . . .
>
> Anyway, you might think that someone else at the kitchen table would notice that I seem to gag on my waffles each morning when this guy shinnies out of Paula's window. But forget it. You could probably drive an eighteen-wheeler right through the living room at breakfast time and no one in my family would even blink.
>
> So I've made a decision. This morning I'm going to alert them just as soon as Romeo next door starts his escape routine. It should be a kick to see how they react.[21]

After being alerted to the spectacle, Scott's dad initially does not catch on to what is happening. When he eventually "gets it," he begins to reach for the telephone to call the police, but Scott explains, "Dad, that guy's been doing that every morning for the last week and a half." Finally realizing that the crime involved is not burglary, Mr. Tauscher gazes at his teenaged daughter Kerry and says, "But Paula's just a little girl. She's your age" (*A Very Touchy Subject*, 8). When it is then explained to the appalled parent that it is not unheard of for fifteen-year-old girls to be sexually active, he immediately proposes sending Kerry to private school. Finally, when Mr. Tauscher gets past that idea ("probably when he remembers what private school costs," Scott cynically thinks) he then considers informing Paula's mother. But it turns out that Paula's divorced mother is a negligent and abusive parent and will be no help at all.

Scott is later obliged to drive Paula to her father's home in Raleigh, North Carolina. Scott's ancient station wagon overheats and dies, and the two teens spend the night together by the roadside. They talk late into the night and find that they have become good friends. Of course, the "guys back home" have their own ideas about what happened:

> Albert slaps me on the back. "Didn't know you had it in you, man."
> "Had what in me?" I ask.
> Albert looks a little surprised. "Well, uh, running away with Paula Finkel. Everybody knows." (178)

Scott tries to explain to his buddies that he was just helping a friend, but his sex-obsessed coworkers refuse to believe this tame story of his adventure with the infamous Paula Finkel.

Genuine friendships across gender lines are precious because they can be so loaded with the possibilities for romantic or sexual involvement, especially between young adults. Although such friendships are often harder to establish, they are all the more rewarding when they are maintained.

Hard Friendships, Exasperating Friends

Friendships are an essential part of life, especially during the formative years, but, like family relationships, they can be difficult and frustrating. Some friendships are harmful or dangerous. Anne Fine's *The Tulip*

Touch is narrated by a well-to-do English girl, Natalie Barnes, who becomes fascinated by a mysterious and emotionally scarred waif. Tulip Pierce lives in a bleak, dirt-poor rural home with her abusive father and a hopelessly depressed mother. Tulip acts out by taking sadistic pleasure in damaging property and playing destructive games with the people of their village. Natalie knows that this behavior is wrong, but Tulip has such a wild, powerful magnetism that Natalie is drawn into her chaotic and destructive life. At first, Tulip's unpleasant little games are funny, as their names suggest: "stinking mackerel" (pretending that someone has a bad odor), "havoc" (small practical jokes), "little visits" (spontaneous visits to stranger's homes), and finally, "wild nights" (arson.)

The novel takes its name from a comment by Natalie's father, who observes that Tulip's outrageous lies often include an imaginative element that make them almost plausible.

> "So I wasn't at school because the police needed one extra person my age and size, for a line-up. They wouldn't say why they'd arrested the girl, but one of them did tell me that he thought she was Polish."
>
> "Ah!" Dad would murmur in unfeigned admiration. "Polish? The perfect Tulip touch!"[22]

The pair become constant companions, and yet neither girl plays a constructive role in the other's life. Tulip plays on Natalie's weaknesses and exploits her. Tulip's destructive impulses grow until she eventually burns down the hotel in which Natalie's family and a large number of guests are staying. She's more a bad habit, a nemesis, than a true friend. The relationship is perverse and clearly harmful to Natalie, and much of story centers on Natalie's struggle to break free of the hold Tulip maintains on her. As Natalie explains, "I needed Tulip. While I trailed around quietly, doing what I was told and being no trouble, Tulip lived my secret life" (*The Tulip Touch*, 81).

Few of the friendships in YA literature approach the destructiveness of that presented in *The Tulip Touch*. Jack Gantos's *What Would Joey Do?* presents a difficult relationship between young preadolescents that ends more happily. In this third of Jack Gantos's trilogy of books about Joey Pigza, a boy with attention-deficit/hyperactivity disorder (ADHD), Joey's condition has improved and his mother agrees to help out Mrs. Lapp, an old friend with a blind daughter, Olivia, by sending Joey to be homeschooled at the Lapp's house.

Joey soon discovers that this will not be a pleasant assignment, finding that he is only the latest in a string of homeschool companions victimized by Olivia's persistent abuse. "Olivia liked to call herself 'blind as a brat!' because she couldn't see to do anything nice. Still, she had twenty-twenty vision for getting me in trouble."[23] Olivia's antics include microwaving Joey's new wristwatch and scribbling Joey's name all over the bathroom walls with a marker. Mrs. Lapp realizes that her daughter is responsible for most of the havoc, but she remains determined to continue homeschooling her daughter.

Olivia begins to have fun with Joey, despite herself. She loves to get out of the house and has little trouble persuading her overprotective mother to let her go off with Joey. "I'll set off a bomb," she tells Joey, and deliberately drops a big glass pickle jar on the kitchen floor. As Olivia expected, Mrs. Lapp's only response is to roll her eyes, sigh, and tells them to take a stroll while she cleans up the devastation (96). Outdoors with Joey, Olivia throws her cane aside and runs recklessly down the street. "'Help!' she hollered. 'A maniac is trying to murder me!' 'That's not true!' I yelled as I passed a woman who was raking leaves. 'I'm a very nice boy!'" When Joey finally catches up to the blind girl, where she has tripped over a fire hydrant and bruised her legs for the umpteenth time, Olivia is laughing and triumphant. "'That was the best thing I've ever done,' she said, wiping dirt from her face. 'Your mom is going to kill me when she sees this bruise,' Joey tells her. Olivia smiles. 'Exactly.'" (103).

Ultimately, Olivia comes to care enough about Joey to explain to him that her bad behavior has nothing to do with him: it's all a calculated plan to get her mother to give up on homeschooling and allow Olivia to attend a school for the blind where she'll feel more comfortable. Joey refuses to participate directly in her sabotage, yet they become true friends.

Jack Gantos gives us a character who has his own set of problems and puts him under even greater stress by pairing him with another kid with her own special "issues," who exploits Joey's weaknesses for her own advantage. This tension permeates the entire story, creating a feeling of being on a high wire. But in the end it becomes apparent that underneath Joey's excitable impulses and Olivia's nastiness there are two very nice kids, and this provides the basis for a humorous and engaging story.

Terry Spencer Hesser's *Kissing Doorknobs* presents another early adolescent plagued by a behavioral condition, in this case obsessive-compulsive disorder (OCD.) In this story, the protagonist herself is the exasperating friend. One symptom of Tara's OCD is a compulsive urge to count, resulting in her need to step over every crack and count each seam in the sidewalk when she walks to and from school. Unfortunately, this prevents her from walking with her longtime friends Keesha, Kristin, and Anna, and this weirdness causes her to lose her friends and become isolated. Months later, after Tara has been helped by a therapist experienced with OCD, Tara is delighted to find that her friends are still there for her when she's ready to try walking with them again.

> "I—I think I can walk with you guys again. I think. I'm not sure. B-But I want to try," I stammered. "Will you let me try?"
>
> Keesha and Anna both smiled so big that I could practically see myself in their braces.
>
> I stepped on every crack I could find. I felt nervous, dizzy, sick, but I did it while Anna and Keesha cheered for me.

Encouraged by this success, Tara decides to confront one of her most secret and humiliating rituals, the one from which the book's title, *Kissing Doorknobs*, derives. Facing down a row of doorknobs in a hardware shop, "'I felt nothing, and jumped for joy.' 'Something tells me this is one ritual I don't want to know about,' said Anna."[24]

Rigid, inflexible behavior is one of the great subjects for comedy. Characters who are inattentive to their social surroundings, who are oblivious to their environment and circumstances, are likely to become the subjects of mockery.[25] The humorous side of Joey Pigza's or Tara Sullivan's dilemma is of the same order. With our contemporary knowledge of psychology and our genius for labeling, we have developed clinical definitions of conditions such as ADHD and OCD. Yet, although Tara's behavior is technically pathological, it really differs only in degree, not in kind, from extreme or inappropriate behaviors we see exhibited every day by acquaintances whom we consider merely eccentric.

In *Hidden Talents*, author David Lubar takes the premise of a group of neurotic adolescent characters in a speculative direction. The story is set in a reform school filled with teenage boys who exhibit a colorful array of psychiatric symptoms: pyromania, kleptomania, habitual lying, ADHD, OCD, and numerous other antisocial behaviors. Protagonist Martin Anderson begins to suspect that the problematic behaviors of many of his classmates at Edgeview Alternative School may be due to paranormal abilities. However, Martin has a difficult time trying to convince his "messed up" new friends that he is on to something. Lubar's clever novel offers an intriguing explanation for apparent psychiatric disorders, laced with a good deal of humor as his "bad boys" cause fires to start, sharp objects to fly about, and other odd occurrences.

Gordon Korman, a prolific author of novels for middle grade readers and young adults, uses the theme of exasperating friendships so regularly in his works that it has become his trademark. Korman's stories usually feature an ordinary teenage boy who soon finds himself stuck with an eccentric friend or two. The particular qualities that make these friends difficult vary: some are overly competitive, some arouse envy because of their undeserved success, while others are annoying because they are chronic screw-ups. The eccentric friend is usually addicted to some sort of compulsive behavior.

Korman's protagonists are invariably pleasant, good-natured, and quintessentially normal young fellows, but they sometimes have unusual problems. Consider Vince Luca, the narrator of Korman's *Son of the Mob*. In that novel, the central conflict concerns Vince's increasingly desperate efforts to dissociate himself from the family "vending machine" business. The novel also features a quirky, unbalanced friendship in the classic Korman mode. Vince's best friend, Alex Tarkanian, seems to have no hope of success with the opposite sex. But Alex insists upon hearing all the details of Vince's dates so that he can experience them vicariously, perversely knowing that he will be made envious and unhappy by any successes Vince might have. *Son of the Mob* opens with Alex advising Vince how he should dress and comport himself on a date:

"Vince, you're not wearing that?" he says.
"Yeah. Why?"

He slaps his forehead. "It's wool! Scratchy! You're taking her to a horror movie! She's going to be all over you! We need one-hundred-percent cotton, or maybe a nice linen-silk blend."[26]

Alex offers another valuable tip: "Don't order the chili! All of our hard work falls apart if your stomach's gurgling with swamp gas!" (*Son of the Mob*, 3).

Semester in the Life of a Garbage Bag features a terrific oddball friend, perhaps the most notable of this character type in the works of Gordon Korman. Raymond Jardine is an eleventh-grade classmate of narrator Sean Delancey, who is a typically pleasant and ordinary Korman protagonist. Jardine, the "garbage bag" of the title, has a persecution complex and is convinced that he never has any luck. His conversation is filled with such remarks as, "Given half a chance, the heavens will open up and dump crud all over Jardine."[27] "Yesterday everything was okay. Not great, but for Jardine, that's the best that can be expected" (*Semester in the Life of a Garbage Bag*, 41). "That's right. Don't kick Jardine when he's down. Wait till he starts to get up. It's time for another exciting, fun-filled episode of Let's Get Jardine" (196). Raymond's habit of addressing himself in the third person by his surname is so ingrained that even his mother calls him "Jardine," and she refers to herself as "Jardine's mother." Much to his own surprise, Sean gradually warms up to Jardine, and finds himself accompanying his eccentric new friend on a series of adventures.

In Korman's *Son of Interflux*, Simon Irving, sixteen, is the son of the wealthy and powerful head of the corporation Interflux, "the largest manufacturer of useless things in the world." Simon's father wants him to join the family business, but Simon prefers to develop his artistic talents at the nearby Nassau County High School for Visual, Literary and Performing Arts. Several of the other art students are quite eccentric, especially Simon's closest friend Philip Baldwin, who has a knack of showing initial promise (never fulfilled) in everything he tries.

Son of Interflux is filled with oddball characters and exasperating relationships. Another of Simon's closest friends, Sam Stavrinidis, is a highly talented artist who insists upon painting camels into every one of his works, driving his teacher, the renowned artist Querada, to despair. Querada himself is wildly eccentric, roaring insults at his favorite students to encourage them. Simon first notices the charms of Wendy Orr, an attractive fellow art student, while she's assaulting him for his unconventional use of student council funds.

Korman's *Don't Care High* features several odd friendships. Paul Abrams, who has relocated from Saskatchewan to New York City, finds himself enrolled in Don Carey High, named after a former sewer czar who reigned as a municipal public works commissioner. The school is more commonly known as Don't Care High, in recognition of the perennial apathy of its student body. Even the school's administrators sometimes slip and publicly refer to the institution by its unfavorable but catchy nickname.

Paul is initially dismayed by the Don't Care environment, but he's even more unsettled by the agitations of classmate Sheldon Pryor, who is on a self-appointed mission to make the place more lively. Pryor enlists newcomer Paul in his crazy scheme of elevating a shy nonentity, Mike Otis, to cult status in order to rouse the student body. In typical Korman fashion, the scheme is successful beyond Pryor's wildest expectations. Bland, unassuming, inarticulate Mike Otis becomes an unwilling celebrity, and Paul is swept along with each of his buddy Sheldon's increasingly wild schemes.

Jason Cardone, the characteristically ordinary protagonist in Korman's *Losing Joe's Place*, has two good friends, Ferguson Peach and Don Champion. Unfortunately, Jason's two pals do not hit it off when he brings the three of them together for a summer adventure in Toronto. Don's uncle, Harry Robb, has offered them jobs in his plastics factory. While Don and Jason labor over the stamping machines, Ferguson endears himself to the plant engineers with his creative suggestions, some of which result in the elimination of his roommates' jobs.

And so it goes, all through the summer. Intent upon their competition, Ferguson and Don both pursue the same girl, Jessica, each telling Jason that he is after Jessica only to annoy his rival. Jason understands their attraction to Jessica, but he is so accustomed to being an observer (and occasional peacemaker) of his pals' competitive antics that it has never occurred to him to go after Jessica himself. Ironically, when the rivals press Jessica to name a favorite, it turns out that she prefers Jason to either of his battling roommates.

Korman likes to pair up characters who get on each other's nerves, much like Oscar and Felix in *The Odd Couple*. He frequently portrays ironic reversals of fortune, with a seeming loser coming out on top, or a preppie champion coming to grief. Korman is a master of the comic YA novel, and each of his many contributions to the genre are meticulously plotted and filled with laugh-out-loud funny scenes. His protagonists are usually regular guys who become forced into close relationships with eccentric characters. Korman piles up increasingly nutty situations that eventually spin out of control. And these difficulties are caused by friends! Think of how much more difficult (and exasperating) the life of a teenager can be when faced by actual adversaries!

Notes

1. Phyllis Reynolds Naylor, *The Grooming of Alice* (New York: Atheneum, 2000), 6.

2. Phyllis Reynolds Naylor, *Achingly Alice* (New York: Atheneum, 1998), 64.

3. Chris Lynch, *Slot Machine* (New York: HarperCollins, 1995), 79.

4. Chris Lynch, *Extreme Elvin* (New York: HarperCollins, 1999), 68.

5. Ron Koertge, *Tiger, Tiger, Burning Bright* (New York: Orchard, 1994), 46.

6. Ron Koertge, *Mariposa Blues* (New York: Joy Street Books, 1991), 33.

7. Bradleyville, Missouri, is the setting of many of Koertge's novels. Like Richard Peck, another transplanted Midwesterner, Koertge draws inspiration from both his Midwestern origins and from his decades of adult residency in California. Peck's *Bel Air Bambi and the Mall Rats* makes overt use of the contrasts between the glitzy Los Angeles area and the sleepy, rural Midwest. Koertge employs the same concept in *Where the Kissing Never Stops*, and reverses direction in *The Harmony Arms* and *Confess-O-Rama*, in both of which a Midwesterner moves to the LA area. In *Boy in the Moon*, California is a literal as well as a symbolic destination for both Frieda and Kevin as they complete high school in Bradleyville.

8. Ron Koertge, *Boy in the Moon* (Boston: Joy Street Books, 1990), 69.

9. *The Harmony Arms* is narrated in the third person. This novel has much to do with filmmaking, and the narrative viewpoint is like that of a camera shooting from just behind the narrator's shoulder.

10. Chapter 6 includes a discussion of some other humorous YA novels featuring same-sex relationships.

11. Ron Koertge, *The Arizona Kid* (Boston: Joy Street Books, 1988), 36.

12. Ron Koertge, *Confess-O-Rama* (New York: Orchard Books, 1996), 67.

13. Thomas Hughes, *Tom Brown's School Days* (Cambridge: Macmillan, 1857).

14. George MacDonald Fraser has authored eleven Flashman novels, beginning with *Flashman: From the Flashman Papers, 1839–1842* (New York: Knopf, 1970).

15. Ellen Conford, *Dear Mom, Get Me Out of Here!* (Boston: Little, Brown, 1992), 7.

16. Catherine Clark, *Wurst Case Scenario* (New York: HarperCollins, 2001), 48.

17. Randy Powell, *Three Clams and an Oyster* (New York: Farrar, Straus & Giroux, 2002), 101.

18. David Klass, *You Don't Know Me* (New York: Frances Foster Books, 2001), 112–13.

19. Daniel Pinkwater, *The Education of Robert Nifkin* (New York: Farrar, Straus & Giroux, 1998), 35–36.

20. Tim Wynne-Jones, "Ick" in *Lord of the Fries and Other Stories* (New York: DK, 1999).

21. Todd Strasser, *A Very Touchy Subject* (New York: Delacorte, 1985), 4.

22. Anne Fine, *The Tulip Touch* (Boston: Little, Brown, 1997), 22.

23. Jack Gantos, *What Would Joey Do?* (New York: Farrar, Straus & Giroux, 2002), 45.

24. Terry Spencer Hesser, *Kissing Doorknobs* (New York: Delacorte, 1998), 135.

25. Henri Bergson, *Laughter: An Essay on the Meaning of the Comic* (Saint Paul, Minn.: Green Integer, 1999), 122.

26. Gordon Korman, *Son of the Mob* (New York: Hyperion, 2002), 2.

27. Gordon Korman, *A Semester in the Life of a Garbage Bag* (New York: Scholastic, 1987), 3.

CHAPTER THREE

~

Bullies

Encounters with bullies are an inevitable, perhaps even an essential part of the experience of growing up. While aggressive competition and selfish behavior are prevalent in the adult world as well, bullying behavior is often more subtle in the offices and boardrooms of adult competition than in the school hallways, playgrounds, and neighborhoods where young people congregate. Adults have access to a wider range of techniques for attempting to dominate others.

Fictional treatment of the overbearing grown-up is often ironic and indirect. Bullying between kids is usually more "in your face," and fiction that centers on this type of behavior is often a good platform for straightforward comedy. The classic bully in YA literature is a boy who is bigger, more aggressive, and often less intelligent than his peers, while the classic victim is scrawny, bookish, and without effective protection from parents or friends. Interesting variations on this stereotype include untypical bullies, victims with unexpected resources, surprising protectors, and characters who are transformed, and perhaps change roles, during a story.

Bully Boys

The comical put-down of a detested adolescent bully is a scenario that lends itself particularly well to the short story. That format provides just the right setting for the introduction of a few characters, and resolution of a single conflict. Many first-rate YA short stories are built around this theme, and Chris Crutcher's brilliant story "A Brief Moment in the Life of Angus Bethune" is a fine example. Angus is not good-looking and he's extremely large, which serves him well on the football field, but causes him grief in most other settings. He's also sensitive about his first name, as he complains to his mother, "You guys named me after a cow."[1] As if that weren't enough, following their divorce each of his unconventional parents has openly taken up with a same-sex partner.

The story centers around the Winter Ball at Lake Michigan High School, where the beautiful Melissa Lefevre is the Winter Ball Queen. Angus has had a crush on Melissa for years, knowing she was far beyond his reach. As a joke, Angus has been elected Winter Ball King. He doesn't know who the culprit is, but someone must have bought a lot of votes to pull it off. With his family's help, Angus determines to make the best of it, enjoy his brief moments alone with Melissa, and to disappoint anyone who thought he would make a fool of himself on the dance floor.

Angus soon discovers that Melissa's wealthy, handsome, but mean-spirited boyfriend, Rick Sanford, had rigged the election. The inebriated Rick mocks the couple before they step into the spotlight for the opening dance. At first Angus and Melissa try to ignore him, but when Rick slanders Angus' parents, implying that he is an AIDS risk to Melissa, Angus throws him to the floor to shut him up. "He's rich and he's rude," Melissa tells Angus. "I'm embarrassed I'm with him . . . It was supposed to be a lesson for me" ("Angus Bethune," 66–67). Unbelievably, beautiful, slender Melissa and big, ugly Angus begin to connect. As she guides him through a slow dance, Melissa confesses to Angus that she's bulemic, and asks if he knows what that is.

> I smile. "I'm a fat kid with faggot parents who's been in therapy on and off for eighteen years," I say. "Yes, I know what that is. It means when you eat too much, you chuck it up so you don't turn out to look like me." (68)

They continue to laugh and talk with genuine affection. Melissa asks Angus to take her home after the dance, but first she guides him through a fast dance, at the end of which she makes clear to Angus and everyone in the hall that she has no worries about the AIDS innuendos Rick had raised. As Angus helps Melissa with her coat and the couple prepares to leave, Rick Sanford confronts them again, screaming with impotent rage. Angus, in his state of euphoria, casually stops the hateful, sodden Rick with a few well-chosen words.

Melissa, the beauty queen, and big, awkward Angus find that, surprisingly, they have a great deal in common. Melissa, too, has problems with her appearance and self-image, since her slender figure has been achieved at the cost of bulimia. Angus's decency and inner solidity—qualities he's picked up from his worthy albeit unconventional parents—make him an appealing character, and when the Prom Queen recognizes his quality, we cheer for this likeable underdog.

Bruce Coville's "Am I Blue?" is another classic YA short story featuring a homophobic bully. Butch Carrigan pummels sixteen-year-old classmate Vincent. "You little fruit," he snarled. "I'll teach you to look at me!"[2] Lying facedown in a puddle, Vincent is helped up by Melvin, an attractive, obviously gay man of about thirty who claims to be Vincent's "fairy godfather."

Vincent learns that now-incorporeal Melvin had met his Maker after being dragged into an alley by strangers and beaten to death because he was gay. Melvin also tells Vincent about "blue day," a fantasy in which every gay person would appear blue for a day. Vincent is given the gift of "gaydar" for a short time, allowing him alone to see homosexuals as blue, and he is surprised at the revelations. Many people, including Vincent himself, are seen to have just a slight tinge of blue. Having been granted three wishes, Vincent then decides to use his first wish to make blue day actually happen "coast to coast" for twenty-four hours, with everyone able to see the blue. The results are spectacular.

All of this has taken place during a weekend, and Vincent has more or less forgotten about his tormentor, Butch Corrigan. As Blue Day is coming to a close and he prepares to return to school, Vincent suddenly knows what he wants for his next wish: to turn Butch Carrigan blue. Fairy godfather Melvin cheerfully agrees to carry out this wish, and shortly returns "grinning like a cat. 'You've still got one wish left, kiddo,' he said with a chuckle. 'Butch Corrigan was already blue as a summer sky when I got there'" ("Am I Blue," 126).

The range and variety of good, humorous, young adult short stories concerning bullies may become evident if we jump from these rough stories about gay-bashing bullies to the gentler short fiction of Canadian author Tim Wynne-Jones. Wynne-Jones is a master of short stories about middle school boys and girls on the brink of puberty and young adulthood. His young characters find magical possibilities within everyday environments, and bullies, like other problems, become manageable when incorporated into the rich perspective that Wynne-Jones brings to his stories.

"Tashkent" is the story of Fletcher, a twelve-year-old boy who has recently returned to school after missing two years because of a serious illness. One day, he pastes the names of many exotic cities on his chest and stomach—Zagreb, Ibadan, Rangoon—and tells his parents that he expects to lose them over the next few days. "The last place left is the first place I'm going to travel when I'm old enough."[3] When questioned by his mother about the areas of his anatomy to which the stickers are applied, Fletcher seriously explains that he hasn't put any in certain places because "that wouldn't be fair."

> "I mean, if I put—let's say—Bilbao on my heel, it would come off the first time I pulled on my sock, right." His mother and father nodded.
> "And if I put Uppsala on my bum—
> "We get the idea," said Mom.
> "Yes," said Dad. "Now it all makes perfect sense."
> Fletcher smiled. He had a winning smile. ("Tashkent," 44)

Fletcher's winning smile soon gets him in trouble. Due to his lengthy illness, Fletcher is the smallest member of his class, about half the size of a large bully named Ted Sawchuk. After his lengthy ordeal, Fletcher can't help smiling at everyone with whom he makes eye contact. In Ted's primitive brain, another male who smiles at their classmate Vivian Weir, whom Ted considers to be "his girl," is cruising for trouble. Of course, Fletcher smiles at Vivian every time he sees her, and worse, from Ted's perspective, Vivian often smiles back.

A few days after Fletcher's return, when only a couple of stickers remain, Ted finally loses his patience and knocks Fletcher down during recess. All their classmates gather around, appalled at this rough treatment of a small, frail boy who had so recently nearly died. As Fletcher struggles to his feet, his friend Shlomo finds a tiny strip of paper on the ground. "Dar-something. . . . Dar es-something. . . . Dar es Salaam," said Fletcher. "Founded by the sultan of Zanzibar in 1866."

Then, with everyone looking really confused and kind of left out and Shlomo whooping with laughter, Fletcher pulled up his sweater to reveal the last place in the world left sticking to him. . . . It was right next to his scar . . .
"What is this garbage?" said Ted. Reaching down, he ripped the last piece of paper off Fletcher's body. "Tashkent," he read. "Who's that, Clark's brother?"
Some people laughed. The crowd kind of eased up.

His anger dissipated by the incongruity of the situation, Ted hands the Tashkent slip back to Fletcher and notices that Fletcher's hand is bleeding. "'You gonna die on us again?' he asked. 'Nope,' said Fletcher. 'I'm just going to travel far, far away'" ("Tashkent," 54).

Some authors of funny stories for an adolescent audience compile a set of linked stories concerning the same characters and locale. This episodic technique can provide the overall impact of a novel, while also allowing an author to take advantage of the special strengths of the short story format within each vignette. Bruce Brooks's *Dolores: Seven Stories about Her* builds up a character portrait of a fiercely independent girl, from age seven to age sixteen. One of the stories, "Do They Mean It?" shows Dolores using her superior wit to outsmart a group of bullying girls who invent malicious gossip about classmates.

Gary Paulsen's *The Schernoff Discoveries* consists of seven linked stories concerning the narrator's junior high school friendship with his geeky, overly intellectual friend Harold Schernoff. Two of the best stories in the compilation involve bullies.

The second episode of *The Schernoff Discoveries*, "Brain over Brawn," describes Harold's typically unorthodox solutions to some common challenges faced by young men. "I know how we can meet girls," he suddenly announces.

"Meeting them isn't the hard part," I said. "It's keeping them around long enough to talk to them. They practically run from us."
"*Exactly*. We must stay in proximity to them until our charms can become evident to them. That is why we're going to take home economics."[4]

Harold's plan proceeds admirably for a while. Although they are teased, it seems a small price to pay for surrounding themselves with a roomful of girls and no other boys to compete with. "Then the football team discovered us." A few of the football players start bullying the boys; they are stuffed into lockers and garbage cans, and little Harold is tossed about like a football. But finally they go too far: Harold's slide rule is broken.

As revenge, Harold uses the skills he learned in home ec class to whip up a big, beautiful chocolate cake loaded with laxatives, which he leaves for the entire football team on the afternoon before a big football game. When it is suggested that this revenge is perhaps too extreme, Harold "took a breath and his eyes grew cold and the smile left him. 'After all, they broke my slide rule. Did they expect me to do nothing?'" (*Schernoff Discoveries*, 21).

In another story in *The Schernoff Discoveries*, "On Making Friends," the two chums face only a single bully rather than an entire football team. But Mike Chimmer is formidable; a stupid and muscular kid from the wrong side of the tracks who seems to have nothing better to do than bully the narrator.

The two friends, along with bully Mike Chimmer, are all pinsetters at the local bowling alley. It was extremely dangerous work, "the worst kind of child labor."

> The men were often drunk and threw very hard, so the pins ricocheted and became four-pound wooden missiles. . . . Bones were broken, setters sometimes knocked unconscious, and a night without serious bruises and bleeding wounds was unusual. . . . All for seven cents a line. (52–53)

The three find themselves working side by side one night, Chimmer in the middle. Chimmer spends the evening viciously harassing his favorite victim, the narrator, punching and slapping, pouring water on him, and upsetting pins that had just been set. When Harold finally tells Chimmer to stop, Chimmer throws Harold down and punches him in the face, breaking Harold's glasses. At this, "screaming a word I'd read in the Mickey Spillane books," the narrator throws himself on the huge bully, and throws a punch towards Chimmer's face "just as a pin screamed over my shoulder and caught him full on the forehead. He went down like a stone" (58–59).

When Chimmer regains consciousness, some twenty minutes later, the narrator expects the worst. But Chimmer never saw the bowling pin that hit him, and thinks he's been hit with a knockout punch. The boys see no reason to correct Chimmer's mistaken assumption, and he never bothers the boys again. Harold later constructs a complex theory to explain how this fortuitous event will affect the evolution of the Chimmer tribe:

"He'll get older and seek a mate and have young and teach his young not to hit people. . . . In time the Chimmers will become a peaceful species."
"How long?"
"Two, perhaps three million years. Certainly not soon enough to help the world now." (62–63)

In many stories involving bullies, a bond formed between victims and opponents creates potential for comic solidarity. However, it is also possible to find humor even in a bullying situation where a victim is isolated without peer support and has little hope of turning the tables on his tormentor. In his entertaining journal entries, young intellectual Adrian Mole takes his own sort of private revenge on the detested Barry Kent by recording the bully's follies.

Tuesday April 7th. Barry Kent is in trouble for drawing a nude woman in Art. Ms. Fossington-Gore said that it wasn't so much the subject matter but his ignorance of basic biological facts that was so upsetting.[5]

Adrian considers his tormenter from an academic perspective:

Tuesday March 3rd SHROVE TUESDAY. I gave Barry Kent his protection money today. I don't see how there can be a God. If there was surely he wouldn't let people like Barry Kent walk about menacing intellectuals? Why are bigger youths unpleasant to smaller youths? . . . When I go to university I may study the problem.
I will have my thesis published and I will send a copy to Barry Kent. Perhaps by then he will have learnt to read. (*Adrian Mole*, 39)

Bully Girls

Female bullies also appear in novels for teens. In Louise Rennison's Angus series, Georgia Nicolson and her "mates" are persecuted by Jackie and Ali, the notorious Bummer twins. The two strapping girls are inseparable and, working as a team, are able to intimidate all their schoolmates.

The Bummers are notoriously fond of cigarettes, and on one occasion Georgia takes advantage of that addiction to distract them. The Bummers suspect that "Nauseating P. Green" has "snitched" on them. They steal her copy of *Hamsters Weekly*, corner her in the lavatory, and knock her eyeglasses to the floor. Georgia bravely succors her classmate by scattering the Bummers' cigarettes across the floor, causing Jackie and Ali to scramble about to recover their precious "fags." As Georgia tells it, the pathetic P. Green[6] is slow to take advantage of the distraction:

> I was like a thing possessed. I leaped over to them and grabbed Jackie's fag packet out of her hand. Then I ran into the loos with it and held it over the toilet. I yelled, "Let her go or the fags get it!"
>
> Jackie was truly worried then and had a sort of reflex action to save her packet of fags. Alison came toward me as well, leaving Nauseating P. Green trembling by herself. I shouted, "Run like the wind, P. Green!!!"
>
> She picked up her glasses and just stood there, blinking like a porky rabbit caught in a car's headlights. Good grief! I tried to give her confidence. "Well, not like the wind, then, but shuffle off as fast as you can."[7]

Perry Nodelman's *Behaving Bradley* introduces a similar pair of bullying sisters. A clean-cut sophomore, Shawn Grubert, the "Grassman," effectively runs Roblin Memorial High School by supplying illegal drugs to many of the students and several of the teachers. Narrator Brad Gold wants to reform the school's code of conduct, and in the process he unwittingly interferes with Grubert's smooth-running operations. The Grassman arranges for two of his best customers, sisters Amanda and Candace, to rough up Brad, who is short, skinny, and a self-confessed all-around wimp.

Brad notes, "They looked like a matched set of lady wrestlers just about to enter the ring and eviscerate the opposition . . ." After Mandy and Candy have delivered their message, punctuated with a few kicks and punches, Brad, from his horizontal perspective, describes their triumphant departure:

Then the two of them stomped off, their heavy footsteps reverberating right through the mall floor and into my bruised and broken body. They strode through the crowd like Attila the Hunette and her twin sister Attila the Other Hunette on their way home from ravaging and pillaging a village or two. A path cleared before them as they went, as sensible shoppers got out of the way and did their best to ignore my battered body lying there on the floor.[8]

Despite his fear of the "Hunettes," Brad doesn't give up his reform program, and the terrible twins continue to threaten him. However, they hadn't counted on his friend Stephanie, a short but sturdy girl who, Brad eventually discovers, happens to be a champion kickboxer (ranked number three in the city of Winnipeg). Before he found out about Stephanie's ability to defend herself, Brad was as concerned for Stephanie as for himself, and so he's startled when she tells him that she has dealt with the fearsome duo. He soon sees the evidence for himself when Mandy and Candy corner him against the wall yet again.

"So, pipsqueak," Candace said, "you think you're like, safe, right? But that little witch of a girlfriend of yours, she isn't always going to be around to protect you, OK?" She'd stuck her face so close to mine that I could smell the dead rat on her breath—or maybe it was just a dead onion—and see every bruised detail of her huge black eye.

"SO, like, you'd better watch your step, OK?" Amanda added, her words a little slurred as they came through the large cut on her lip. (*Behaving Bradley*, 182)

As Amanda and Candy hobble off, Brad marvels at the prowess of his diminutive friend Stephanie, who was clearly responsible for the black eye, the cut lip, and the hobbling. "What a woman!" he reflects admiringly, as he pulls himself together after another beating (183).

Richard Peck's Newbery-winning *A Year Down Yonder* begins with a story about a female bully. Fifteen-year-old Mary Alice has been sent to live with her grandmother in rural Illinois. Grandma soon brings her to the small local school, warning Mary Alice to avoid "that big girl with the dirty hair." After silently looking over a gray horse tied at the front of the school, Grandma departs with a warning:

"Steer clear of her if you can. Watch your back if you can't."

"What's wrong with her?"

"She's a Burdick."[9]

Mary Alice is seated next to Mildred Burdick, who sneers at the "rich Chicago girl" for a few moments, then turns to extortion:

> "Ya owe me a buck. . . . And I ain't afraid of your grandma. Ya oughtta see mine. Mine drinks straight from the bottle and wears tar all over to keep off the fleas. And my paw's meaner than a snake. He's tougher than any of them Chicago gangsters. He's worse than Pretty Boy Floyd, and lots uglier."
>
> I didn't doubt it. (*A Year Down Yonder*, 13)

After school, Mildred mounts the gray horse ("I have to say, Mildred's horse was better looking than she was") and follows Mary Alice home. Mary Alice notes that Grandma is sitting on the porch "almost like she was waiting for us." Despite Mildred's demand for the dollar, Grandma is quite friendly to the big girl, offering her food and chatting away, then stepping out of the kitchen on pretense of fetching additional snacks. As Grandma returns, Mary Alice is startled to observe Mildred's horse trotting away, with the boots Grandma had instructed Mildred to remove tied around its neck. Sometime later, when Mildred finally realizes something is amiss and races outside, the horse is long gone. Grandma latches the door behind Mildred and sits down with Mary Alice.

Mary Alice fears that Grandma's trick will "get her killed" when Mildred returns to school. But Grandma explains that such fears are groundless: the horse belongs to another family that lives "seven miles in the other direction," and will return to its rightful owners. Mildred's father is a notorious horse thief, but he won't be able to steal another horse "until he gets out of the penitentiary." Grandma "can't picture Mildred walkin' five miles both ways for an education."

> ". . . Barefoot," I said.
>
> "Barefoot," Grandma said. "I can't fight all your battles for you, but I can give you a level start."
>
> A silence fell while I thought that over. Then I said, "And you acted real nice to her too, Grandma. You gave her buttermilk and that big slab of corn bread."

"Oh, well." Grandma waved herself away. "Didn't want to send her off hungry. I knew she had a long walk ahead of her." (18)

For a nice contrast in tactics, we might compare Grandma Dowdel's efficient disposal of Mildred Burdick with a scene from *Alice, I Think*, in which Alice MacLeod's mother takes on a delinquent girl who has been bullying her daughter:

> My mother launched herself at Linda, grabbed her by the lapels of her jean jacket, and threw her on the ground. On the ground, if you can believe it! Linda kicked viciously until she knocked my mother down with her. They pummeled each other like a couple of kindergartners in a fight over who gets to eat the Play-Doh, only it wasn't children, it was my pink-and-purple mother and the worst girl in town rolling around in the parking lot of the Smithers Grocery Giant.[10]

When a policeman arrives, Alice adds to the confusion by pretending she had nothing to do with the incident:

> "Well, is that your mother over there?" he asked, pointing to my tear-stained mother, who stared at me with this horrified look.
> "Oh. Her. Well, yes. I guess so." (*Alice, I Think*, 42)

"That was our mother-daughter Saturday at the mall," Alice concludes (43).

Tough Girls

Unlike Alice MacLeod, Richard Peck's Blossom Culp is a girl who can take care of herself. Peck has a knack for generating comedy from situations in which bullies of either sex are undone by clever females. In *Ghosts I Have Been*, the irrepressible Blossom Culp tangles with a classic bully named Les Dawson and uses her wits to defeat him.

As Blossom describes him, Les is "a bully of more brawn than brain" who was in her grade after being "left back several semesters."[11] As a Halloween prank, Les and his gang of troublemakers plan to overturn some of the outhouses still in use by residents of Bluff City. Blossom decides to hide in Old Man Leverette's privy dressed as a ghost and startle

Dawson's gang when they arrive to tip it over. Unfortunately, Blossom interrupts Leverette himself using the facility, and she has to do some fast talking to convince him of her own good intentions.

With Old Man Leverette now part of her scheme, Blossom returns to the privy and the gang soon arrives to push it over. Between Blossom's ghostly performance and Old Man Leverette's shotgun charge of rock salt, the gang is thoroughly frightened and Les takes a full load square in his backside as he struggles over a fence. As Blossom tells it:

> Les Dawson did not come to school till noon. I have an idea that his kin spent many hours picking rock salt out of him. A morning recess without Les was as good as Christmas for the smaller kids, for Les never missed a day of stealing their pennies and putting their lunch buckets in trees. When he did come to school, he was in a meaner frame of mind than usual. (*Ghosts*, 18)

Blossom soon falls afoul of Les, who "could have felled me with one blow. But who knew better than me how tender his rear must be, pocked with rock salt as it was? I kicked him hard where it would be most instructive" (20).

Richard Peck is also responsible for what is probably the funniest bully story ever written, "Priscilla and the Wimps." Again, a schoolgirl, Priscilla Roseberry, brings about the downfall of a formidable male bully. Unlike Blossom Culp, Priscilla is a substantial girl: "Priscilla was, hands down, the largest student in our particular institution of learning. I'm not talking fat. I'm talking big. Even beautiful, in a bionic way."[12]

Priscilla was a loner, except for her close friend, pint-sized Melvin Detweiler. She was perhaps the only student in the school who was unaware of the sinister extortionist Monk Klutter, and his gang of henchmen, Klutter's Kobras, who helped to enforce Monk's collections. Every boy in the school was oppressed by the gang. Girls were generally left alone, but Priscilla's magnificent obliviousness to the gang was unique. "Priscilla was sort of above everything, if you'll pardon a pun. And very calm, as only the very big can be."

One fateful winter afternoon, at the end of the school day, one of Klutter's Kobras goes after Melvin. Priscilla is nearby, and it doesn't take her long to dispose of the Kobra. "Who's your leader, wimp?" she demands. Amazed, he meekly replies, "Monk Klutter." "Never heard of him," Priscilla mentions. "Send him to see me." Monk soon comes along to handle the case personally and makes the mistake of laying a hand on Melvin ("Priscilla and the Wimps," 44–45). Suffice it to say that Melvin Detweiler won't be bothered again by the bullies, although the spectacular ending won't be divulged here. This classic is one of the great short stories in young adult literature and confirms author Richard Peck's reputation as a master storyteller and humorist. "Priscilla and the Wimps" can be found in several anthologies.[13]

In his first YA novel, Carl Hiaasen presents an equally satisfying encounter between a notorious bully and a formidable girl who decides to befriend one of the bully's selected victims. Hiaasen, renowned for his racy adult novels, packs *Hoot* with classic Hiaasen touches, including guerrilla warfare between developers and environmentalists in South Florida, and a deliciously ironic fate for each of the "bad guys."

Among these is the bully Dana Matherson, an unregenerate juvenile delinquent who loses no time in roughing up new kid Roy Eberhardt. Each school day, Dana sits behind Roy on the bus and chokes and punches him throughout the trip. Roy is finally saved from this abuse when Beatrice Leep, a large girl he has befriended, takes the seat next to Dana and without saying a word, intimidates the bully into keeping his hands to himself. However, Dana keeps looking for opportunities to corner Roy. He finally catches Roy alone in the gym, drags him into a dark closet, and applies his trademark chokehold.

> This is it, Roy thought. The dumb goon is really going to kill me. Roy felt hot tears rolling down his cheeks.
> Sorry Mom. Maybe you and Dad can try again . . .
> Suddenly the door of the utility closet flew open, and the weight on Roy's chest seemed to vaporize. He opened his eyes just as Dana Matherson was being lifted away, arms flailing, a stunned expression on his pug face.[14]

Roy later discovers that Beatrice has "left Dana Matherson stripped down to his underpants and trussed to the flag pole in front of the administration building at Trace Middle School" (*Hoot*, 111).

Unexpected Sparks

The undoing of a male bully by a female classmate is a fictional premise that rarely fails to please. But what if things go wrong? Graham Salisbury's short story, "Frankie Diamond Is Robbing Us Blind" takes a humorous twist on the theme of female protector versus male bully.
Several undersized Hawaiian sixth graders known as the "ShortBoyz"
are being robbed by Frankie Diamond, a slick, handsome eighth grader.
Usually accompanied by the sinister Andrade brothers "who I once saw
in the backseat of a police car,"[15] Frankie extorts a lion's share of snacks
taken from the kids in each encounter.

After one of these robberies, the ShortBoyz enlist a tough older girl,
Lynette Piper, to protect them. Lynnette, herself an eighth grader, but
unacquainted with Frankie Diamond, begins escorting the ShortBoyz
to and from school. A few days later, the confrontation finally arrives.
Frankie and his remoras, the Andrade brothers, are spotted in the dis-
tance, and Lynnette is alerted. "'So that's Frankie Diamond,' Lynnette
said. 'I've seen him around but didn't know his name. He's cute.' Joey
mutters, 'I didn't like the sound of that'" ("Frankie Diamond," 135).

However, Lynnette plays her agreed role, and when Frankie grabs a
bag of snacks from one of the boys, she snatches it back, "quick as a
toad's tongue," holding it behind her until it is retrieved by one of the
ShortBoyz. But then Frankie and Lynnette begin an odd stand-off, eye
to eye, chest to chest, bumping one another. "It wasn't about the bag
anymore. Now it was about something else." They became "lost in each
other's eyes, never once blinking . . ."

> Then something weird happened. Frankie and Lynnette stopped bang-
> ing into each other and stood with their chests and eyes glued to each
> other . . . and I knew my plan had just died.
>   Frankie grinned his shark-white teeth. Lynnette let that hidden smile
> loose.
>   And the Andrade brothers walked away. (140)

Frankie and Lynnette depart arm in arm, with a generous tribute of
snacks, and Joey observes that the ShortBoyz' problem "had just dou-
bled." The sixth graders never anticipated the sparks that ignited between eighth graders Frankie and Lynnette. Salisbury's story is a good

illustration of one of the unexpected complications that can develop in the matrix of relationships between bully, victim, and bodyguard.

Another sort of sparks are ignited in David Lubar's novel, *Hidden Talents*, which features a colorful bully with the deliciously apt name, Bloodbath. (His full name is Lester Bloodbath, but he prefers to be addressed only by his sinister surname.) Bloodbath's brutality is terrifying, but sometimes funny, as when he stuffs Torchie "the human flame" into a small closet already occupied by Waylon, nicknamed "Hindenburg" because of his prodigious gaseous emissions. Torchie is believed to be a pyromaniac, but it turns out that he has a "gift" for unintentionally causing nearby flammable objects to spontaneously ignite. On this occasion, Bloodbath is inspired in the pairing of his victims: the prospect of being locked in a tight place with the odiferous Hindenburg frightens Torchie, "sparking" his uncontrolled gift for combustion. The spectacular result of a locked door being blown off its hinges and propelled across the corridor is explosively funny, and as good an example of a bully-generating humor as literature is likely to provide.[16]

Notes

1. Chris Crutcher, "A Brief Moment in the Life of Angus Bethune," in *Connections: Short Stories by Outstanding Writers for Young Adults*, ed. Don Gallo (New York: Delacorte, 1989), 55.

2. Bruce Coville, "Am I Blue?" in *Odder Than Ever* (San Diego: Harcourt Brace, 1999), 115; also in *Am I Blue? Coming Out from the Silence*, ed. Marion Dane Bauer (New York: HarperCollins, 1994).

3. Tim Wynne-Jones, "Tashkent," in *Some of the Kinder Planets* (Toronto: Groundwood, 1993), 46.

4. Gary Paulsen, *The Schernoff Discoveries* (New York: Delacorte, 1997), 11–12.

5. Sue Townsend, *The Adrian Mole Diaries* (New York: Grove, 1986), 56.

6. (Lovely name, P. Green, with its suggestion of "pea green.")

7. Louise Rennison, *On the Bright Side, I'm Now the Girlfriend of a Sex God; Further Confessions of Georgia Nicolson* (New York: HarperCollins, 2001), 189.

8. Perry Nodelman, *Behaving Bradley* (New York: Simon & Schuster, 1998), 98–99.

9. Richard Peck, *A Year Down Yonder* (New York: Dial, 1998), 10.

10. Susan Juby, *Alice, I Think* (New York: HarperTempest, 2003), 40.

11. Richard Peck, *Ghosts I Have Been* (New York: Viking, 1977), 7.

12. Richard Peck, "Priscilla and the Wimps," in *Sixteen: Short Stories by Outstanding Writers for Young Adults*, ed. Don Gallo (New York: Delacorte, 1984), 43.

13. The story first appeared in Don Gallo's *Sixteen*, and is also included in *Who Do You Think You Are: Stories of Friends and Enemies*, ed. Hazel Rochman (Boston: Little, Brown, 1993); also in Richard Peck, *Past Perfect, Present Tense: New and Collected Stories* (New York: Dial, 2004).

14. Carl Hiaasen, *Hoot* (New York: Knopf, 2002), 109.

15. Graham Salisbury, "Frankie Diamond Is Robbing Us Blind," in *Island Boyz* (New York: Wendy Lamb Books, 2002), 119.

16. David Lubar, *Hidden Talents* (New York: Tom Doherty Associates, 1999).

CHAPTER FOUR

~

Authorities and Adversaries

In addition to putting up with their parents, teenagers must cope with a seemingly endless stream of adult authority figures: teachers, counselors, coaches, law enforcement officers, ministers, employers, and on and on. Sometimes it must seem that the whole world is trying to tell them what to do and how to behave. The efforts young people make to outwit and outmaneuver these omnipresent adults, whether successful or not, are great fodder for intergenerational comedy.

School

Teachers and Administrators
With the exception of their parents, school teachers and administrators are the authority figures most frequently encountered by young adults. Much of the fiction geared toward young adults is set during the summer holiday, and many stories about teens are set entirely outside of school. Nevertheless, the necessity of spending one hundred and eighty days of each year in school ensures that secondary school experiences are central in the lives of most kids. Authors of fiction for adolescents use humor in stories about secondary schools of every type: rural and urban, public and parochial, large and small, contemporary and historical. Some of the most unconventional educational authorities are found in home and alternative schools.

Homeschooling has been the setting for some very funny stories. Susan Juby's *Alice, I Think* describes Alice MacLeod's difficulties in socializing with peers after relative isolation during years of homeschooling. Her parents began to have doubts about the practice following a Home-Based Learner's Picnic where they discovered that most homeschooled kids

> weren't exactly what my dad called "paragons of normalcy." A disturbing number of them were still breast-feeding at an age when most kids are taking up smoking. One boy wore antlers all afternoon. His sister's eyes rolled around in her head. But Fleet and Arrow were practically normal compared to the religious homeschooled kids . . . one of the religious parents told my mother I was a demon spawn after I told her daughter that girls were allowed to wear pants.[1]

Alice further notes, "The reality is that what I've been doing is self-schooling. Sure my mom and dad take turns pretending to teach me," but her mother is mainly teaching political correctness, and her father "supposedly teaches me science and math, although mostly what we do is drink coffee and read *Popular Science* and *Omni*" (*Alice, I Think*,15).

Ms. Wyman of James Howe's *The Misfits* has a colorful personality, and narrator Bobby Goodspeed explains that she knows how to use it to maintain complete control of the eighth graders of Paintbrush Falls Middle School.

> She's so sweet sometimes you can swear you smell muffins baking. But here is the bad news about Ms. Wyman: if you cross her, watch out. That smiley face of hers'll fall off like a mask that's popped its elastic, and underneath is a dragon lady. And *that* Ms. Wyman, I swear, wouldn't blink at removing your liver with her bare hands and eating it with a spoon.[2]

The liver and muffin metaphors are repeated at strategic intervals in the novel:

> As soon as we get inside Ms. Wyman's room we put a lid on our laughter because she's got this look on her face like she has been sharpening her knife and fork and just waiting for our livers to arrive. When we hand in our late passes, she does a quick change into her muffin-baking self, all gooey smiles. (*The Misfits*, 132)

Ms. Wyman's Jekyll-and-Hyde personality, and the consistent use of the muffin-baking and liver-eating metaphors to describe her moods resonate throughout the novel.

In contrast to the formidable Ms. Wyman, Mr. Fogelman, an eighth-grade English teacher in Gordon Korman's *No More Dead Dogs*, becomes a study in frustration. He loves to assign his favorite children's classic from the 1950s, *Old Shep, My Pal*, and he's appalled when Wallace Wallace writes a disparaging review. Wallace thinks that the story is really lame, especially because of the overused cliché of the faithful dog dying at the end. "What a heartbreaking surprise ending!" insists Fogelman. Wallace disagrees:

> "I wasn't surprised," I said. "I knew Old Shep was going to die before I started page one."
> "Don't be ridiculous," the teacher snapped. "How?"
> I shrugged. "Because the dog always dies. Go to the library and pick out a book with an award sticker and a dog on the cover. Trust me, that dog is going down."

When Mr. Fogelman demurs, Wallace's classmates quickly cite Old Yeller, Sounder, and Bristle Face. Then Wallace adds, "Don't forget *Where the Red Fern Grows* . . . the double whammy—two dogs die in that one."[3]

Wallace, who is constitutionally unable to tell a lie, refuses to write a positive review of the book, despite being placed in detention by Mr. Fogelman until he complies. Then Fogelman, who is also the school's theater director, decides to dramatize (what else?) *Old Shep, My Pal* for the school's annual play. Wallace, who had no previous interest in drama, finds himself spending his detention hours in the auditorium where Fogelman's theatrical presentation of *Old Shep, My Pal* is being rehearsed. Bit by bit, Wallace's critiques of the novel and his suggestions for improvements in the dialogue and action insinuate themselves into the production. Finally, when the announcements are printed, he shares the billing with Mr. Fogelman as codirector of what is now a musical production "loosely based" on *Old Shep, My Pal*, and featuring skateboards, a moped, a remote control dog, and local rock band, The Dead Mangoes. The arc of the story is neatly expressed by Mr. Fogelman's rising frustration through perhaps two-thirds of the novel, until he finally surrenders, embraces chaos, and has a good time with the play after all.

Humor involving school teachers is also prevalent in British YA literature, as in the following trio of popular English series. The earliest, Sue Townsend's *Adrian Mole Diaries*, has some wonderful passages about Adrian's school experiences. The headmaster of Adrian's school is "Popeye" Scruton, famous for his gimlet eyes. Scruton is politically conservative, which puts him at odds with a student body largely drawn from the lower classes and suffering under Prime Minister Thatcher's policies.

Thursday February 18th
This morning the whole school was ordered to go to the assembly hall. Mr. Scruton got up on the stage and acted like the films of Hitler. He said in all his long years of teaching he had never come across an act of such serious vandalism. Everybody went dead quiet and wondered what had happened. Scruton said that somebody had entered his office and drawn a moustache on Margaret Thatcher and written "Three million unemployed" in her cleavage.[4]

Louise Rennison's Georgia Nicolson is one of many fictional teen diarists who owe a debt to Sue Townsend's brilliant *Adrian Mole Diaries*. Georgia's comments on, and interactions with her teachers are quite funny, although usually lacking the darker, satirical edge of the class and generational warfare described by Adrian Mole a generation earlier. Georgia is amused by Herr Kamyer, calling him the school's "rogue male."[5] Much of the fourth Georgia Nicolson novel, *Dancing in My Nuddy-Pants*, surrounds a field trip to Paris. Here Rennison has great fun with a trilingual situation. Herr Kamyer, who speaks mediocre English and no French, is determined to be helpful in providing the girls a rich cultural experience. He does provide them a rich experience.

2:15 PM
Herr Kamyer has been showing us how to ask for things in shops . . . he keeps going up to French people and asking for things, which is hilarious in the extreme as: a) no one has a clue what he is talking about and b) they wouldn't give him anything anyway, because he is not French.
Oh, I tell a lie. He did manage to get something. He went into the tourist information center for a map. "I vill be back in a moment, girls, *mit* der map and ve vill proceed to the Champs Elysées."

He came out ten minutes later dithering like a loon with a souvenir walking stick but no map. As I pointed out to Jools, "The tragic thing is that they speak English in the tourist information center."[6]

The fifth entry in J. K. Rowling's series, *Harry Potter and the Order of the Phoenix*, includes a scene in which beloved Professor McGonagall finds a perfect situation for the application of her sharp, dry wit. McGonagall has been harassed by the odious Dolores Umbridge, a toadlike bureaucrat who has been striving to take over Hogwarts School. Umbridge has finally managed to displace the revered Professor Dumbledore and has appointed herself headmistress. Harry and his friends are wondering how Professor McGonagall will react.

> "Our new—Headmistress—" Professor McGonagall pronounced the word with the same look on her face that Aunt Petunia had whenever she was contemplating a particularly stubborn bit of dirt "—has asked the Heads of Houses to tell their students that cheating will be punished most severely—because, of course, your examination results will reflect upon the Headmistress's new regime at the school—"
>
> Professor McGonagall gave a tiny sigh; Harry saw the nostrils of her sharp nose flare.
>
> "—however, that is no reason not to do your very best. You have your own futures to think about."[7]

Coaches and Gym Instructors

In many schools, the gym teacher is also the coach of some of the varsity athletic teams. This can be problematic for a student who is not into sports or is not physically fit, since coaches tend to take athletics very seriously. Encounters between these students and gym teacher/coaches have enlivened many YA novels. Coach Spline in Daniel Pinkwater's *The Education of Robert Nifkin* is just the kind of crass, bullying coach and gym teacher/coach that out of shape kids fear. On the first day of phys ed Robert meets his new "teacher":

> "Give me ten laps, fatty," Coach Spline growled. He was wearing sweats and had a crew cut and a face that looked like a rotten tomato.
>
> "Now?"
>
> "Right now!" he bellowed, spraying me with spit. "Right now! Go! Go! Go! Go!"

> I ran ten laps around the gym, wearing my street clothes and carrying my briefcase and program cards.
>
> "Now haul your fat little butt out of here," Coach Spline said.[8]

Later that day, his first in high school, Robert transfers from gym to R.O.T.C. When Sergeant Gunter asks him why he wants to join the R.O.T.C., Robert blurts out, "Because Coach Spline is a bastard?" The Sergeant replies, "It is not appropriate for a cadet in Riverview High R.O.T.C. to refer to a member of the faculty as a bastard . . . he is not a bastard. He is a Fascist bastard" (*The Education of Robert Nifkin*, 21). Robert soon discovers that Sergeant Gunter is a fervent Marxist, but the sergeant's antiauthoritarian rhetoric does not seem excessive when applied to Coach Spline.

An excessive glorification of sports has become institutionalized at a high administrative level in Chris Lynch's *Slot Machine*. Brother Jackson, the Dean of Men at Elvin Bishop's Catholic high school, presides as a kind of godfather over brutal team sports and sadistic coaches and revels in the achievements of his illegally trained sports teams. Brother Jackson has built a macho culture in which sports are worshipped above all other endeavors, and he is indirectly responsible for the repulsive caste system and organized hazing that take place each year at summer camp.

After running the gauntlet of athletic possibilities and being discarded by a series of coaches, Elvin eventually finds his way to the Arts Sector, and immediately takes a liking to the nonathletic Brothers who preside there. After a herd of jocks has broken the windows of the Arts classroom and called them "faggots" and other obscenities, the Brothers bring out a piñata.

> The Art Brothers had gotten together to build it, and it was professional. Papier-maché, bigger than life-size. It had angel's wings, and an angelic expression looking heavenward. And it had Arnold Schwarzenegger muscles, shoulder pads, a baseball cap on backward. With one had it was leaning on a baseball bat, and with the other it was grabbing its crotch.
>
> It was a dead ringer for Brother Jackson.[9]

When it comes to team sports, girls are no longer expected to remain on the sidelines as spectators or cheerleaders. However, in Mariah Frederick's novel, *The True Meaning of Cleavage*, Jess Horvath is totally disinterested in athletics, and her friendship with Sari Aaronsohn is rooted in their common dislike for team sports:

> Sari and I have been best friends since seventh grade. We had the same gym class, and we were always the last two picked for every team. Me because I was bad, Sari because she just didn't care. One game, the teacher made Sari be goalie, and she let the ball roll right into the goal. The other team started jumping around and slapping hands. The teacher immediately made her sit down on the bench next to me. I held my hand up, and we slapped hands.[10]

It is ironic that a mutual distaste for team sports—which are supposed to promote teamwork and bonding—is exactly what brings Jess and Sari together. As with the Art Sector staff and students in Chris Lynch's *Slot Machine*, art is Jess's substitute for sports. She is dismayed at having to navigate past a volleyball game to reach the art studio.

> The art studio is next to the gym. When I get to the fifth floor, there's a class going on, and I nearly get my head taken off by a volleyball.
>
> I wait for a lull in the game so I can cross the gym. I totally don't get sports. All these people running after a ball, shrieking, "I got it, I got it!" Got what? What do you have? One team commits the ultimate sin of letting the ball drop. They all groan while the other side jumps up and down and slaps hands. I take advantage of the break to race into the art room. (*The True Meaning of Cleavage*, 97)

Jess's attitude toward sports is funny because it's so directly and unabashedly opposed to the normative view that strenuous exercise is a Good Thing, and that team sports are an enjoyable way of achieving physical fitness. Jess's lack of interest in helping her teammates maintain the altitude of a volleyball may seem odd to some of her peers, but they haven't met Tara Sullivan. In Terry Spencer Hesser's *Kissing Doorknobs*, Tara doesn't merely ignore the flight of the volleyball; she listens to it.

> The ball was served and then, as usual, instead of paying attention to the game, I found myself counting the number of times I heard the ball make contact with the floor, a fist, or even the occasional head . . .

"*Tara!*" The ball grazed my ear and fell at my feet, and the other team scored a point and cheered.

Wendy went ballistic. "*That's the last time! That's it! What's up with you, Tara! You didn't even try to hit the ball!*" Her face was red with anger . . . *Why didn't you even try to hit the ball?*"

"Because," I replied, and the gymnasium went silent. "Because, what's the point?" I asked.

"*What's the point?*" Wendy's eyes were slitted with hatred. "*What's the point?*" I could feel the entire class's eyes on us.

"Yeah. I don't see the point. If I hit it back to them, they'll just hit it back to us. So why not just keep it, as long as they insist on hitting it over here?"

Even though they were on my team, Keesha, Kristin and Anna laughed until they cried. Wendy ran out screaming at everyone and eventually got a note sent home about her bad behavior.[11]

Tara, who suffers from obsessive-compulsive disorder (OCD) genuinely finds counting ball sounds more compelling than playing the game. Like many scenes in *Kissing Doorknobs*, this one is both hilarious and disturbing in its presentation of extreme incongruities resulting from collisions of Tara's OCD perspective with the conventional world of her classmates.

Counselors and Psychologists

Adolescence being a time of confusion, exploration, and enormous personal development, it is not surprising that encounters with school psychologists are a frequent feature of YA literature. In humorous situations, the mental health professional himself may be unexceptional, serving quietly and competently as a sounding board for a protagonist who is bouncing off the walls. "Special Ed" Vanness is such a figure in Jack Gantos's *Joey Pigza Swallowed the Key*, and Mr. Verplaz plays a similar role in Arthur Slade's *Tribes*, novels about troubled early and late adolescents, respectively.

There are rich possibilities for humor when the counselor himself is made the object of comedy. As a trained professional, the school "shrink" is expected to be not merely a mature adult, but a person of exceptional wisdom and moral strength. The reaction of a teen protagonist to a counselor who turns out to have as many "issues" as his client has been the grist for some priceless scenes in YA literature.

Megan McCafferty's novel, *Sloppy Firsts*, features a "teeny bopper" counselor whom Jessica is unable to respect.

> Mrs. Glick called me out of Trig to meet Brandi, the school's pseudo shrink. Her nameplate says "Professional Counselor," which I figure means she's a few credits short of a legit Ph.D. She probably couldn't find enough evidence for her doctoral thesis to prove that hugs are indeed better than drugs.[12]

In Susan Juby's *Alice, I Think*, fifteen-year-old Alice MacLeod, who has been homeschooled most of her life, is about to enter the public school system. She is counseled at the Teens in Transition Club and will be enrolled in the Alternative Solutions School. Upon hearing the names of these two institutions, Alice's father observes that the people who named them have an "absolute flair for acronyms" (*Alice, I Think*, 32).

Alice mentions that her first counselor at TIT, Mrs. Frieson, "cracked up during one of my sessions" (7) losing her composure when Alice explained her fear of peer interactions by describing henpecking incidents she had observed on her neighbor's poultry farm. "Mrs. F. sort of screamed and said that chickens didn't have peers" (8).

Alice's next counselor is a young fellow named Bob whose appearance—he has a small goatee and dresses entirely in black—causes Alice to think of him as "Death Lord Bob" (11). He spends most of their sessions telling Alice about his own problems:

> I am sort of enjoying Bob's very indirect counseling style. He's trying hard not to pull a Mrs. F. and scar me for life by telling me what he really thinks. I appreciate the effort. I really do. But I can't help him out. I mean, what if I opened up and it caused him to pull a crackup like Mrs. F.? I couldn't live with myself. (52)

Author Daniel Pinkwater has given young adult literature a couple of its least professional but most hilarious mental health practitioners. In *Alan Mendelsohn, the Boy from Mars*, Leonard Neeble is referred to a private therapist. Dr. Prince is completely out of his mind and provides many entertaining scenes in the novel. In a typical scene, Dr. Prince yells reassurance to his client: "'Don't worry about a thing,' he shouted down the hall as we headed for the elevator. 'I've cured people twice as crazy as you!'"[13] Dr. Prince's nutty behavior continues outside the office as he throws a tantrum in the Bermuda Triangle Chili Parlor when told they're out of corn muffins, and a bit later the psychiatrist begins crying with frustration when a biker who claims to be a native of the planet Venus gets the better of him in a metaphysical discussion:

> The brothers of the Laughing Alligator escorted Dr. Prince, who kept saying, "Crazy as a coot! Crazy as a coot!" out of the Bermuda Triangle Chili Parlor. They hoisted him onto a motorcycle and roared off into the darkness . . . Alan Mendelsohn and I walked back to the bus station. We didn't say much. Seeing Dr. Prince go nuts was a little upsetting for both of us. (*Alan Mendelsohn*, 141)

In Pinkwater's *Young Adult Novel*, a brilliant satire of the genre, the Wild Dada Ducks, a group of five weird, nerdy teenage boys, lose sight of the boundaries between art and real life, with hilarious results. That novella was followed by two short sequels, "Dead End Dada" and "The Dada Boys in Collitch."[14] "Dead End Dada" offers a superb satire of an untrustworthy psychiatrist, "the treacherous Dr. Cookie Mendoza."

The vice-principal of Himmler High School, Mr. Gerstenblut, hates the Ducks because of their persistent nonconformity, most recently demonstrated by their simultaneous arrival at school with shaved heads. Besides suspending them from school, which he had done on several previous occasions, this time Gerstenblut also insists that they each be evaluated by the Board of Education psychiatrist before being readmitted to school.

The following day, the boys gather outside Dr. Mendoza's office for their five consecutive fifteen-minute appointments. Despite their conversion from Dada to Zen, the boys are still known to one another as Charles the Cat, The Indiana Zephyr, Captain Colossal, Igor, and The Honorable Venustiano Carranza (President of Mexico). From the waiting room, they can clearly hear every word spoken in the office, and thus they overhear Dr. Mendoza encouraging the student who preceded them (Richard F. Scott, of 5235 Pearl Street) to admit to the practice of masturbation, which she describes as a healthy and natural pastime. Taking a cue, the Ducks each report themselves to be frequent practitioners of this activity. Soon afterward, they are called into Gerstenblut's office.

"I have here the official report from Dr. Cookie Mendoza," the Executioner said. "She says the five of you are vicious little perverts, and utterly preoccupied with unwholesome practices. I could have told her that."[15]

Dr. Cookie recommends a number of harsh disciplinary penalties, all of which Gerstenblut gleefully imposes. Although presented in context of an over-the-top satire, Dr. Cookie's treachery hits a nerve. It must be all too tempting for a school psychiatrist to deliver judgments that will please harried school teachers and administrators, rather than advocating for the adolescent whose real needs may be awkward or inconvenient for the educational bureaucracy.

Arthur Slade's clever and quirky novel *Tribes* features a good therapist in a grimly humorous novel about an older teen. Mr. Verplaz is a skilled, sensitive, and caring psychologist, not at all like Brandi or Death Lord Bob or Cookie Mendoza. The humor of the scenes between Percy and Verplaz comes not from the therapist's behavior, but rather from the unusual speech of his troubled patient. Percy first learns that he is being sent to the counselor when he hears a commanding voice from the school entrance:

"Percy Montmount, come here."
    It was the leader of all the Groverly High strata. He-Whose-First-Name-Is-Too-Sacred-to-Speak.
    Principal Michaels.[16]

When the Principal tells him to see Mr. Verplaz, Percy muses, "The school therapist. Again. He was a singularly valuable hominid. 'Of course, sir. I will visit the shaman—I mean Mr. Verplaz'" (*Tribes*, 16).

Before his appointment, Percy characterizes Mr. Verplaz as "the school shaman, He-Who-Lives-on-the-Top-Floor" (50). Percy describes Mr. Verplaz: "His eyes were spectacular, the oversized orbs of a well-groomed lemur, evolved to soak up moonlight" (87). Although he knows that most people are alarmed by his anthropological jargon "('Mom was more comfortable if I used teen vernacular')" (22), Percy does not tone himself down for the therapist:

"Do you know why you're here?"
    "I was in a fight, so Groverly's patriarch ordered me to attend."
    Mr. Verplaz smiled. "Are you angry with Mr. Michaels?"

"No."

"Then tell me, what is the real reason you are here?" This was another tool of *Homo shaman therapist*—a skin bag stuffed with questions.

"Apparently the Teacher Tribe is concerned about my behavior."

"Do you understand why?"

"They are hired to assimilate me. It's their duty." (88)

With the help of Mr. Verplaz, Percy is eventually able to put down the anthropological persona that he had wrapped about himself to avoid confronting the real problems he needed to face.

Employers and Landlords

Employers

The fast-food industry employs millions of adolescents and can provide a colorful setting for young adult sagas. M. T. Anderson's novel *Burger Wuss* is one of the best. Early in the novel, Anthony and his girlfriend, Diana, enjoy making fun of fast-food merchandising:

> I remember her saying that she was sick of the O'Dermott's Happy Lunch, man, and wasn't it about time to deal with reality and do the Desolate Lunch instead, with games on the box like "Can you help Kermit get to safety?" and the answer is "No," and "Can you connect the dots?" and the answer is "No" . . . and inside for a prize there is broken things or dust.[17]

When Turner, the local stud, lures Diana away from him, Anthony concocts an elaborate revenge plot, which requires that he take a counter job at the detested Kermit O'Dermott's alongside his rival. Unfortunately, the revenge of this nerd misfires badly, and Turner heaps a series of further humiliations on Anthony.

Some of the "flavor" of Anthony's life as a burger flipper can be conveyed by the pep talks he regularly gets from Mike, his manager:

> "We're going to have a little talk about team spirit. Would you come into the office?"
>
> I went into the office.
>
> "Anthony . . . we have a problem. We have a problem, don't we?"
>
> "No. No, sir."

"Yes, Anthony. A problem is exactly what we are having. Let's look at you for a second, Anthony. Let's look at the person you are. You're a person who can't be relied on, because you won't go and get the shake mix . . . You're a person whose uniform is wet. Who wants to see a wet uniform? People will think, 'Look at that boy, I bet he wets the nuggets.'" (*Burger Wuss*, 95)

Although most of his schemes for getting even with Turner backfire, Anthony does manage to strike a few blows against the fast-food industry by kidnapping the condiment troll from rival Burger Queen and spoiling a promotional film shoot at his local O'Dermott's.

Catherine Clark is another notable chronicler of teen jobs in the fast-food industry. *Truth or Dairy* and its sequel, *Wurst Case Scenario*, describe the working side of campus frozen yogurt and bagel shops. The latter novel takes its title from the premise of an animal rights activist and vegetarian from Boulder, Colorado, who goes off to college in the intense meat-and-cheese culture of Wisconsin. On her first trip to the college town, Courtney notices that nearly "all the stores advertised 'Cheese' and 'Sausage' and 'Bratwurst' in their windows." She and her family laugh at the misspelling of the word "bagel" at a place called "Bagle Finagle,"[18] but that's just where Courtney ends up working, after considering the options.

Job search really sucked. Everything's already taken, or I'm not qualified, or I don't want to dress up like Helga and wear horns on my head and serve German potato salad on roller skates at the Vivacious Viking. (*Wurst Case Scenario*, 43)

Bagle Finagle is a corporate chain, and Jennifer, the manager of the local franchise, falls into the humorless persona of fast-food managers everywhere as she tries to restrain the giddy impulses of her young crew. "We cracked up laughing and then got a dirty look from Jennifer. She does that a lot. Glaring at people" (50). More rules and restrictions are introduced:

Working for Jennifer is killing me. Today she started this new stupid system where there's a board with our names on it, and we have to mark down where we are "at any given time." Like, even when we go to the bathroom. She has this board and when you leave your "post" you have to put a "code" on it, and a "time estimate." Like I'm telling people what I'm in the bathroom for? Is she insane? (98)

Gail Gauthier's *Saving the Planet & Stuff* offers an inside look at a publishing office, from the viewpoint of Michael Racine, an inexperienced summer intern. *The Earth's Wife* is an environmental magazine produced in an office where the politics are fierce and often funny. On Michael's first day, Amber, a girl who has worked in the office for a while, tells him:

> "It's like being in the midst of a pack of animals. . . . 'This one' wants 'that one's' job. 'This one' wants 'that one' fired. 'This one' doesn't get along with 'that one,' and now, this year, 'this one' is 'involved' with 'that one.' I would name names, but gossiping is so unprofessional."[19]

In contrast to the teens slaving at detested minimum wage jobs, those in Joan Bauer's novels often enjoy their work. In *Rules of the Road*, Jenna Boller performs several different jobs for Madeline Gladstone, the crotchety old president of Gladstone's Shoe Stores, and Jenna relishes them all. She begins as an outstanding sales clerk in one of the Gladstone Shoe outlets, where she is discovered by Mrs. Gladstone and hired to be her driver and companion on a road tour to visit outlets in the Midwest and then attend the annual stockholder's meeting in Texas. Jenna's initial impression of Mrs. Gladstone: "She was very short but made up for it like one of those little yippy dogs who barks at anything."[20]

Jenna finds that Mrs. Gladstone's bark is worse than her bite. Over the course of the road trip, the pair become a team. Along with her talent for getting along with grumpy bosses, Jenna enjoys the work itself. Throughout *Rules of the Road*, she scatters brief, humorous comments that give us an insight into her enthusiasm for her job. The novel opens with this action scene:

> I leaped onto the sliding ladder in the back room of Gladstone's Shoe Store of Chicago, gave it a shove, and glided fast toward the end of the floor to ceiling shelves of shoeboxes. My keen retailer's eye found the chocolate loafers, size 13, I slid the ladder to the Nikes . . . [and] rode the ladder to the door one-handed. Children, do not try this at home. I am a shoe professional. (*Rules of the Road*, 1)

When Mrs. Gladstone turns Jenna loose in the Kansas City store, she sells "five pairs of quality shoes in under ten minutes . . . I blew on my shoehorn to cool it down, tossed it in the air in a little twirl, and put it back in my pocket" (112–13).

Jenna Boller's zestful embrace of her job as a shoe salesman in *Rules of the Road* is paralleled by Hope Yancey's enthusiasm for her job as a waitress in Bauer's later novel, *Hope Was Here*. Hope enjoys being a waitress and talks about the job very much in the way that Jenna Boller talks about selling shoes:

> A kid throws his spoon at his baby sister. I'm there to catch it before disaster. I hand it to his mother, who looks at me gratefully. Full-service waitressing. We feed, protect, and defend.[21]

Hope has amusing insights into the behavior of diner patrons that could only come from long intimacy with a job one truly loves.

> In minutes, I got every kind of sitter at the counter. I love watching people sit down. There are ploppers, slammers, sliders, swivelers, and my personal favorite, flutterers, who pose suspended above the seat and move up and down over it before finally lighting. (*Hope Was Here*, 61)

Many teens find themselves overscheduled and stretched too thin when they add a part-time job to school and extracurricular activities. One way around that problem is to work *instead of* attending school. The hero of Daniel Pinkwater's *The Education of Robert Nifkin*, while skipping his classes at Riverview High School, finds himself occasionally employed to assist in the delivery of furniture whose provenance has been altered to make it appear antique and valuable. This casual work experience helps Robert learn valuable life lessons, despite his delinquency. An older teen, Kenny Papescu, offers Robert a few to help move a heavy piece of furniture:

> "What are we delivering?" I asked.
> "La Mesa de los Pecados Capitales," Kenny said.
> "Huh?"
> "The Table of the Seven Deadly Sins." It's a work of art, painted by Heironymus Bosch in the fifteenth century . . . We're taking it to a guy in the suburbs." (*The Education of Robert Nifkin*, 83)

The "guy in the suburbs" is wealthy Miles Greenthorpe, who has become a local legend as a result of his frenetic late night TV appearances as a retailing czar of major discount appliances. "Miles was famous for jumping around and waving his arms and yelling and getting spit on the camera lenses" (87). Greenthorpe is a classic nouveau riche and an easy mark for the fraudulent alterations by Kenny's father.

Kenny tells Robert that he helped his father paint the table, before they coated it with six coats of bowling-alley polyurethane. "It looks great," Miles Greenthorpe exclaims. Miles gives each of the boys a crisp $100 bill, and moreover, asks them to give his attractive daughter a ride to an appointment. During the ride, Pamela Greenthorpe flirts with Robert and kisses him (90). Needless to say, all this hardly encourages Robert to return to his dreaded classes at Riverview High.

Another teen with little experience on the inside of high school classrooms is put to work in Susan Juby's *Alice, I Think*. Before long, a quirky employer finds herself saddled with an even quirkier new employee. Alice, a teen with no friends who has been homeschooled most of her life, gets her first job at a local New Age/used bookstore, where her mother, a middle-aged hippie, is the assistant manager. The bookstore is more or less the hobby of a local woman.

> Corinne, the owner of Mountain Lighthouse Brambleberry Books, trained me for about five minutes. Then she had to go and look after her chronic fatigue, fibromyalgia, and multiple chemical sensitivity disorder. Unfortunately for someone who owns a bookstore, Corinne is allergic to books and just about everything else in her store, including her customers and the native arts and crafts in the corner. (*Alice, I Think*, 84)

Corinne has an unusual response to her customers:

> If anyone gets too close, to ask a question or whatever, she starts to wheeze and holds out an arm and asks them to please step back. Then, with the back of one gloved hand against her veiled mouth, she gestures frantically like some futuristic Bedouin traffic cop for one of the other bookstore employees to come and help. (84–85)

Alice's favorite part of the job is her self-appointed role as security guard. Convinced that many of the bookstore's clientele are shoplifters, she spies on them obsessively. On one occasion, while she is kneeling to peer through a gap in a lower shelf to keep a suspect in view, another customer, not expecting anyone to be kneeling in the aisle, trips over her, precipitating a spectacular crash of books and bodies that exposes Alice's snooping.

Alice ultimately manages to get herself fired from this most laid-back of jobs by perversely lighting up several Buddhist Temple Blend incense sticks in the unventilated storage room just before she knew Corinne would be entering. After being fired, Alice decides "to leave the mirrors I had brought in for surveilling. . . . It was my grand and noble gesture" (121).

Landlords

Readers couldn't ask for a funnier landlord character than Plotnick of Gordon Korman's *Losing Joe's Place*. Joe Cardone will be away from his prized downtown Toronto apartment all summer, and his younger brother, Jason, has agreed to housesit and pay rent during Joe's absence. Jason and his two best friends, Don and Ferguson, are excited about spending the summer in Toronto rather than in their small Ontario hometown.

Their landlord is Plotnick, a colorful character who owns the deli downstairs from the apartment, and one of the very finest of Gordon Korman's eccentric personalities. The building is located on a badly paved street, allowing Plotnick to retrieve the occasional detached hubcap:

> An enormous clang rocked the neighborhood, and suddenly a shiny, spinning hubcap was airborne. In a single motion, Plotnick reached under the counter, produced a butterfly net, and was out the door. He threw himself heroically in the path of the hurtling cap, and netted it with a delicate flick of the wrist. We joined in the applause.
>
> Flushed with triumph, Plotnick waddled back into the deli, rushed to the griddle to flip a pancake, and stopped to examine his prize. "Very good condition," he said with satisfaction; he slapped on a sticker that read $19.95, and tossed the hubcap into the playpen with the rest.[22]

Plotnick is always trying to make a buck. When one of the boys puts a foot through a rotten board of the building's decrepit staircase, Plotnick makes him pay for a new flight of stairs. And a new banister. And new carpeting. When Jason is convalescing at home, Plotnick thoughtfully sends up a bowl of chicken soup, along with a bill for $1.75.

Lucy Frank's *Just Ask Iris* presents another comical battle between landlord and tenants, but this time the residents are the winners. Twelve-year-old Iris Diaz-Pinkowitz lives in a shabby, broken-down, six-floor tenement in New York. The elevator has been out of service for several months, inconveniencing everyone on the upper floors, including Will Gladd, a wheelchair-confined teenage boy on the third floor.

One day, a sharp, well-dressed woman from the rental management company arrives. Iris is struck by the woman's appearance and behavior.

> What was she doing here, with that alligator briefcase, and that suit that looked like it cost a thousand dollars, and those long red nails, and those four-inch heels? I couldn't decide whether she looked beautiful or mean, or both. Her legs were skinnier than mine . . . [and] she had a loud, mean voice . . .
>
> Uh-oh. She'd caught me staring. "Do you live in this building? What's your name?" she demanded, as if she were my teacher, or the principal, or the truant officer.
>
> Now I knew who she reminded me of! Cruella De Vil, the evil lady in *101 Dalmations*.[23]

"Cruella" browbeats the resident manager, or "super," Mr. Ocasio, demanding to know why the elevator is broken and the basement is filthy. He replies that Mrs. Witherspoon in 6B has a lot of cats and flushes their litter down the toilet, which hardens the pipes, floods the basement and elevator shaft, affecting drainage throughout the building. Cruella warns him that she will make an inspection after lunch, and he had better have the problems fixed.

Fearing that Mrs. Witherspoon will be evicted and her cats impounded, Iris springs into action! She races upstairs to 6B and finds the "Cat Lady" attempting to barricade her apartment with heavy furniture. Iris begs her to consider a more practical course of action. She manages to enlist several of her fellow residents in a plan to capture and box up the thirty-plus cats and kittens in 6B and hide them throughout the building until after the inspection. The Cat Lady agrees, but only if Iris first explains the plan to the cats. So Iris addresses the assembled felines and then turns to Mrs. Witherspoon, "trying not to look as stupid as I felt. 'How was that?' I said." "'Very good,' she said. 'But you don't need to talk to them in that high, squeaky voice. You can talk to them normally'" (171).

The plan succeeds as the residents cooperate to protect one of their own from the detested landlord and his overdressed representative. Even Will, in his wheelchair, helps by keeping watch and manning the telephone. By the time Cruella returns, 6B has been aired out and most of the cats have been packed up and distributed to other apartments. But a few of the most uncooperative cats remain, and Iris fears that Cruella will notice "a cat on top of the wardrobe. I prayed she wouldn't spot it. There was a lump under the bedspread that had to be a cat" (186).

Yolanda Alvarez from 5B provides a welcome distraction by bringing Cuca, her extremely rude parrot, upstairs. Iris opens the cage: "'Dirty bird!' I said. 'Cuca's a dirty bird!'"

> "Kiss my little green ass!" he screamed, flying to the top of the refrigerator. "*Awwwk!* Ends greasy buildup! *Myowwww!*" I ducked as he flew over me. "And it's a high fly ball to center field! *Mrrrarrr!* Operators are standing by!" Cruella swung her briefcase at him as he flapped past her head. "*Raaaaarrr!* Step OUT of the vehicle! Partly cloudy, chance of late-day showers! *Meouwwww! RARRRRRRR! Myeww! BRRKK!* I NEED A HUG!" (191)

Cruella flees the scene. Led by Iris and Will, the residents have protected Mrs. Witherspoon and foiled the landlord's evil minion. The story ends on a high note: the elevator is repaired, most of the cats are adopted by the newly united tenants, and the helpful Cuca is returned to his cage.

Local Authorities, Civil and Otherwise

Teens sometimes feel that law enforcement authorities "have it in for them." The authorities often say that they need to "send a message," and "teach kids a lesson." Sometimes a youth who has lost fear of his parents and teachers is more impressed by the formality of a courtroom presided over by a formidable judge.

Don Trembath's *The Tuesday Café* features a grimly humorous scene between a no-nonsense local judge and Harper Winslow, a fifteen-year-old boy charged with "arson causing property damage." Although he did set a little fire in a school wastebasket and is technically on record as a three-time offender, Harper is not really a habitual delinquent. His previous offenses are pretty tame: at age eight he hid from his parents in the spare bedroom long enough that they called the police, and when he was finally discovered under a bed calmly reading a comic book, the police charged him with mischief. Later he was wrongly accused of a theft, and although he was innocent and the case had been dismissed, somehow it was still on his record. However, the judge is not interested in excuses or explanations.

Harper describes the judge as "an older man with a wooden face that looked like it hadn't worn a smile in about fifty years. His eyes were small and jet black, and just about everyone who stood before him squirmed when he looked at them."[24] As he stares at Harper, his face gets darker and darker. "And you've been charged three times with serious crimes," said the judge. Harper tries to explain:

> "Actually two, sir," I said to the judge. "The theft charge was dropped. It was a mistake."
> "So that makes it okay then?" said the judge. He was really starting to get upset.
> "I was just—"
> "Don't you *just* anything in this courtroom, young man!" He was hot now. He slammed his gavel down so hard the glass of water he had on his desk tipped on its side and the water ran over the edge.
> "Now look what you've done!" he cried, leaping to his feet. (*The Tuesday Café*, 7)

The judge is fuming and Harper observes, "His lips were shaking, he was so mad." The judge soon works himself up into another outburst:

> "And you've just gone and tried to *burn it all down!*" Ka-boom! went the gavel again. I jumped about a foot in the air. "You should be *ashamed of yourself, Harper Winslow!* . . . I don't sense a bit of remorse in you. That whole school could be a pile of ashes right now and I don't think you'd care, would you? *Would you?*"
> "Yes, I would care, sir," I said. I wasn't kidding either. I was scared to death. (9)

The judge's intimidating display—whether spontaneous or calculated —is successful in getting the boy's attention. The judge wields absolute authority in his courtroom, so that even when he loses his temper, and no matter how unfair his pronouncements may seem, he is not to be questioned.

In Carl Hiaasen's *Hoot*, a variety of authority figures and local officials are bedeviled by teen environmental activists. Mother Paula's All-American Pancake House has selected a site in central Florida for a new restaurant franchise. The site happens to include the homes of several breeding pairs of highly endangered burrowing owls.

The resistance begins with small acts of vandalism: survey stakes are removed and the tires of a trailer carrying portable toilets are deflated. Officer David Delinko is called to the scene and, hearing a splash, inspects one of the toilets with his flashlight. A moment later, the policeman makes a mad dash out of the latrine and tells Curly, the construction foreman:

> "They put alligators in your potties, sir. Real live alligators."
> "More than one?"
> "Yes, sir."
> Curly was flabbergasted. "Are they . . . big gators?"
> Officer Delinko shrugged, nodding toward the Travelin' Johnnys. "I imagine all of 'em look big," he said, "when they're swimming under your butt."[25]

The inability of the foreman and the local police to prevent these acts of vandalism comes to the attention of Chuck E. Muckle, Vice President for Corporate Relations at Mother Paula's All-American Pancake House, Inc. Muckle rants and raves during each of his phone conversations with Curly, abusing and threatening the hapless foreman. In the novel's climactic scene, Muckle's carefully choreographed corporate relations event is upstaged by a group of (mostly teenaged) environmentalists, and the choleric executive completely loses control and tries to throttle a journalist. Muckle's young adversaries profit from the public exposure of their opponent's true character and emotional instability to save the burrowing owls.

Other Authorities and Adversaries

Authorities and Adversaries in Historical and Regional Fiction
Novels with a small town or rural atmosphere and a regional flavor often provide good opportunities for conflict between protagonists and local authorities. In a relatively isolated village, small town, or frontier

area, justice is often administered informally. Similarly, historical novels frequently allow us a glimpse of systems predating our own well-established judicial bureaucracies.

Karen Hesse's *Letters from Rifka* is a well-researched historical novel, based on U.S. immigration history and the author's personal interviews with her Aunt Lucy, herself an early twentieth-century Jewish immigrant. Although filled with harrowing escapes from deadly peril, Hesse's novel is enlivened by a rich vein of humor.

Rifka Nebrot, a Russian Jewish girl, is bedeviled by authorities all through the story. First her family barely escapes from Russian guards who would have, at the very least, prevented them from leaving the country and forced Rifka's brother to return to the army he had deserted. When her family has finally crossed Europe, a case of ringworm quarantines Rifka in Belgium for many months. Finally Rifka is allowed on board a ship to America, but she still has two worries: first, although her ringworm has healed, her hair has not begun to grow back. She learns that this could cause her to be turned back, on the grounds that she would be unmarriageable. She is also worried about Ilya, a seven-year-old Russian boy she has befriended during her journey. He speaks Russian with Rifka, but he is afraid of nearly everyone else and has learned no English. The immigration officials may send him back as well if they conclude that he is deaf, dumb, or incapable of literacy.

Rifka persuades Ilya to read aloud from a Russian edition of Pushkin's poetry, and Mr. Fargate, the immigration official, is persuaded that Ilya may enter the country. Then he turns his attention to Rifka, expressing his concern about her lack of hair. Rifka avoids exposing her head and instead boasts of her linguistic abilities and the work she did on board:

> "Not very modest, is she?" Mr. Fargate observed, and everyone laughed . . .
>
> "I still worry about her hair," Mr. Fargate said.
>
> I looked Mr. Fargate right in the eye. "I do not need hair to get a good life," I said.
>
> "Maybe right now you don't," Mr. Fargate answered, "But what about when you wish to marry?"
>
> "If I wish to marry, Mr. Fargate," I said—can you believe I spoke like this to an American official, Tovah?—"if I wish to marry, I will do so with or without hair."
>
> I heard Mama gasp. This much English she understood.[26]

Rifka continues her assertive speech, until Fargate finally concludes:

> "No wonder the boy never talked. She talks enough for both of them."
> Now, I thought, it would be clever to keep quiet.
> "Well, Miss Nebrot," Mr. Fargate said, "After giving the matter some consideration, I think you are correct. Whether you wish to marry or not is no business of mine. He turned to Doctor Askin. "Heaven help the man she does marry." (*Letters from Rifka*, 141)

A decade after Rifka's immigration in 1919, the United States and many other countries experienced the Great Depression. The Depression era provides a rich background for antiauthoritarian humor. Two prolific authors named Peck have penned engaging regional tales in which "the common man" triumphs over pompous and overbearing small town officials. Richard Peck's *A Long Way from Chicago* includes of a series of vignettes about the formidable Grandma Dowdel and her unique manner of resolving justice in her rural Illinois town. One of those tales, "A One-Woman Crime Wave" features Grandma's hilarious one-woman triumph over sheriff O. B. Dickerson and all of his deputies. Robert Newton Peck's *Horse Thief*, set in rural Florida during the Depression, sets up the villainous judge Elberton Carvul Hoad and his dim-witted son, deputy Futrell Hoad, for richly deserved ridicule. In this engaging story, a young man tries to rescue his beloved rodeo horses from the Judge's plan to sell them for dog food. The "mad-dog mean" judge and his "brains of a dung beetle" son are just two among a host of colorful characters in this atmospheric regional novel.

Wicked Uncles

Although the evil stepmother is the most notorious of bad relations in folktales, in the world of humorous YA literature it seems that wicked uncles, and occasionally, wicked aunts, are encountered more frequently. That most famous of recent fictional characters, Harry Potter, has been raised in the family of his Aunt Petunia Dursley, but now that he is able to attend Hogwarts each school year, he must endure the Dursleys only during holidays. "He was back with the Dursleys for the summer, back to being treated like a dog that had rolled in something smelly."[27] The Dursley's mistreatment of Harry Potter is largely motivated by their fear and dislike of the uncanny magical talents Harry has inherited from his deceased parents.

The Dursleys confine Harry to a closet under the stairs, make him do all the housework, and blatantly spoil their own son while treating Harry like a slave. Harry gets back at the Dursleys in many amusing ways, most spectacularly by departing from an upstairs window of their house directly into a flying automobile in *Harry Potter and the Chamber of Secrets*. In turn, the Dursleys tell their neighbors that Harry attends "St. Brutus's Secure Centre for Incurably Criminal Boys."[28]

Another popular fantasy series, Lemony Snicket's A Series of Unfortunate Events, also features a hateful uncle. However, the villain in this instance is a more distant relative of his victims. The three Baudelaire children, Violet, fourteen, Klaus, twelve, and Sunny, a toddler, have been left orphans when their house burns down, presumably killing their parents. Mr. Poe, the rather dim-witted banker in charge of arranging their guardianship, assigns them to live not with any of their close relatives, but rather with the relative who happens to live closest, even though he is unknown to the children. This happens to be Count Olaf, "either a third cousin four times removed, or a fourth cousin three times removed. He is not your closest relative on the family tree, but he is the closest geographically," Mr. Poe explains.[29] Count Olaf is a horrible guardian, who mistreats the children and ceaselessly plots to steal the inheritance that will go directly to Violet when she comes of age.

> The three siblings survived living with Count Olaf, but just barely, and since then Olaf had followed them everywhere, usually accompanied by one or more of his sinister and ugly associates. No matter who was caring for the Baudelaires, Count Olaf was always right behind them, performing such dastardly deeds that I can scarcely list them all: kidnapping, murder, nasty phone calls, disguises, poison, hypnosis, and atrocious cooking are just some of the adversities the Baudelaire orphans survived at his hands. Even worse, Count Olaf had a bad habit of avoiding capture, so he was always sure to turn up again. It is truly awful that this keeps happening, but that is how the story goes.[30]

Deb Gliori's *Pure Dead Magic* features a wicked uncle with the delicious name, Don Lucifer di s'Embowelli Borgia. Like Count Olaf, villainous Don Lucifer is an over-the-top villain who plots to steal the inheritance of his nephew and nieces before they reach the age when they can control it directly.

In Philip Pullman's *Count Karlstein*, the odious Count has been appointed guardian of two English girls, Lucy, twelve, and Charlotte, ten, to whom he is only very distantly related. Pullman's short melodrama is filled with chance events, hairbreadth escapes, and a variety of comic characters and situations. Count Karlstein himself is a bit over the top as a caped villain: a gaunt, cold, humorless old miser whom we love to hate.

Jean Ferris's *Love among the Walnuts* features a pair of dastardly uncles in a more contemporary, yet fantastic setting. *Love among the Walnuts* has an unusual atmosphere, somewhat akin to Farmer's *The Ear, the Eye, and the Arm*, Louis Sachar's *Holes*, and also to Ferris's own later novel, *Once upon a Marigold*. Like Shakespeare's late romances, these stories are comic in their happy resolution, but are also filled with strange elements from the genres of mystery, fantasy, and romance. The exaggerated malice of quirky villains, the whimsicality of antiheroic protagonists, sudden reversals of fortune, and a rich and strange dreamlike atmosphere are some of the chief elements.

Evil uncles often resemble old-fashioned stage villains, like the handlebar-mustachioed Snidely Whiplash in his cape and top hat chortling, "Har, har, my beauty, I've got you now" as he ties Nell Fenwick to the railroad tracks.[31] Patricia Wrede has fun with the convention in several satirical takes on the wicked uncle theme throughout her Enchanted Forest stories.

The second novel of Wrede's Enchanted Forest series, *Searching for Dragons*, features an outstanding wicked uncle episode. It begins when the major domo announces "His Royal Highness, Crown Prince Jorillam of Merimbee . . . and his Royal Highness's uncle and guardian, Prince Rupert." Young Prince Jorillam, who is about ten-years-old, explains, "the whole reason we came was so he could leave me in the forest and go home and take over my kingdom."[32] Uncle Rupert is embarrassed, but explains that his club, The Right Honorable Wicked Stepmothers' Traveling, Drinking, and Debating Society, requires that he do some dastardly deed. He sighs, "I've been a member of the Men's Auxiliary for the past fifteen years."

"That would be for wicked stepfathers?" Mendanbar guessed.

"Yes, though we don't get many of those," Prince Rupert said. "Mostly, it's Wicked Uncles . . . If I don't do something really wicked soon, I'll get kicked out of the club. I only have until sunset tomorrow." (*Searching for Dragons*, 183–84)

Fortunately, King Mendanbar is able to oblige his guests. As an alternative to being abandoned in the forest, Prince Jorillam asks to be thrown in a dungeon. Mendanbar's Enchanted Castle is just the place, with numerous empty dungeons guaranteed to fascinate the young prince. Mendanbar orders his steward to "see that His Royal Highness, here, is made comfortable in one of the dungeons" (186). When the young prince is let out, he complains that the dungeon was not equipped with a torture rack or populated by rats (225).

In "Utensile Strength," a short story about the Enchanted Forest, Wrede presents another wicked uncle, the pompously self-titled Rothben The Great, who is "turned into an enormous poached egg" by a clout on the head from his annoyed niece, who just happens to be wielding the Frying Pan of Doom.[33] Nobody does wicked uncles better than Patricia C. Wrede.

Notes

1. Susan Juby, *Alice, I Think* (New York: HarperCollins, 2003), 14.

2. James Howe, *The Misfits* (New York: Atheneum, 2001), 17.

3. Gordon Korman, *No More Dead Dogs* (New York: Hyperion, 2000), 5.

4. Sue Townsend, *The Adrian Mole Diaries* (New York: Grove, 1986), 154.

5. Louise Rennison, *Angus, Thongs and Full-frontal Snogging: Confessions of Georgia Nicolson*. New York: HarperCollins, 1999, 90.

6. Louise Rennison, *Dancing in My Nuddy-Pants: Even Further Confessions of Georgia Nicolson* (New York: HarperTempest, 2003), 125.

7. J. K. Rowling, *Harry Potter and the Order of the Phoenix* (New York: Scholastic, 2003), 625.

8. Daniel Pinkwater, *The Education of Robert Nifkin* (New York: Farrar, Straus & Giroux, 1998), 16–17.

9. Chris Lynch, *Slot Machine* (New York: HarperCollins, 1995), 234–35.

10. Mariah Fredericks, *The True Meaning of Cleavage* (New York: Atheneum, 2003), 4.

11. Terry Spencer Hesser, *Kissing Doorknobs* (New York: Delacorte, 1998), 20–21.

12. Megan McCafferty, *Sloppy Firsts* (New York: Crown, 2001), 19.

13. Daniel Pinkwater, *Alan Mendelsohn, the Boy from Mars* (New York: Dutton, 1979), 127.

14. All three stories are collected and still in print as *Young Adults* (New York: Tor, 1991).

15. Daniel Pinkwater, "Dead End Dada" in *Young Adults* (New York: Tor, 1991), 137.

16. Arthur Slade, *Tribes* (New York: Wendy Lamb Books, 2002), 13.

17. M. T. Anderson, *Burger Wuss* (Cambridge, Mass.: Candlewick, 1999), 24.

18. Catherine Clark, *Wurst Case Scenario* (New York: HarperCollins, 2001), 11.

19. Gail Gauthier, *Saving the Planet & Stuff* (New York: Putnam, 2003), 87–88.

20. Joan Bauer, *Rules of the Road* (New York: Putnam, 1998), 4.

21. Joan Bauer, *Hope Was Here* (New York: Putnam, 2000), 36.

22. Gordon Korman, *Losing Joe's Place* (New York: Scholastic, 1990), 30–31.

23. Lucy Frank, *Just Ask Iris* (New York: Atheneum, 2001), 157.

24. Don Trembath, *The Tuesday Café* (Victoria, BC: Orca, 1996), 3.

25. Carl Hiaasen, *Hoot* (New York: Knopf, 2002), 27.

26. Karen Hesse, *Letters from Rifka* (New York: Holt, 1992), 138–39.

27. J. K. Rowling, *Harry Potter and the Chamber of Secrets* (New York: Arthur A. Levine Books, 1999), 5.

28. J. K. Rowling, *Harry Potter and the Order of the Phoenix* (New York: Scholastic, 2003), 15.

29. Lemony Snicket, *The Bad Beginning* (New York: HarperCollins, 1999), 15.

30. Lemony Snicket, *The Austere Academy* (New York: HarperCollins, 2000), 2–3.

31. Snidely Whiplash was one of the characters in "The Adventures of Rocky and Bullwinkle" cartoons, which first appeared in 1959.

32. Patricia C. Wrede, *Searching for Dragons: The Enchanted Forest Chronicles* (San Diego: Harcourt Brace, 1991), 182.

33. Patricia C. Wrede, "Utensile Strength," in Patricia C. Wrede, *Book of Enchantments* (San Diego, Harcourt Brace, 1996), 217–19.

CHAPTER FIVE

~

What's Wrong with Me?

Adolescents often feel that they are being persecuted and their lives are out of control. Sometimes this is a realistic assessment of the situation, but it could also be a hormonally driven overreaction to minor or temporary nuisances, such as mild acne, a changing voice, or being grounded for the weekend. Many YA novels have mined humor from these teen angst situations. Al Capsella, the hero of three humorous YA novels by Australian author Judith Clarke, offers a perceptive insight on the trials of adolescence:

> Being fourteen is scary. It's like being in a fairy tale; you never know what you will find in the mirror when you wake up in the morning: not just pimples or a hole in your front teeth, but something different and strange, like your nose growing big or your eyes getting small, things that can't change back again, so you know you're going to look like that for the rest of your life.[1]

Al notices physical changes daily and he doesn't know where it's all going to end. And this has merely to do with facial appearance! Al has not addressed all the other physical and psychological changes he can expect during his adolescence. Even "just pimples," as Al noted, can dramatically impact a teen's self-confidence and quality of life.

Weighty Matters

Some YA literature brings out the inherent humor in these episodes. Pete Hautman's short story, "Hot Lava" features a witty, extended comparison of the narrator's emerging pimple to a volcanic eruption, as well as to the build-up of his feelings for a girl he admires. Nick Bishop, the narrator of Ron Koertge's novel, *The Boy in the Moon*, compares his acne scars to the surface of the moon and uses self-deprecating humor to try to come to terms with his unsightly condition. Both narrators offer lyrical and wryly humorous reflections upon this unpromising topic. In both stories, the use of vast geothermal and astronomical forces as overwrought metaphors for a teen's skin "eruptions" humorously overstates what are real, but perhaps not cosmic, problems.

Ron Koertge has a knack of writing with grace and humor about teens suffering from debilitating conditions. Hector, a sixteen-year-old paraplegic in Koertge's *Confess-O-Rama*, makes frequent wisecracks about his confinement to a wheelchair and presents an unfailingly cheerful face to the world. Koertge's *Stoner & Spaz* presents a pair of teens with serious problems whose lives intersect. "Stoner" is drug-addicted Colleen Minou, "Spaz" is Ben Bancroft, partially crippled by cerebral palsy (CP) but also emotionally crippled by his self-imposed isolation from his peers. Ben appreciates Colleen's brutal directness.

> "Ed would kill you if he caught you coming on to me."
> "I would be so stoked if Ed thought that. I never came on to anybody in my life."
> "Oh, bullshit. Isn't there, like, some spaz dating club or something? How about that blind chick, Doris? You guys would be perfect. She can't see you limp, and you could feel her up whenever you wanted."[2]

Colleen applies the same rough humor to herself. When Ben asks her about her rehab experience, she replies, "Well, I asked God to remove all character defects and shortcomings, and He said He'd have to get back to me on that because there are only so many hours in a day" (*Stoner & Spaz*, 136).

Ben and Colleen are frank and funny about Ben's CP. This has helped Ben to come to terms with his physical affliction. Like Hector's paralysis, Ben's CP can't be wished away, and Ben must learn to accept the condition as a part of his life. However, Ben realizes that his prig-gish personality is something he *can* change. Humor helps him to emerge from the deep ruts of his snobbish attitudes and solitary habits, and to mark his progress toward a healthier adolescent social life. Chris Crutcher is another author noted for his ability to produce tough, realistic YA novels in which his characters face daunting chal-lenges with courage and humor. Sarah Byrnes of Crutcher's *Staying Fat for Sarah Byrnes* has been scarred by burn injuries to her face and hands. Her agony is made all the worse by the knowledge that her father, with whom she is still living, deliberately caused her injuries, drove off Sarah's mother, and refused to allow any reconstructive surgery. Despite these terrible circumstances and her abysmal appearance, Sarah man-ages to engage in bleak humor about her condition. Her friend, Eric (aka Moby), explains how he and Sarah came up with the name of their underground newspaper, *Crispy Pork Rinds*: "Don't you get it? Sarah Byrnes is crispy, I'm a porker, and rinds are the part that's left—that no one pays attention to. We print the news the regular newspa-per misses."[3]

Sarah Byrnes uses black humor to help her face a life that would oth-erwise be unbearably painful. It can also be said that author Chris Crutcher has artfully infused Moby's narration and Sarah's speech with wit and humor to maintain reader involvement in a novel that takes his characters and his readers through some very dark episodes before a satisfying resolution is finally achieved. Thus, in a well-written novel, humorous narration and dialogue function simultaneously on two lev-els. While the humor must be a believable component of the particular character's thoughts and speech, it also serves as an authorial device to sustain reader interest.

Disfiguring injuries such as those suffered by Sarah Byrnes fortu-nately are rare. Far more common are those variations in body size and shape, which, even if well within "normal" range, nonetheless deviate sufficiently from the ideal to cause distress to self-conscious adolescents and provoke teasing from their peers. In our culture, overweight boys and girls can be subjected to ridicule and criticism, causing sometimes permanent damage to an already diminished adolescent self-image.

Some YA novels feature a female protagonist who uses humor as a way of coping with her physical imperfections. Barbara Wersba wrote an outstanding trilogy of novels about an overweight teenage girl. *Fat, A Love Story* (1987), *Love Is the Crooked Thing* (1987) and *Beautiful Losers* (1988) tell the story of Rita Formica, who at age sixteen falls in love with the thirty-two-year-old Arnold Bromberg. Rita describes herself as "five foot three and weighing over two hundred pounds."[4] Rita has an honest, funny way of expressing herself, as here when she describes her eating habits:

> My idea of food has always been different from other people's. Other people seem to consume meat and vegetables, dairy products and fruit, whole grains and starches—whereas my concept of food, to put it plainly, is junk. Cookies, candy, and potato chips. Pizza and strawberry shortcake. Malteds, french fries, Sara Lee cakes. Gummy bears. (*Love Is the Crooked Thing*, 20)

Other chunky but spunky heroines have been brought to life in more recent YA literature. Fifteen-year-old Virginia Shreves of Carolyn Mackler's *The Earth, My Butt, and Other Big, Round Things* feels like a failure because she is the only one in her family who is not slender, good-looking, and accomplished. Virginia makes an unimpressive appearance, being overweight, with plain features and no shining talents. Because her mother is always trying to make her over, telling her how to dress and accessorize, Virginia decides to cultivate a "look," although it's not what her mother had in mind. Over her mother's protests, she goes to Seattle and returns with an eyebrow ring. She then dyes her hair purple, chooses her own clothes instead of the ones her mother likes, takes up kickboxing, and comes to terms with her physique. Virginia, with her wry, skeptical sense of humor, observes, "People refer to me as plump, as if being likened to a vine-ripened tomato is some kind of compliment."[5] The book's title is that of an autobiographical article Virginia has written for the first issue of a new webzine she has launched with some friends. In her article, she is remarkably frank about her body:

> I've never been a fan of my butt. Too big, too round, blah, blah, blah. But when grooving outside the MTV studios in Times Square, it's much more fun to shake your booty when you actually HAVE a booty to shake, not just a bony excuse for a rear end. (*The Earth, My Butt, and Other Big, Round Things*, 239)

Virginia's concerns about her "big booty" seem mild when compared to the weight problems of Myrtle Parcittadino, the protagonist of Rebecca O'Connell's unique, quirky novel *Myrtle of Willendorf*. Myrtle describes herself as five foot four and grossly overweight. Through high school and her first year of college, Myrtle's love affair with food leads to a weight gain that results in her being marginalized and outside the mainstream of adolescent social life. In high school, Myrtle's pagan friend, Margie, had introduced her to the famous Venus of Willendorf fertility figure and other symbols of female value, but Myrtle was unable to take Margie and her earnest feminism seriously. Now in college, Myrtle is a sad, but witty narrator.

> In Bio 101, I was learning that paramecia can reproduce sexually, too. This really bothered me.
>
> I was the only living creature on the face of the Earth who didn't get to pair off and mate. I was below protozoa on the scale of social evolution. I was literally less romantically adept than pond scum.
>
> I couldn't take this kind of stress. I would have to stop and get an ice cream on my way back to the house I shared with Jada.[6]

Myrtle can be quite funny about her size, speaking of her "dirigible body" (*Myrtle of Willendorf*, 39) and inventing other wordplay:

> Margie said it. Goddess-energy can influence the physical sphere. Well, that was nice for the Goddess, but right now I didn't even have the energy to influence my physical rear. (75)

Myrtle appreciates her friends' jokes, too. Crying and upset, she tells her gay friend, Sam Horton:

> "They said I was a nympho-psycho-lesbo."
> Good ol' Sam. He kept a straight face. "That's ridiculous," he told me. "You're not a lesbo."

Myrtle laughs so hard she needs a handful of napkins to clean her face (88).

In the end, Myrtle refuses to be diminished, or to be seen as merely a fat girl who should quietly hide herself away from the view of "normal" people. A talented artist, Myrtle can lavishly express herself on canvas. Naked, she confronts herself directly in a mirror and produces a startling, dramatic, and characteristically witty self-portrait she entitles "Myrtle of Willendorf." The painting is hung in a popular campus café/gallery and is later purchased by the Office of Women's Studies. Myrtle then reconnects with her old friend Margie, sending her a clipping of a local newspaper story about the success of "Myrtle of Willendorf." Myrtle has finally made a true and uniquely personal connection with "the goddess" who embodies female strength and potency by using her wit as well as her talent to accept and even celebrate the primal aspect of her rotund female body.

Myrtle of Willendorf could not be a successful novel without its humor. One can hardly imagine a less promising heroine for a conventional "problem novel" than a depressed, grossly obese young woman who feels she has no hope of ever dating or being loved. Like Koertge's *Stoner & Spaz* and Crutcher's *Staying Fat for Sarah Byrnes*, O'Connell's novel employs humor with powerful effect to make us care deeply for a character we might otherwise merely pity.

We might "broadly" divide overweight girls into two types: the Rubenesque and the Amazonian. The former are simply overweight; the latter are vertically imposing as well. In a boy, the second condition is generally preferable, since it suggests the manly quality of strength. However, for girls, being both stout and tall is usually not a desirable body type.

Ellie Morgan of Joan Bauer's *Squashed* is a bit taller than average, at five foot seven, and describes herself as "twenty pounds overweight."[7] Her efforts to lose weight are comically juxtaposed with her simultaneous obsession to grow a record-breaking giant pumpkin she has named Max. "I weighed 144 pounds and was dreaming about chocolate chip cheesecake. Max weighed 430 pounds and was dreaming about victory" (*Squashed*, 40). Ellie is a humorous narrator: "I had great skin, but twenty pounds too much of it . . . My life was passing in front of my eyes, and it was pudgy" (5).

Another of Joan Bauer's gutsy heroines, Jena Boller of *Rules of the Road*, is of truly Amazonian proportions. Like Ellie Morgan of *Squashed*, overweight Jenna is a bit circumspect about her weight, as when describing her new driver's license:

Jenna Boller
Eyes: Brown
Hair: Red
Height: 5'11"
Weight: None of your business[8]

Jenna compares her own appearance unfavorably to that of her sister Faith, who is much more attractive by conventional standards.

> Faith always seemed put together—her head matched her neck; her long legs matched the rest of her body. I felt like I'd been glued together with surplus parts—my shoulders were big and bony, my legs were long and skinny. I had a swan-thin neck that held my round head in place. (*Rules of the Road*, 16)

During the road trip that furnishes the novel's title, Jenna receives valuable beauty tips and learns how to use her height to advantage, especially when confronting the diminutive villain, Elden Gladstone: "I stood super tall and looked down at Elden like he was fertilizer" (125).

Iris Hoving of Beverly Keller's *The Amazon Papers* is like Ellie Morgan and Jenna Boller in many ways. She's tall, at five foot ten and a conscientious first (and only) child. Like Jenna, she's a practical young woman who hasn't given much thought to fashion or glamour. When she impulsively tries heavy makeup for the first time, a friend tells her, "Well, you . . . look kind of like a raccoon with a high fever."[9] Iris is funny about her own minimal approach to grooming.

> I aimed a brush at my hair, which had recently been whacked at an EIGHT DOLLARS NO WAITING NO APPOINTMENT NO MAKING A SCENE ON THE PREMISES OVER THE RESULT place. (*Amazon Papers*, 13)

Iris is a bit self-conscious about her height, but unlike Jenna Boller, who would like to lose a few pounds, Iris is otherwise comfortable with her body. However, she is concerned that her interests in sports and automotive mechanics, combined with her considerable height, will make it hard for her to attract a suitable boyfriend.

> I realize that at almost sixteen, five feet ten, with all the feminine wiles of an Amazon, I could emerge untouched from spring break at Ft. Lauderdale.
> Not that guys ignore me. I can put my finger on an engine problem . . .
> Of course, there have been those who think of me as more than one of the boys. They tend to be under five feet five, long on enthusiasm but short on subtlety—as if, because I'm tall and strong and capable, I'm to be approached like the north face of the Matterhorn. I think of it as the

Mount Everest Syndrome, the male's urge to conquer something monumental. (26)

Most of Iris's troubles into in this very funny novel follow from her powerful hormonal response to Foster Prizer, "lean and dangerous looking, with his black curly hair, blue eyes, and earring, and the cheekbones of a Tartar" (8). As her friend Zelma puts it, "Foster has a way of making women do crazy things" (74). By the end of her adventurous week as head of the household, Iris has to wonder if she's as level-headed as she had always supposed herself to be. "I never dreamed you had a wild streak in you, Iris," Aunt Blanche tells her (145).

In *My Cup Runneth Over*, author Cherry Whytock introduces us to Angelica Cookson Potts, a.k.a. "Angel," a large girl from a wealthy family living in the upscale London suburb of Kensington. Angel reflects that each of her friends are obsessed with their own various physical imperfections:

> It's funny, isn't it, what people worry about? I mean, if I had Mercedes's amazing figure, would I worry about piffling little braces? NO, I WOULD NOT. But then I wouldn't think that I wasn't talented or that people wouldn't always really like me if I was Minnie. And I certainly wouldn't worry if I had one or two TINY pimples if I was Portia. I wonder why we all worry about the things we think are wrong with us instead of trying to think about our good points—funny that.[10]

Angel describes herself, variously, as "a great, big gallumphing whale" (*My Cup Runneth Over*, 142), "a vast blob" (144), and "a giant heffalump" (114). She's self-conscious about her large breasts: "I hunch my shoulders to try and hide the beastly boulders" (23). Perhaps the key self-description is Angel's reference to "my big, wobbly, out-of-control body" (139). Just so. Like Al Capsella's lament with which we opened this chapter—when he worries that the next time he looks in the mirror his nose might be bigger or his eyes smaller—Angel feels that her body has a mind of its own.

> Things went badly wrong about two and a half years ago when I was twelve. I went to bed all innocent and sweet with my teddy bear and my picture of Brad Pitt, as you do, and suddenly during the night, BOOM!—

bosoms. Not those nice, well-shaped pert little numbers that I had hoped for, but HUMUNGOUS, great barrage balloons that started under my arms and seemed to end somewhere near my navel. . . . Then the rest of my body decided it wanted to match my boobs, and there I was—a great, big, walloping whale with a wobble rating of about a zillion. (3)

Angel's good-humored tolerance of the surprises her body has imposed upon her carry her through. With the right outfit, and after being fitted for some well-chosen "underpinnings" by "Mrs. Born-in-a-Corset" at Harrod's lingerie department, Angel finds that she can project statuesque glamour at a fashion show she had been dreading.

Big Mouth & Ugly Girl, the first YA novel by prolific adult market author Joyce Carol Oates, offers a unique perspective of the psyche of a big, tall girl. Like Rebecca O'Connell's Myrtle, Ursula Riggs has a quirky, unique way of looking at herself and at the world. But unlike the other large-sized girls we have discussed, Ursula appreciates her Amazonian proportions: "It felt good, too, to be almost as tall as my dad (who was six feet three, weighed over two hundred pounds), so he'd have to treat me more like an equal than just a child."[11]

Ursula has a special name and an entire persona for herself: Ugly Girl. Oates employs an unusual narrative technique in this novel: half of the chapters are narrated by Ursula, always in first person; the remainder are narrated in the third person, often with an omniscient view of the thoughts of the other main character, Matt Donaghy (Big Mouth). Other YA novels have been narrated alternately by two or more main characters: Gordon Korman's *No More Dead Dogs* has several alternating narrators, and Todd Strasser often uses the technique. However, *Big Mouth & Ugly Girl* has an interesting tilt toward Ugly Girl—Ursula—because only her perspective is rendered in the first person. It must be so, to bring out Ursula's unusual habit of speaking about herself in the third person as Ugly Girl.

> Strange: that stuff that used to bother me in the middle school, had the power to make me hide away and cry, didn't bother me at all now. Since that day I woke up and knew I wasn't an ugly girl. I was Ugly Girl.
> I laughed, and it wasn't a nice feminine laugh like my mom encourages. It was a real laugh, deep in the gut. I would never be ashamed of my body again; I would be proud of it. (*Ugly Girl*, 9–10)

So deeply is this image embedded in Ursula's mind that she almost forgets that it is unknown to others: "I half expected them to call me Ugly Girl. It surprised me sometimes, that no one knew about Ugly Girl. She was my secret, even from Matt" (240). The Ugly Girl persona is more than just a label. Ursula also has a special vocabulary for Ugly Girl's emotional states: "It was Ugly Girl who was susceptible to "moods"—these ranged from Inky Black to Fiery Red" (12). While not laugh-out-loud funny, *Big Mouth & Ugly Girl* has a distinctive humorous aspect. The Ugly Girl persona is serious and purposeful; Ursula dons it as if it were armor: "Ugly girl, warrior woman. Going her own way" (86).

Big girls, and strong young women who do not present traditional feminine appearance or behavior, are often subjected to crude suggestions that they are lesbian (insinuating that this is shameful). The female protagonists of *Big Mouth & Ugly Girl* and *Myrtle of Willendorf* are each persecuted by gossip and taunts concerning their sexual orientation. Myrtle, Ursula, and many of the YA protagonists discussed here do sometimes question their own sexual identity, reminding us that developing a clear sexual identity (and orientation) is an integral part of the adolescent's complex developmental process.

At one point Ursula draws whistles and a call of "Hey there, sexy!" from a pair of "tough-looking girls" in leather and with spiky dyed hair. She thinks to herself, "They were Ugly Girls, too" (121). An Ugly Girl is not defined by her sexual orientation, but by her personality, style, and behavior. Even when everyone in school has seen that she and Matt are a couple, Ursula remains "intimidating, especially now with her glaring blond hair, and her manner that differed so from most girls' soft-melting, sunny-cheery smiles" (259).

Although not labeled a lesbian, Elizabeth Clarry of Jaclyn Moriarty's *Feeling Sorry for Celia* represents another kind of adolescent girl with concerns about her feminine identity. Elizabeth is a long-distance runner whose intense training regimen keeps her extremely thin. She has never had a boyfriend and is constantly reminded of her perceived unattractiveness because her closest friend, Celia, is such a boy magnet. In this funny epistolary novel, Elizabeth's journal entries and the quirky notes stuck on the fridge by her mother are interspersed with purported memoranda from imaginary organizations such as The Cold Hard Truth Association and The Young Romance Society. Like Jenna Boller and

Iris Hoving, Elizabeth is an overly responsible young woman helping her single mother. And like Iris, Elizabeth surprises herself by finally loosening up and allowing herself to have fun, in spite of her responsibilities and insecurities.

Another long-distance runner, sixteen-year-old Jessica Darling of Megan McCafferty's *Sloppy Firsts*, is so dedicated to her sport that her habitual running not only burns off body fat, but also interferes with her menstrual cycle. Jessie's track coach and her doctor have talked to her about amenorrhea, a common condition that can affect female athletes. But Jessie's imagination runs wild:

> I've been extra edgy about my no-show menstrual cycle. What if there's something seriously wrong with me? What if I picked up an as-of-yet undiscovered crazy cow virus by eating an undercooked cheeseburger? What if I'm a bizarro, *Ripley's Believe It or Not!* girl-boy hybrid, mere moments away from popping a set of nads between my legs? What if I'm a genetically mutated by-product of an intergalactic liaison between my mother and an alien's proboscis?[12]

McCafferty's overwrought narrator has been described as a female Holden Caulfield. Jessie's sleepless, hyperactive manner, extreme sense of alienation, and sharp, satirical wit give *Sloppy Firsts* a distinctly edgy tone. Although Jessica is very hard on her classmates and her family, she's even harder on herself, describing herself as "Boobless, neurotic, PMS-y" (*Sloppy Firsts*, 70), and as "the average almost-sixteen-year-old honor student with no best friend or boyfriend and bigger bumps on her face than in her bra" (21).

We've considered the image problems of both fat and thin girls. With characteristically raw humor, Jessica considers the plight of the beautiful:

> Bridget is always zeroing in on the hugeness of models' asses. This is because Bridget herself is an aspiring model who is convinced she has a huge ass. This is the burden of being beautiful. In Psych class I learned that the hotter you are, the more paranoid you are about the way you look. That's because born beauties get so much pretty-girl praise that their appearance becomes crucial to their oh-so-delicate self-worth.
> Boo-freaking-hoo. (9)

For a boy, being overweight does not diminish self-worth as much as it does for girls. Chris Crutcher has presented some heavyweight boys whose prowess at sports, combined with a healthy sense of humor, has helped them endure teasing and other negativity concerning their hefty bodies. The hero of Crutcher's "A Brief Moment in the Life of Angus Bethune" is a well-adjusted young man who uses his extra pounds to advantage on and off the football field. Eric Calhoune of *Staying Fat for Sarah Byrnes* is a similar protagonist: smart, witty, and a good athlete. When Eric complains about the fat genes he inherited from his overweight father, his mother tells him he's not fat but "big and solid."

"Big and solid as twelve pounds of mashed potatoes in an eight-pound bag," I said. "If you dressed me up in an orange-and-red sweater, you could ride me around the world in eighty days."

"And you have a much better sense of humor than your father," she said. (*Staying Fat for Sarah Byrnes*, 2)

Rather than being hurt by the nickname "Moby," Eric has come to embrace it:

"You know, Mark, people call me Moby because I'm a chunko swimmer. I could get pissed; you know, threaten to go after anyone who calls me that. . . . I truly believe I could get people to quit calling me Moby, but I could never stop what they think when they see me in a tank suit, and I couldn't stop what they'd say about me if I went around with a chip on my shoulder. . . . Besides, folks calling me Moby is pretty funny, don't you think?" (196–97)

Crutcher's chunky protagonists face teasing and ridicule with grace and humor. Other comic YA novels with overweight male protagonists include *Slot Machine* and *Extreme Elvin* by Chris Lynch; Daniel Pinkwater's *Alan Mendelsohn, the Boy from Mars* and *The Education of Robert Nifkin*; and James Howe's *The Misfits*. None of the young men featured in these stories are strong and athletic like Chris Crutcher's oversized heroes, so they are unable to turn their size directly to advantage. Instead, each uses his wits and develops a healthy sense of humor to compensate for the problems he is caused by being fat.

Euphemisms can help. Leonard Neeble, of Pinkwater's *Alan Mendelsohn, the Boy from Mars*, keeps reminding us that he is "not actually fat but portly. That's what it says on the label when I get clothes in the department store: boy's portly."[13] When the plus-sized Elvin Bishop in Lynch's *Extreme Elvin* needs new clothes for a school dance, his friends take him to the Big and Tall store and pretend it's because he's tall. Frankie asks Elvin, "You been drinking giraffe milk, El? Listen, we got to get you into the Big and *Tall* shop." "I better duck on the way in," Elvin says. Mikie tells the salesman, "He'd like to see some of your finest tall-people pants."[14]

K. L. Going's remarkable first novel, *Fat Kid Rules the World*, portrays a fat adolescent who sees his salvation not in losing weight, but through achievement in an arena where his size is not a disadvantage. At six foot one with a nonathletic, 300-pound body, Troy Billings is depressed. As the story opens, he is standing at the edge of a subway platform, staring at the tracks and the oncoming train,

> trying to decide whether people would laugh if I jumped. Would it be funny if the Fat Kid got splattered by a subway train? Is that funny? I'm not being facetious; I really want to know. Like it or not, apparently there's something funny about fat people. Something unpredictable.[15]

Just as Ursula Riggs sees herself as "Ugly Girl," Troy identifies himself in the third person as "Fat Kid." As he continues to stare at the subway tracks, he imagines the derisive phrase on a movie marquee:

> I want to picture myself flying dramatically through the air but realize I wouldn't have the muscle power to launch my body. Instead, I would plummet straight down . . . FAT KID MESSES UP—coming soon to a theater near you.
> I start to laugh. Suddenly there's something funny about it. I swear to God. There really is. (*Fat Kid Rules the World*, 2)

Troy is able to laugh at himself, but only in this bitter, self-despising way. Then he meets Curt MacCrae, a scrawny, filthy, punk rock genius who had been sleeping in the underground subway station. Only after Curt has taken an interest in him and given him something to care about is Troy capable of a less self-destructive view of himself.

Troy does not lose weight, but he does begin to immerse himself in music, practicing his drums with a furious energy to reach the level that Curt has asked of him. Troy is beginning to have a life. But when the pair finally take the stage for their first live performance, Troy "loses it" in an unforgettable scene:

> I'm staring into the audience, knowing I cannot lift my fat arms in front of all these perfect, competent, skinny people. I can*not* pretend to be a rock star. My nauseous stomach lurches as if I've just crested the top of a mammoth roller coaster. I can taste the bile in my mouth and then . . .
> I am Mount Vesuvius.
> Everything I've eaten for a week erupts. Canned ravioli, leftover pizza, Ben and Jerry's ice cream, mashed potatoes, Twinkies, Sprite, pretzels, bean burritos. I am the mother of all volcanoes.
> There is stunned silence. Absolute and total silence. There's vomit everywhere, covering the stage like Pompeii. I wait for the laughter, and decide that when it comes, I will die. I will stop my heart by sheer force of will.
> Then I hear it. Someone *is* laughing. It's Curt. He stares, wide-eyed, grinning like he's just seen the best show on earth.
> "Holy shit," he says. He turns to the stunned crowd.
> "How's that for punk rock?" he asks them. He grins, then says it again louder with bother middle fingers extended. "How's that for fucking punk rock? Now that was a very new thing." He screeches his guitar and the crowd goes nuts. (133)

Drugged-out Curt has the most astonishing social instincts. Here he has found a way to transform Troy's humiliation into a celebration. Troy's development as an accomplished musician, and more importantly, his new found self-esteem, help him get past his "volcanic" first performance, by taking the focus off of his body size, self-pity, and depression. In this exceptional novel, weight loss is not presented as the antidote to an overweight teen's depression.

A number of funny YA novels have depicted boys with an undersized, ectomorphic body type. Most famously, Harry Potter is described as being quite thin: "Perhaps it had something to do with living in a dark cupboard, but Harry had always been small and skinny for his age . . . Dudley was about four times bigger than he was."[16] Harry happens to be a star in the sport of Quidditch, so at Hogwarts his small size is not important, since neither wizardry nor the role of a Quidditch seeker are much dependent upon size or strength. Athleticism confers status among young men, enabling both undersized boys like Harry Potter and oversized boys like Chris Crutcher's heavyweights to achieve status and boost self-esteem through their prowess.

Joan Bauer's *Stand Tall* is the story of an extremely elongated seventh grader without athletic skills. Tree Benton is over six feet three and as skinny as a rail. He takes a lot of teasing over his sticklike shape and feels a kinship with a great white oak tree growing in the middle of the local park. Contemplating the huge tree, he reflects:

> He'd gotten used to the name. Considered the white oak . . .
> So he learned how roots could go as deep in the ground as a tree's branches grow tall. . . . How being a tree is the best thing going in the plant world. People expect trees to be strong and steady and give good shade.
> Tallness is packed with great expectations.[17]

But then a dog rudely interrupts his reverie.

> Fang ran up to the white oak, lifted his leg, and peed on the noble gray bark.
> Tree sighed deep; cold air came out.
> Being a tree isn't easy. (*Stand Tall*, 7)

Unlike his father and older brothers, Tree is not good at sports. He makes a valiant attempt at basketball, but just doesn't have any talent for the sport. "'Trust your instincts,' they told him. Tree tried. But his basic instinct was to avoid sports altogether" (24–25).

Anthony of M. T. Anderson's *Burger Wuss* and Bradley Gold of Perry Nodelman's *Behaving Bradley* both exemplify the scrawny, "ninety-eight-pound weakling" protagonist. Each relies upon his wits—and his wit—to combat physically imposing opponents. Anthony is the chosen victim of local stud, Turner, while Brad is oppressed by an odious teacher as well as by the muscular twin bullies, Mandy and Candy. Brad has another physical problem besides his lack of muscular development and athleticism: for Brad, every day is a bad hair day, and he keeps a baseball cap on his head at all times. When he finally works up the nerve to tell Stephanie, the girl he has been admiring, that he is at-tracted to her, she replies, "Hey, you're not so bad yourself. . . . If you'd lose that dumb baseball cap, you'd be really kinda cute."[18]

Brad's bad hair is a potential embarrassment he hopes to hide. A more intimate and embarrassing physical defect is revealed in Chris Lynch's *Slot Machine*. In a letter from summer camp, Elvin Bishop tries to relate a humiliating experience from a humorous perspective:

> You remember my MOLE, don't you, Mom? I guess I haven't had a chance to show you my MOLE lately, but picture it just like when I was a baby, only five *hundred* times larger and bluer. Well, due to my MOLE, all my disrob-ings . . . have become popular activities. They are by far the most unifying community events here, much bigger than movie night or campfire time, although they are similar in that the guys do all link arms and sing songs at my MOLE, Mom. It's just a shame that it's only gargantuan and blue and fuzzy and not hot as well, or I'm sure there'd be marshmallows involved.[19]

Like the wisecracking protagonists of Chris Crutcher and Ron Ko-ertge, Chris Lynch's Elvin Bishop is a witty, likeable narrator. When a novel is narrated in the first person by a witty protagonist, the narra-tor's sense of humor and the author's are usually essentially the same: Elvin Bishop's wit is also Chris Lynch's wit. The various male protago-nists of Chris Crutcher, Chris Lynch, Ron Koertge, and Gordon Kor-man, and the (mostly) female protagonists of Joan Bauer, tend to dis-play the same style of comedic discourse as their respective authors.

Dim Narrators

To identify comic YA literature in which this is clearly not the case, we must turn to works in which the narrator's wit is notably inferior to that of the author who created him. Each of M. T. Anderson's clever, satirical novels feature a narrator of this sort. The narrators of Anderson's *Burger Wuss* and *Feed* are both quite ordinary young fellows who always turn up a day late and a dollar short. Their essential dullness and timidity, their failure to seize the moment, condemns them each as hapless losers. An-derson's mordant wit is situational rather than directly presented by these narrators.

Thirsty, Anderson's first novel, features his most pathetic narrator. Chris[20] is a young man who is evolving into a vampire. His vampirism is aroused by his awakening adolescence, and much of the novel's humor derives from the interplay between mundane adolescent awkwardness and vampire lore. When Chris experiences his first strong surge of vampirism, his newly protruding canines destroy his dental braces, to the dismay and suspicion of his orthodontist. When he tries to kiss a girl, his fangs protrude and he flees, "screaming petulantly, 'No! No! No! Oh, thit, thit, thit, thit, *thit!*'"[21]

Chris is someone things happen to; a victim. When on one occasion he acts boldly by carrying out a solo mission to destroy Tch'muchgar, the Vampire Lord, it turns out that he was a complete dupe and had no idea what the mission was really designed to accomplish. Chris's reflections upon his dreadful fate are ploddingly prosaic: "I can't believe that I'm a half-vampire . . . I can't understand why they hate me so much" (*Thirsty*, 139). Chris's friend Tom assures him that his appearance is acceptable to girls. "Look, Chris. Seriously. You're not a monster" (37–38). The joke—that Chris is in fact becoming exactly that, a monster—is accessible only to the reader, not to Chris or to the other characters within the novel.

Chris unwittingly generates humor by indiscriminately mixing powerful vampire legends with mundane contemporary details, as in this observation:

> It is said that the spirit Tch'muchgar in prehistoric times ravaged the land with an army of Darkness, and that his dominion extended over the whole expanse of mountain and forest now covered by the 508 and 413 area codes.

Chris goes on to tell us that shining beings from the Forces of Light had descended "to tell the Pompossitticut tribe what rituals should be done each year in special ritual sites to keep Tch'muchgar locked away forever . . . Unfortunately there is now a White Hen Pantry and a Texaco station standing on one of the ritual sites" (10).

In short, although Chris's narration is often quite funny, it is rarely so by his own intent. Just as Chet the Celestial Being uses Chris to carry out the Tch'muchgar mission, author M. T. Anderson uses the clueless protagonist to mouth startling oxymorons and non sequiturs that Chris himself doesn't seem to realize are funny. Chris's adolescent self-absorption in the midst of horror is nicely demonstrated by his response to a terrifying prophecy:

> "Tch'muchgar the Vampire Lord will return and probably conquer most if not all of North America. Then he will most likely start to use mankind as cattle. Keep a few around as studs to corral and breed. Cripple their children. Lock each one in its dark little cubbyhole for easy storage until it starts to mature. Keep the race fed on a protein-rich diet. Then kill them, one by one, and drink their blood."
> I shuffle from one leg to the other.
> "Okay," I say. "And me?" (47)

Anderson's prevailing technique is *bathos*, "a ludicrous descent from the elevated to the commonplace."[22] Chris's obliviousness to this aspect of his narrative contributes strongly to the novel's savage irony. Chris continuously asks, "What's wrong with me?" and "Why is this happening to me?" In another context, such existential angst could elevate a hero to the tragic stature of a Hamlet or an Oedipus, but in Anderson's dark novel, Chris is merely whiny and pathetic. He is the inversion of YA fantasy heroes like Harry Potter or sexy werewolf Vivian Gandillon of Annette Curtis Klause's *Blood and Chocolate*, who accept and grow into the powers that develop in them during adolescence. Chris is only horrified by his own vampirism and is utterly incapable of embracing it forcefully. M. T. Anderson is one of the most clever authors of fiction for young adults today, in part because his narrators are among the least clever of young protagonists.

Unintentional humor and irony can also be generated by narrators other than those who are unsophisticated or unsympathetic. Percy Mountmont of Arthur Slade's *Tribes* is as brilliant a narrator as Chris of Anderson's *Feed* is a dull-witted one. Percy's affected academic jargon and his posturing as a field anthropologist taking notes on his "primitive" classmates and teachers is superbly performed and frequently hilarious. One could not ask for a wittier narrator. And yet Percy is fooling himself throughout. His insistence that his father has died turns out to be a wall of self-delusion he has erected against the betrayal he felt at his father's departure from the household. His first romantic episode with a girl is ruined by his clinical reference to her "mammae." Indeed,

Percy's self-assumed role as an adult anthropologist is his way of making virtue of his weaknesses: an overly intellectual personality, a frail, nonathletic physique, and an emotional loss he is unable to face directly.

The varied ways in which characters try to deal with shortcomings is the basis of much of the humor in young adult novels. Sometimes the comedy is overt, as in the novels of Joan Bauer, whose protagonists joke openly about their own excessive height or weight. In other narratives, readers may relish the humor in a situation despite a protagonist's inability to perceive his own weaknesses or appreciate the lighter side of his difficulties.

What Am I Doing in This Family?

Sometimes a teen is more embarrassed by his parents than by his own imperfections. Virginia Clarke's wonderful (and recently reprinted) novel *The Heroic Life of Al Capsella* portrays a family in which the characters are annoyed rather than amused by one another's foibles, and yet the personality clashes and generational ironies make for a fine comedy. Teenage Al is becoming aware of strong peer pressure to appear "normal."

> When I was a little kid, I never thought about myself or other people this way, worrying about whether they were normal, or strange . . . I was happier when I thought in this simple way. Since I've gone on to high school, being normal has become a matter of importance: All of us are secretly worried that we might not be normal, that there might be something a bit odd about us, something that *shows*, that other kids can point to and laugh about. (*Heroic Life of Al Capsella*, 4)

Al is mortified by his parents, particularly his eccentric mother. She is an author of romance novels, who does her writing late at night and then wanders about during the day in tatty old outfits salvaged from thrift shops. She is unlike the mothers of any of his friends. Her bohemian lifestyle and behavior contrast sharply with the neat, suburban routines of the neighbors. Al feels that he already has enough to worry about with regard to establishing his own normalcy, and it doesn't seem fair that his parents should cause him even more much anxiety.

Having normal parents is part of it. No one wants visible parents—unless they are pop stars or football players. Parents should be perfectly ordinary and unobtrusive, quiet and orderly, well dressed and polite, hardworking, and as wealthy as possible. Like children in the olden days, they should be seen and not heard. . . . The Capsellas are a real liability. (6)

Then Al has an experience that changes his outlook. During a school holiday, he and his mother travel to spend a few days with her parents, whom he hasn't seen in some years. Since his grandparents, Neddy and Teddy, live near Sidney, Al has visions of spending some quality time on Bondi Beach. However, it turns out that Neddy and Teddy have not been to Sidney for thirty years, and they have no desire to leave their excruciatingly neat, suburban home. Their routines are stifling and unvarying: Teddy opens the windows each day from 5:15 to 5:25 A.M., and again from 6:45 to 6:55 P.M. He takes a walk at 9:15 every morning, scrubs and polishes his gleaming white shoes every night, and everyone goes to bed at 10:00 P.M. Al's grandparents are fearful of their few ethnic neighbors, and they rant about the supposed "good old days" when everyone in their suburb was white.

The word "normal" as defined by his grandparents causes Al to see that they aren't really so "normal" as they suppose; they merely label everything abnormal that does not conform to their own extremely narrow experiences and views. After spending only a couple of days with Neddy and Teddy, both Al and his mother are nervous wrecks, and Al is beginning to understand the origins of his mother's eccentricities. "I was terribly glad to be going," Al says, and then as their taxi pulls away, he sighs, "I'll never use that word again." "What word?" his mother asks, "Normal," he replies (152).

Ron Koertge's early novel, *Where the Kissing Never Stops*, features another teen who is embarrassed by his mother. Seventeen-year-old Walker Davis is ashamed that his mother has taken a job as an exotic dancer, following the premature death of her husband. Walker criticizes his mother in their private conversations and goes to great lengths to conceal his mother's profession from his new girlfriend, Rachel.

As an only child living with his widowed mother, Walker is hyper-responsible and feels pressured to be the man of the family. When he finally builds up the nerve to tell Rachel that his mother is an exotic dancer, not a waitress, she replies, "I knew all that." Moreover, she tells him, "Probably almost everybody" knows.

> "How come nobody ever said anything to me before?"
> She shrugged. "So they'll kid you tomorrow."
> "They'd kid me. They'd kid me tomorrow. And that's what it would amount to—kidding. All this time and nobody really cared but me."[23]

Another protagonist embarrassed by his family, Vince Luca of Gordon Korman's *Son of the Mob*, wants to stay out of the family "vending machine" business. But events conspire to frustrate his good intentions. One promising relationship is ruined when Vince and his date discover a small-time crook bleeding in the trunk of the car. Vince later becomes romantically involved with Kendra Bightly, whose father "Agent Bite Me" has bugged the Luca residence in an attempt to gain evidence with which to prosecute Vince's father. Vince's repeated excuses to Kendra whenever she suggests meeting one another's parents nearly destroys their romance.

Each of these comedies involves a rather ordinary son playing the role of the "straight man" who is embarrassed by eccentric or unusual parents. Rather than asking, "What's wrong with me?" Al Capsella, Walker Davis, and Vince Luca must ask themselves, "What am I doing in this family?" and "Was I adopted?"

It can be just as difficult to live with a parent who is a public hero and a paragon of virtue. Steve York of Rob Thomas's *Rats Saw God* has exactly the opposite problem from that of the trio just mentioned. Steve's father is a famous astronaut; a handsome, fit, clean-cut military officer and all-American hero. Rather than competing with this paragon, Steve becomes a rebel, immersing himself in a narcotic haze and failing in school. The burden of living up to the heroic Alan York is stressful for the entire family and this, combined with a setback in his love life, results in Steve's emotional freefall.

Steve is self-deprecating and ironical about himself. "I'm 'gifted.' I know this because I was tested in junior high. Twelve of us so designated were isolated in separate classes, taught Latin phrases, allowed to use expensive telescopes, taken on field trips to ballets, and labeled complete geeks by our classmates." Steve counteracts this image by having both ears pierced and wearing big hoops: "When I combine the look with a doo rag, I'm a regular pirate."[24] Steve persistently refers to his celebrated father as "the astronaut," making him an object rather than a person. When parents are embarrassingly odd, like Mr. and Mrs. Capsella, or annoyingly perfect, like Steve York's father, their offspring face special challenges. But challenges are also opportunities! Opportunities for growth and for healing laughter that eases the growing pains. Virginia Shreves, daughter of an impossibly perfect mother, puts it well: "I'm realizing that sometimes it's easier to laugh off annoying Mom-isms than get angry at them" (*The Earth, My Butt, and Other Big, Round Things*, 242). Whether adversity is caused by external factors—such as a difficult parent—or by one's own shortcomings, an ability to step back and view problems with some degree of humorous detachment is essential to the growth of a self-conscious adolescent into a healthy adult.

Notes

1. Judith Clarke, *The Heroic Life of Al Capsella* (New York: Holt, 1988), 39.

2. Ron Koertge, *Stoner & Spaz* (Cambridge, Mass.: Candlewick, 2002), 29.

3. Chris Crutcher, *Staying Fat for Sarah Byrnes* (New York: Greenwillow, 1993), 12.

4. Barbara Wersba, *Love Is the Crooked Thing* (New York: Harper & Row, 1987), 6.

5. Carolyn Mackler, *The Earth, My Butt, and Other Big, Round Things* (Cambridge, Mass.: Candlewick, 2003), 18.

6. Rebecca O'Connell, *Myrtle of Willendorf* (Asheville, N.C.: Front Street, 2000), 16–17.

7. Joan Bauer, *Squashed* (New York: Delacorte, 1992), 31, 3.

8. Joan Bauer, *Rules of the Road* (New York: Putnam, 1998), 7.

9. Beverly Keller, *The Amazon Papers* (San Diego: Browndeer Press, 1996), 45.

10. Cherry Whitock, *My Cup Runneth Over: The Life of Angelica Cookson Potts* (New York: Simon & Schuster, 2003), 125.

11. Joyce Carol Oates, *Big Mouth & Ugly Girl* (New York: HarperTempest, 2002), 11.

12. Megan McCafferty, *Sloppy Firsts* (New York: Crown, 2001), 69.

13. Daniel Pinkwater, *Alan Mendelson, the Boy from Mars* (New York: Dutton, 1979), 5.

14. Chris Lynch, *Extreme Elvin* (New York: HarperCollins, 1999), 17.

15. K. L. Going, *Fat Kid Rules the World* (New York: Putnam, 2003), 1.

16. J. K. Rowling, *Harry Potter and the Sorcerer's Stone* (New York: A. A. Levine, 1998), 20.

17. Joan Bauer, *Stand Tall* (New York: Putnam, 2002), 4–5.

18. Perry Nodelman, *Behaving Bradley* (New York: Simon & Schuster, 1998), 172.

19. Chris Lynch, *Slot Machine* (New York: HarperCollins, 1995), 49.

20. M. T. Anderson's narrators never seem to have surnames.

21. M. T. Anderson, *Thirsty* (Cambridge, Mass.: Candlewick, 1997), 214.

22. *Oxford English Dictionary Online* (New York: Oxford University Press, 2004), http://dictionary.oed.com/entrance.dtl (12 November 2004).

23. Ron Koertge, *Where the Kissing Never Stops* (Boston: Atlantic Monthly, 1986), 206.

24. Rob Thomas, *Rats Saw God* (New York: Simon & Schuster, 1996), 9.

CHAPTER SIX

~

Could This Be Love?

"Romance" can mean many things in literature. It may be used to describe romantic love between two people, as the generic term for the popular fiction in the Romance sections of libraries and bookstores, or it may refer to the traditional literary form that includes Arthurian and Grail legends and other medieval epics and ballads.

Light Romance

Love and romance in humorous literature geared to a young adult audience can encompass any of the above definitions. Romantic love is a major preoccupation in the adolescent experience, and the established authors of humorous and primarily realistic fiction for teens—Joan Bauer, Anne Fine, Ron Koertge, and many others—deal with love and romance in most of their works. Some authors, such as Ellen Conford and Meg Cabot, specialize in humorous fiction that has the tone of popular romance novels. Their works are light romantic comedies, such as Conford's *If This Is Love, I'll Take Spaghetti*, and Cabot's *Princess in Love*. Finally, authors of humorous fantasy, among them Jean Ferris, Patrice Kindl, Gail Carson Levine, and Diana Wynne Jones, have written romance novels that resemble a more traditional literary form. Ferris's *Once upon a Marigold*, Kindl's *Owl in Love*, Levine's *Ella Enchanted*, and Jones's *Castle in the Air* use romantic backdrops to portray a young couple who must battle fantastic obstacles before they can be united.

Several writers have earned a reputation for fiction that is both humorous and romantic. Lynn Hall and Phyllis Reynolds Naylor have both written series aimed primarily at young women. Hall has written four novels featuring Dagmar Shultz, a plucky protagonist whose wholesome, small-town surroundings assure us that positive family values will prevail. However, Dagmar is a feisty teen who challenges family and community conventions just enough to be mischievous and keep people on their toes. The comedy usually arises from the revelation of an emotion such as a crush on a boy, or jealousy toward a rival, which Dagmar does not want to admit. In *Dagmar Schultz and the Green-Eyed Monster*, thirteen-year-old Dagmar's jealousy toward rival Ashley Fingerhut leads to comical antics that are resolved in the end by the warmhearted tolerance of Dagmar's family and community. In *Dagmar Schultz and the Angel Edna*, the ghost of a deceased relative returns and constrains the gregarious Dagmar with her old-fashioned notions of morality; and in *Dagmar Schultz and the Powers of Darkness*, Dagmar gets help with her love life from the assistant meat manager at the local supermarket, who happens to be "the only warlock in Strawberry Point, Iowa."[1]

Richard Peck's Blossom Culp novels, and Thom Eberhardt's recent *Rat Boys: A Dating Experiment* are wonderful novels with protagonists much like Dagmar Schultz: funny teenage girls in small, Midwestern towns who use supernatural forces to create mischief and get the attention of boys. Phyllis Naylor's enormously popular Alice series is similar to Hall's Dagmar Schultz novels in its basic premise of a young girl maturing into a woman against a background of strong family values and warm humor. The Alice series eschews the supernatural elements favored by Peck, Eberhardt, and Hall.

Phyllis Reynolds Naylor's books are lengthier and not as consistently funny as those of Lynn Hall. While Hall's novels are primarily comedies about puberty and first love, Naylor's Alice novels are realistic stories about growing up that include some humor. When Naylor presents information and instruction to her young readers, she usually injects a good dose of humor. Naylor tackles tough subjects, such as death, divorce, and abusive behavior, using optimism and humor to show how even the most serious problems can be faced and overcome.

Ellen Conford has authored many humorous and romantic novels and stories, among them *A Royal Pain*, a precursor to Meg Cabot's recent Princess Diaries series. Kansas high schooler Abby Adams is forced to leave her familiar Midwestern surroundings to begin a new life as Princess Florinda XIV of Saxony-Coburn, when it is revealed that Abby and another baby were accidentally switched at birth. Abby's new life as a princess is strange but not altogether unpleasant, until she discovers that she is expected to marry the creepy Prince Casimir on her upcoming sixteenth birthday. While fending off Casimir, Abby develops a crush on hunky skier-journalist Geoffrey Torunga, who naturally rescues Abby in this romantic comedy. Conford's short story collections, *If This Is Love, I'll Take Spaghetti* and *I Love You, I Hate You, Get Lost!* each contain several funny love stories. Conford's humor is situational; she artfully spins funny stories out of circumstances involving relatively unexceptional teenagers in ordinary settings.

Joan Bauer and Gordon Korman, two of the best known authors of humorous YA literature, both write primarily for middle teens. The protagonists of both authors are typically sixteen or seventeen years of age, and naturally romance is an important element of many, although not all, of their novels. Bauer's *Rules of the Road* and *Stand Tall*, and Korman's *Don't Care High* and *No Coins, Please* are largely devoid of romance. Both authors write wholesome fiction that rarely contains references to physical intimacies beyond kissing, although Korman's recent *Son of the Mob* is distinctly bawdier than most of the author's previous novels.

Romance plays a more dominant role in *Thwonk!* than in Joan Bauer's other books. This novel is also uncharacteristic of Bauer in its inclusion of the fantasy element of a talking, arrow-shooting cupid. The competition for a desirable male is the source of much of the humor in *Thwonk!* and in the author's first novel, *Squashed*. In that book, despite a lack of glamour, Ellie Morgan wins the attention of handsome newcomer Wes by demonstrating her knowledge of agriculture in contrast to the beautiful but woefully ignorant cheerleader Sharrell Upton, who cannot name the season in which corn is planted despite her title of Sweet Corn Coquette. Bonding over shared activities is a hallmark of Bauer's fiction: *Backwater*'s Ivy Breedlove meets a handsome young forest ranger in the wilderness, and Hope Yancey of *Hope Was Here* gets to know Braverman in the kitchen where both work. A strong Protestant ethic runs through Bauer's fiction, and young people who love their work gravitate toward one another.

Gordon Korman's settings are realistic, and most of his characters are believable urban or suburban teens, but he makes extensive use of exaggeration and overstatement for humorous effect. The students of *Don't Care High* are outrageously apathetic, Artie Gellar of *No Coins, Please* has an extreme talent for making money, Professor Querada of *Son of Interflux* takes eccentricity to a level of near insanity, Raymond Jardine of *Semester in the Life of a Garbage Bag* never has any luck, and Wallace Wallace of *No More Dead Dogs* never tells a lie.

In keeping with this tendency to depict humorous extremes, Korman's most striking technique in romantic situations is a predilection for sudden, dramatic mood swings from love to hate and back again. Often the shift will be ironically timed so that just as one partner turns back toward a relationship, the other pulls away. Wendy Orr finds Simon Irving infuriating throughout *Son of Interflux*, but just when she finally warms up to him, Simon has a petty tantrum and cuts short their first date. *Son of the Mob* features a Romeo and Juliet affair, in which Vince and Kendra perversely desire one another all the more fervently when they learn that their fathers are mortal enemies. In *Losing Joe's Place*, Jason watches his two roommates compete for Jessica all summer, but in the end Jessica chooses Jason over both of the boys who had pursued her.

In Korman's *No More Dead Dogs*, Rachel writes periodic letters to Julia Roberts detailing her irritation with the annoying Wallace Wallace, until Julia finally replies:

Dear Rachel,

I've starred in enough romantic comedies to know one when I see it. Take my word for it—you are crazy about this guy Wallace. Don't let him get away.

Yours truly, Julia Roberts[2]

Not until receiving this letter does Rachel finally realize that she loves Wallace. The last time she had seen him before reading Julia's letter, Rachel had punched Wallace in the stomach, so she will need to use a bit of ingenuity to get back on his good side.

Writing of and from the Heart

Authors Todd Strasser and Randy Powell are both noted for the provocative titles of their realistic novels involving older teens. Randy Powell's novels, including *Is Kissing a Girl Who Smokes Like Licking an Ashtray?*, *The Whistling Toilets*, *Tribute to Another Dead Rock Star*, and *Three Clams and an Oyster*, are atmospheric and introspective, partaking strongly of the overcast Seattle ambience in which Powell has spent his life. Although most of Powell's novels feature romantic situations, the author rarely presents a romance in full bloom. He writes of fringes and edges, of the beginnings and endings of relationships. Powell's sense of humor, like his romantic sensibility, tends to be understated.

Todd Strasser's novels are generally more realistic and straightforward than one might suppose from such quirky titles as *Girl Gives Birth to Own Prom Date* and *How I Spent My Last Night on Earth*. Strasser's protagonists are usually boys of sixteen or seventeen. However, Strasser has also been quite successful with female narration. *Girl Gives Birth to Own Prom Date* is alternately narrated by a high school girl and boy, respectively, and *How I Spent My Last Night on Earth* is entirely female-narrated by Allegra "Legs" Hanover.

Strasser is more explicit in his handling of adolescent sexuality than the previous authors discussed. *A Very Touchy Subject* is quite open about teen sexuality, and *How I Spent My Last Night on Earth* is an extremely sexy novel. Fearing that a giant asteroid is about to strike the earth, teens camp out on the beach for what may be their last night on Earth. Allegra's boyfriend and her best friend lose their virginity together, and Allegra spends the night with a handsome biker she has just met. It turns out that the asteroid misses and the world does not end, but this setting certainly provides Strasser with a great opportunity for his characters to cast off their usual inhibitions.

Few YA authors have given us more good fiction both humorous and romantic than Ron Koertge. From his first novel, *Where the Kissing*

Never Stops, in 1986, to *Stoner & Spaz*, in 2002, Koertge has authored a string of YA novels in which humor is always, and romance is nearly always, present. At least three of Koertge's novels present initial sexual experiences. *The Arizona Kid* and *Boy in the Moon* each features a tender and humorously awkward scene in which both teen partners lose their virginity together. Colleen Minou of *Stoner & Spaz* is far past virginity, nevertheless her gentle lovemaking with Ben Bancroft is presented romantically, inasmuch as their relationship is so different from the rough life she had been living as the girlfriend of a drug dealer. In other novels, including *The Harmony Arms*, *Confess-O-Rama*, and *Where the Kissing Never Stops*, Koertge presents a developing romantic relationship between the protagonist and a girlfriend that does not go so far as the bedroom.

In all of these novels, Koertge's characters use humor to ease tensions, including nervous little jokes about proper use of condoms in the three novels in which the characters do engage in intercourse. Koertge is one of the most skilled authors of witty YA dialogue. His novels are filled with sharp observations and clever one-liners which sum up a situation with admirable wit and brevity.

The novels of Francesca Lia Block present sexuality even more overtly than do the works of Strasser and Koertge. Block's lush, poetic language is cast over all subjects, magically transforming every object and experience, from food to clothing, into sexuality. Block's romanticism and her sense of humor are intertwined in a sensual banquet. In Block's sensational first novel, *Weetzie Bat*, when My Secret Agent Lover Man doesn't want a baby, Weetzie turns to her friends Dirk and Duck. Soon there is a result:

> Weetzie was pregnant. She felt like a Christmas package. Like a cat full of kittens. Like an Easter basket of pastel chocolate-malt eggs and solid-milk-chocolate bunnies, and yellow daffodils and dollhouse-sized jelly-bean eggs.[3]

No one else writes like that. In this characteristically lush and extravagant passage, humor, love, and sensuality are inseparable.

Some have described Francesca Lia Block's stories as modern fairy tales. Other authors of modern fairy tales bring different kinds of humor and romance to their stories. In some of her many fantasy novels, Diana Wynne Jones offers conjunctions of humor and romance quite different from those of Block. Jones achieves much of her effect through clever plotting. A nice romantic touch is achieved in the Chrestomanci novels.

In *The Lives of Christopher Chant*, young Christopher travels to another world and meets a goddess, the Living Asheth, actually a girl of about his own age who is bored in her isolation as a divinity. Christopher brings her some series fiction about an English schoolgirl named Millie: *Millie Goes to School, Millie of Lowood House*, and so on. "Surefire slush," Christopher's friend Oneir tells him. "Does your sister really like these?" Christopher asks incredulously. "'Wallows in them,' said Oneir. 'She reads them over and over again and cries every time.'"[4] Indeed, the Goddess adores the Millie books, and Christopher is compelled to return with the remainder of the series. At the end of *The Lives of Christopher Chant*, the Goddess has joined Christopher in his own world and, to her delight, plans are made to send her to just the sort of private school described in the Millie books. In fact, the Goddess has even changed her name to Millie.

The romantic aspect of all this is that in the sequel, *Charmed Life*, we meet a man with the title of Chrestomanci who is married to a woman named Millie, and we realize that these are the same persons, now all grown up with children of their own, whom we last met as Christopher and the Goddess. Jones never spells this out for her readers; the characters are simply there. It is entirely characteristic of Jones's sophisticated, multilayered storytelling to make fun of pulp, schoolgirl series fiction, while also using a favorite character's genuine affection for that same sentimental fiction to advance a very romantic story.

A similar lifelong romance is presented in Hilary McKay's charming novel *The Exiles in Love*. The exiles are the four Conroy sisters, who previously appeared in *The Exiles* and *The Exiles at Home*. Ten-year-old Rachel, one of the younger sisters, is quite taken with a French teenager, Philippe, who stays with the English family for a week. She frequently tells Philippe, and anyone else who will listen, that she plans to marry him. Philippe, suave and gallant, knows just how to respond.

"Philippe," said Rachel that first afternoon, "will you marry me?"

"Let the poor boy get his coat off at least," said Mr. Conroy.

Philippe, who had just stepped through the door, stooped down to look at Rachel properly.

"But certainly," he said, straightening up. "How very kind! I should be charmed!"

"Rachel," said Naomi at teatime, "what about all the others you've said you're going to marry?"

"*Tous les autres?*" asked Philippe, sounding extremely shocked. "I am not the first?"

"Graham in Cumbria," said Naomi. "Martin-the-Good, who lives next door, Alan Adair from the butcher's . . ."

"And they have all agreed?" asked Philippe.

"No," said Rachel. "They just haven't said they wouldn't. And you are by far the best."

"I am so pleased to hear it."

"I shall keep them as spares."

"You won't need spares," said Philippe, twinkling at Ruth, "if you marry me!"[5]

Each chapter of the novel begins with a few lines of dialogue that appear to be occurring at a later time, looking back fondly on the past actions being described. Finally, at the very end of the novel, the meaning of this dialogue becomes clear: the other three Conroy sisters are gathering at a church to celebrate the wedding of Rachel and Philippe! Both Jones and McKay achieve a warm, humorously romantic effect by first engaging the reader's interest in a pair of young characters, and then unexpectedly revealing that there is more to be told of that relationship than one might have supposed.

From this survey of some of the authors who have distinguished themselves in producing YA literature that is both humorous and romantic, let's turn to a consideration of some typical romantic situations whose comic possibilities have been explored in YA novels.

Bad Dates

YA literature is filled with accounts of disastrous dating experiences. It's a classic situation because there is usually considerable tension between a pair of self-conscious young people who are just getting to know one another, each trying to make a good impression. Novels that describe a dating disaster, but then go on to show the protagonist laughing about it later and living to date again, are enormously reassuring to adolescents.

Sometimes a date goes wrong for reasons beyond the control of either party. In Gordon Korman's *Son of the Mob* Vince Luca's date with sexy Angela O'Bannon comes to an abrupt end when they open the trunk of Vince's car to grab a beach blanket, only to find that the blanket is wrapped around the bloody body of a small-time mobster Vince recognizes as Jimmy "Rat" Ratelli. Angela is horrified.

> "He's dead! He's dead! Oh, my God, Vince, he's dead!"
> "He's not dead." For some reason, the only thing I can think of is that old dead parrot skit on Monty Python. "He's—resting."[6]

After Angela has gone home in a huff, Vince is able to free Jimmy Rat, who "looks disdainfully" back at Vince's Mazda. "Damn foreign cars. No trunk space at all" (*Son of the Mob*, 11). This opening scene works superbly to introduce the central conflict of the novel: Vince's discomfort with the notorious family business that permeates every aspect of his life.

In Bev Keller's *The Amazon Papers*, a calamitous dating experience— also involving an automobile—results in a series of comical mishaps. Iris Hoving is a sensible fifteen-year-old girl whose mother has left her in charge of the family home and two lively young nephews. Flattered at being asked out by handsome Foster Prizer, Iris volunteers the use of her mother's car when Foster's fifteen-year-old hearse won't start. Iris knows that this is risky and muses, "Maybe Foster had a way of driving a woman's brains right out her ears."[7]

Foster takes Iris to a "raunchy" pool hall on the edge of town, and the date quickly deteriorates. Within minutes, Foster is kicked out of the hall, and Iris is injured by the spiked heel of Foster's former girlfriend. With her date nowhere in sight and unable to drive herself, Iris is forced to leave her mother's car at the pool hall. By the time she returns to reclaim the vehicle, it has been stripped of "hubcaps, radio, window glass . . ." (*Amazon Papers*, 75).

Iris's disastrous date with Foster, like Vince Luca's date with Angela O'Bannon in *Son of the Mob*, goes wrong due to circumstances beyond their control, and not because either party has malicious intentions. All of the characters in Keller's hilarious comedy of errors are likeable, and Iris even becomes friends with Zelma, the girl whose spiked heel nearly broke her foot.

However, sometimes a date turns out badly because one of the parties has an agenda to use the other person. In Meg Cabot's *The Princess Diaries*, freshman Mia has a crush on handsome senior Josh Richter. She doesn't expect anything to come of her infatuation. However, shortly after Mia is "outed" as a princess, Josh suddenly breaks up with his longtime girlfriend and asks Mia to the big Fall dance. Dazzled by this unexpected success, Mia gratefully accepts and is soon frenzied with anticipation of her "dream" date. She doesn't even mind that her armed bodyguard, Lars, will have to be present throughout. But Josh turns out to be a lout. He arrives late, and then at the restaurant pompously insists upon ordering filet mignon for everyone at the table, never noticing that Mia (a well-known vegetarian) is reduced to eating salad and rolls. Then he drinks himself into a stupor. However, these are mere preliminaries to his main purpose: Josh has invited paparazzi to photograph him escorting Mia. Temporarily eluding Lars, he drags her to the top of the stairway outside the dance hall, and "smashed his mouth up against mine," as Mia tells it, while camera flashes go off all around.[8]

In the manner of diary novels, Mia commits all this to her journal while hiding in a stall of the ladies' room. She is completely humiliated. But this *is* a comedy! Mia's friends persuade her to stay at the dance and she has a wonderful evening after all. Josh Richter does not bother her again.

> I have a feeling Lars might have used one of his special nerve-paralyzing holds on Josh, because the next time I saw him, Josh was slumped over at the Pacific Islander display table with his forehead resting on a model of Krakatoa. (*Princess Diaries*, 231)

The grotesquely awful dating episode in David Klass's *You Don't Know Me* arises out of somewhat similar circumstances. Like Mia, John is a novice at socializing with the opposite sex, and he is thrilled to have landed a date with a popular and beautiful classmate. Unfortunately for John, Gloria, like Josh Richter, turns out to be the sort of wealthy, decadent, spoiled person who uses others for her own amusement. Gloria's idea of fun is to lure an unsuspecting date to her basement, encourage him to remove most of his clothing, and then to make sure that her choleric, fanatically protective father hears suspicious noises in the basement and comes charging in to save her "honor." John escapes a battering by Gloria's berserk father—barely—by painfully squeezing himself out through a cat door, but then has to make his way home on a frosty winter evening without shoes, shirt, or jacket.[9] This humiliating yet funny episode is characteristic of the black comedy tone sustained in Klass's novel.

Parents and Dating

Parents who are merely quirky, rather than violent, appear more frequently in adolescent dating situations. Ron Koertge's Confess-O-Rama includes a humorous mismatch of characters when Tony and his anxious mother go out with Jordan Archer and her father, both eccentric Southern California artists. Irrepressible Jordan wants to know all the details surrounding the demise of each of Mrs. Candelaria's four deceased husbands. Jordan's father, a health fanatic, is so shaken to learn that all four of this relatively young woman's husbands have expired, that he begins driving wildly through heavy traffic until abruptly pulling into a health food store. There he has his pulse checked, and a bit later, insists that everyone eat a banana to maintain their potassium levels.[10] Although she has the weirder parent, Jordan is totally relaxed about her father's goofiness, while Tony is easily embarrassed.

A protagonist's frantic efforts to hide an embarrassing fact about his home or parents often backfires. One of the funniest treatments of this situation is Kate Gilmore's Enter Three Witches. High schooler Bren West lives with four weird women: his mother, Miranda, a powerful witch; Miranda's mother, Rose, a fortune-teller; tenant Louise La Reine, a voodoo priestess who tends a flock of black chickens for purposes Bren doesn't like to think about; and Madame Lavatky, an aging soprano who continues to wear theatrical costumes and makeup, and still strains to hit high C. The house itself is strange and spooky: an old mansion, it already had twelve-foot ceilings, but that wasn't enough for Miranda, who removed an upper floor to give herself a twenty-foot-high tower studio in which to practice her dark arts.

When Bren begins dating Erika, his clumsy efforts to keep her away from his unconventional mother and home only increase her curiosity. Erika comes across an ad for "Madame Rose, Spiritual Advisor," and realizing that the address is the same as Bren's, pays a visit to Madame Rose to get a look at Bren's household and its occupants. There Erika gets the full treatment: a spooky séance with Bren's grandmother, followed by eerie encounters with Miranda and Louise. "Well, now you know," groans Bren.

> "Now I know, and I think it's all amazing and wonderful," she said. "How could you think I wouldn't, Bren? Did you think I was some kind of nitwit who wanted everything to be like a TV cereal commercial?"
> Bren lifted his head and smiled uncertainly. "Never," he said. "Not for a minute, but, you know, there's normal, and there's different enough to be interesting, and then there's my place."[11]

Susan Juby's *Alice, I Think* includes a hilarious encounter of Alice's family with a young man who comes to visit for a weekend. Fifteen-year-old Alice, who had been homeschooled for most of her life, doesn't get out much and has absolutely no experience with boys. So she is stunned when a cute boy, Aubrey, takes an interest in her. She is a bit put off by his personality—he almost never stops talking about himself—but she allows him to schedule a visit. Alice and her parents are nervous about having a hormonally active young man in the house, but as it turns out, they needn't be concerned about his possible advances toward Alice, since "he could never stop talking long enough to do anything that physical."[12] *Alice, I Think* may be one of the funniest YA novels ever written. Its offbeat humor arises from Alice's outsider perspective, her droll narration and, not least, from the involvement of her eccentric family in most of her numerous misadventures.

Tongue-Tied Teens

One of the most common problems in young romance is the fear of revealing an attraction to the other person. Sometimes teens fear that a friendship will be damaged by their declaration of romantic feelings, possibly resulting in the object of their affections avoiding them. In other instances, the lover may simply fear rejection. It's a tense situation for many adolescents, and thus a prime opportunity for comic relief. Author David Lubar, known for his quirky sense of humor, provides a unique setting for a declaration of love in his novel *Dunk*. This title refers to the carnival attraction in which a loud-mouthed clown, known as a "Bozo," shouts insults at passers-by and offers them a chance to dunk him into a pool of water, for a price. Lubar's protagonist, fifteen-year-old Chad Turner, becomes fascinated with this strange performance and is eventually offered a chance at donning the greasepaint of a Bozo. Near the end of Chad's first shift, he spots Gwen, a girl he has long admired but has been too shy to approach. From the microphone at which he has been yelling insults at passers-by, Chad finally works up the nerve to declare himself. Gwen, not knowing that Chad has taken up this strange occupation, is startled at being hailed by a clown. All ends well, as Chad finds that the attraction is mutual.

> "Don't go away," I said to her, as I headed off to remove my makeup.
> "Don't worry, Chad," she said. "I'm not running off with any other clowns."[13]

In his everyday persona, Chad couldn't work up the nerve to approach Gwen other than as a casual friend. But in the Bozo role, Chad was required to put on a bold public disguise, in which he was able to approach Gwen romantically. This scene, so goofy on the surface, rings true because of its psychological realism. Sometimes a comic scene may offer the most compact and memorable way of conveying the essence of a dramatic conflict.

The passing of written notes, often anonymous, is a technique often used by shy admirers. A number of YA novels have presented humorous twists on this practice. James Howe's *The Misfits* features a complex mystery of anonymous note-passing that leads to considerable confusion among a group of seventh graders, some of whom have not yet figured out their gender preferences.

In *Feeling Sorry for Celia*, author Jaclyn Moriarty has created a splendid comic mystery of note-passing. The entire novel is epistolary in various forms: a collage of journal entries, faxes, pen pal letters, notes left on the refrigerator, and memos from imaginary societies such as The Cold Hard Truth Association. The anonymous notes that Elizabeth finds in her bag after her school bus rides thus fit nicely into this pastiche of written communications.

It all begins when Elizabeth finds a note of condolence in her bag: "Dear Elizabeth, I'm incredibly sorry about your dog dying. From a stranger."[14] After some of her subsequent bus journeys, she finds additional notes. The second apologizes for writing her an anonymous note, and is signed, "A Stranger (Who Catches Your Bus)" (*Feeling Sorry*, 150). A few days later, a third note:

> Dear Elizabeth,
> I just realized that the note I left the other day was also an anonymous note.
> I'm sorry for leaving an anonymous note apologizing for leaving an anonymous note.
> A STRANGER WHO CATCHES YOUR BUS (156)

This sort of thing continues for some time. Eventually, Elizabeth is able to narrow the possible perpetrators down to five boys who attend nearby Brookfield School who sit together in the back of the bus every day. Then a breakthrough! The anonymous boy writes that he's too shy to speak to Elizabeth, but he'll let her know who he is by wearing a black cap the next morning. As Elizabeth reports to her friend:

> He left me a note yesterday saying that he'd wear a black cap on the bus.
> So this MORNING I'm all excited and nervous when I get on the bus.
> I look down the back at the Brookfield boys, as casual as I could.
> And guess what?
> Every single one of them was wearing a black cap. (188)

Of course, then Elizabeth starts getting anonymous notes apologizing for the dirty trick with the hats. In fact, there is a multiple layering of notes and letters. Elizabeth's pen pal Christina finds that she is a classmate of the anonymous note writer, and so Elizabeth and Christina exchange letters discussing this bashful "mystery boy." Meanwhile, The Society of Amateur Detectives weighs in with memoranda chiding Elizabeth on her lack of perspicacity in solving the note mystery. *Feeling*

Sorry for Celia is a cleverly plotted novel that sustains a high level of humorous interest by gradually revealing romantic secrets and surprises, entirely through a variety of epistolary forms.

In extreme cases, difficulty in revealing one's romantic feelings may derive from more than mere shyness, but rather from a more fundamental inability to be oneself. Seventeen-year-old Josh Swenson of Janet Tashjian's *Gospel According to Larry* has been romantically attracted to his neighbor and classmate Beth for years, but has never told her that he wants to be more than a friend. While mulling over various schemes to take his relationship with Beth to that new level, Josh has secretly become a national celebrity as "Larry," the pseudonym under which he posts his wildly popular "sermons" against consumerism.

Beth, an ardent admirer of the mysterious Larry, marvels at his knack of addressing topics of current relevance to her own life. But when Josh is discovered to be Larry, Beth is disturbed that he has been using their private conversations as material for Larry's sermons. She tells Josh that she had been romantically interested in him "since the ninth grade," but that their chance to have a romantic relationship had been ruined by his secretiveness. The novel is characterized by a series of heavy ironies, in which all of Larry's considerable cleverness works against his real interests and desires.

Ned Vizzini's novel *Be More Chill* presents another self-conscious protagonist unable to be himself. Jeremy Heere is a geeky high school boy who loves the beautiful Christine Caniglia from afar, not daring to ask her out. With little hope of becoming socially adept on his own, he purchases a dangerous, illegal new product called a squip, a microchip that "sits in your brain and assists you . . . it tells you how to be cool all the time."[15] The squip's internal dialogues with Jeremy are quite funny; it wants him to play the field and becomes morose when Jeremy remains fixated upon Christine. The squip has warned Jeremy that it will malfunction if drugs are in his system; when Jeremy gets high it begins babbling in Spanish:

TU ESTÁS EN UNA SITUACIÓN MUY PELIGROSO.
  "What the—?"
  ¡ALARMA ROJA, JEREMY! ¡ALARMA ROJA! (*Be More Chill*, 195)

With the aid of his squip, Jeremy achieves some social success and even begins to develop a relationship with Christine. But he eventually discovers that surrendering control of his own judgment and inhibitions to the persuasive squip is not such a good bargain after all. Some shortcuts to coolness create more problems than they solve.

Impossible Love

Romantic obstacles may be exciting, or merely frustrating, and both the excitement and the frustration can be treated with humor. One type of "impossible love" situation is the Romeo and Juliet scenario, in which two young people fall in love, but because of some dispute between their families, their union cannot gain social approval.

Diana Wynne Jones's *Magicians of Caprona* includes a light-hearted Romeo and Juliet subplot that suits the novel perfectly, since it is set in a mythical Italian city-state with the feel of Shakespeare's Verona.

One of the episodes of Lloyd Alexander's *Gypsy Rizka* offers another humorous variation on the Romeo and Juliet theme. Mayor Pumpa and Mr. Podskalny are rivals in the village. The mayor's daughter and cloth merchant's son fall in love, but they know that their parents will never approve. Through the linked vignettes of *Gypsy Rizka*, young Rizka maintains balance in the village. Like Grandma Dowdel in Richard Peck's *A Long Way from Chicago* and *A Year Down Yonder*, Rizka is an eccentric, somewhat disreputable fringe member of village society. But through her clever resolutions of the village's disputes, Rizka fine-tunes social relationships within the village in ways that satisfy her own sense of justice (as well as her sense of humor) and ultimately maintain civic harmony.

Exactly at the point when both pairs of grieving parents are agreeing, "I'd rather see them married than eaten by bears or at the bottom of a boiling mud puddle,"[16] Rizka fortuitously "finds" the young couple in the caves and presents them to the parents who have just been heard by numerous witnesses to have bestowed their blessings upon the union.

Gordon Korman's *Son of the Mob* varies a bit from the Romeo and Juliet theme in that there's not quite a full family feud. FBI Agent Bightly is after the entire Luca family, but the rest of the Bightly family is uninvolved. At least, they are not intentionally involved. It turns out that the agent's teenage daughter, Kendra, a karaoke enthusiast, once unwittingly destroyed a crucial piece of evidence against the Luca family by recording one of her singing performances on a cassette her father had left in the kitchen (*Son of the Mob*, 242–43).

Both Vince and Kendra are stimulated by the taboos they are breaking. Vince kisses Kendra for the first time when he learns that Kendra's father is none other than the FBI "Agent Bite Me," so named by Mr. Luca. When Kendra finally discovers why Vince has kept her away from his parents, to Vince's astonishment and delight she becomes passionate rather than angry:

> Turns out that Kendra thinks we're some kind of cops-and-robbers Romeo and Juliet—star-crossed lovers from families that are mortal enemies . . . it ratchets up the intensity level of our relationship about five-hundred percent. Hey, if I knew this was going to happen, I would have told her about Anthony Luca on day one. (*Son of the Mob*, 166)

Yet another kind of impossible love is that which could never happen except through some sort of artificial manipulation. In Joan Bauer's *Thwonk!* A. J. McCreary finds a cupid named Jonathan who reluctantly grants her wish that the best-looking boy in her school, Peter Terris, be made to fall in love with her. Sure enough, Peter dumps his longtime girlfriend and becomes enamored of A. J. But the victory is hollow: in the first place, Peter and A. J. have little in common.

> "Peter," I tried again, "what kind of things do you like to do? I mean, I love to go to museums and just spend time around all that good, rich art that's lasted for centuries. I love sitting in front of it and seeing it from every angle. You can learn a lot about yourself that way."
> "I kind of like to hang out," Peter said.[17]

A. J. is embarrassed when Peter's unnatural infatuation with her creates some uncomfortable situations, such as when Peter begins announcing his love for A. J. with joyous shouts in public places:

> Peter was singing me a love song, for crying out loud, a lame, pathetic love song in front of half the school.
> "I love youuuuuuuuuuu!" he crooned.

> I shut my eyes in supreme agony.
> "Open them, my friend," ordered Jonathan. "Observe the fulfillment
> of your wish." (*Thwonk!*, 146)

After several such public scenes, her cupid is able to convince A. J. that it was foolish to trick someone with whom she had nothing in common to fall in love with her.

Gail Carson Levine's *The Wish* plays upon a similar concept: Wilma, a lonely eighth grader, is granted her wish to become the most popular kid at her school. She later realizes that the conditions are limited to the exact words of her request: she will be popular *only* with the students at her middle school, during the remaining few weeks before they graduate. She begins dating Jared, the one boy who had liked her before her artificial popularity, and she is thrilled and relieved to discover that he still likes her after her wish has expired.

The near-impossibility of steadfastness in loving someone who swings from the heights to the depths of school popularity is a theme of Jerry Spinelli's *Stargirl*. The novel presents a classic social dilemma, as protagonist Leo Borlock is forced to choose between his love of Stargirl and his desire to be accepted by his peers. The crowd behavior of the students, as their comfort zones are disrupted by Stargirl's extroverted individuality, is both funny and disturbing. Dyan Sheldon's *Tall, Thin and Blonde* presents a similar situation with the genders reversed, as high school freshman Jenny Kaliski ponders a choice between school popularity and a developing relationship with a weird, fascinating young man.

One distinct obstacle to romance between a young man and a young woman is the eventuality that the pair do not share a heterosexual orientation. Sometimes this encumbrance does not become evident until late in the game. Jessica Darling of Megan McCafferty's *Sloppy Firsts* has a crush on handsome senior Paul Parlipiano. After months of admiring him from afar, she finally manages to be alone with him at a beach party. Unfortunately, her boldness in approaching the object of her dreams has been inspired by a great deal of alcohol. Immediately after confessing her undying love, Jessica passes out.

> I woke up this morning on Sara's bedroom floor with no memory of anything after that. Unfortunately, Sara gleefully filled in the Grand Canyon-sized gap in my memory.

All you really need to know is this one horrifying thing:
I puked on Paul Parlipiano's shoes.
After I pledged my love, but before I passed out . . .
I will be forever immortalized in Paul Parlipiano's mind as The Drunk
Girl Who Puked on My Shoes.[18]

Soon afterward, Jessica is startled to learn that Paul is gay and thus
out of her reach regardless of her behavior. A friend tells Jessica that
Paul came out to his family over Thanksgiving, and the family tried to
be quietly supportive. "But yesterday Mrs. Parlipiano ran into a neighbor at Super-Foodtown and broke down right in front of the deli
counter. 'My son is gay!'" (*Sloppy Firsts*, 248).

Ellen Wittlinger's *Hard Love* is a much more somber novel, yet not
without its humorous moments. John (Gio) Galardi knows from the
start that his friend Marisol is gay, and yet he is unable to prevent himself from falling in love with her. There's a tough humor in the novel;
when John asks Marisol to his junior prom she replies that he should
find someone feminine who would enjoy the event.

I shrugged. "There's nobody I really want to go with anyway. Most of the
girls in my school are such . . . girls."
"Gio, you are radically confused."
"I know."[19]

John is attracted to tough, independent-minded women, and he finds
his friend Brian's "constant talk about girls and sex" tiring. "Maybe it's
weird, but I'm not interested in it . . . I guess guys my age are supposed to
be like Brian, lusting after pouty lips and big boobs" (*Hard Love*, 19).
When John and Marisol go their separate ways, he asks her if their relationship was important to her, even though she could not reciprocate his
romantic feelings. "She laughed a little then, trying to lighten things up.
'Of course it was! You know you're the only boyfriend I ever had!'" (221).

Same-Sex Attraction

An increasing number of novels for teens are addressing the issues of
homosexuality and romance between same-sex partners. This literature
is particularly valuable for young people who may be uncertain about

their own sexual orientation, or who have experienced attraction to someone of the same sex. These young adults are often seeking a better understanding of their own feelings and the challenges likely to be encountered by gay people in an often hostile society. Stories with gay characters and themes are also informative for family, friends, and teachers of gay, ambivalent, or uncertain adolescents. Issues surrounding homosexuality and gay culture are being "mainstreamed" to a much greater extent than in the past. And aside from the bibliotherapeutic uses of fiction lies the simple fact that same-sex attraction is a rather common element of the human experience. As such, this aspect of life should be adequately represented in the arts.

In view of the widespread prejudice and intolerance that has long been directed against same-sex relationships, presentation of gay characters and situations in good, honest works of literature enriches all of us, regardless of age or orientation, by expanding our appreciation and empathy for the diversity of human attachments. Like other touchy adolescent themes, homosexuality can often be presented most effectively when accompanied by a healthy dose of laughter.

Ron Koertge's *Arizona Kid* was praised in 1988 for presenting a gay man in a completely positive context. Sixteen-year-old Billy Kennedy has left his Midwest home to spend the summer in Tucson with Uncle Wes, his father's brother. Although Billy's father has discussed Uncle Wes's sexual orientation with him, Billy has never spent time in a gay household. As Billy and Wes gradually come to know and trust one another, humor is vital in easing tensions between them. Their friendship and mutual trust eventually extends to the touchiest of subjects, including their respective love lives. Billy finds Wes to be an extraordinarily perceptive confidant.

Billy's regard for his uncle is nicely demonstrated in the train platform scenes that serve as "bookends" to the novel. When Billy arrives in Tucson, he passes out from anxiety, lack of sleep, and the sudden shock of Arizona summer heat. When he awakens a few moments later, he discovers that he's being comforted by his Uncle:

> My *gay* uncle. In whose lap I had my head.
> "Holy shit!" I yelled as I shot to my feet and stood gasping between the sinks in the train station's men's room.
> "I think," Wes reassured a porter and a couple of other people who'd been watching, "it's safe to say he's regained consciousness."[20]

In the final scene, Billy embraces Uncle Wes before he boards the train: "I'll pat you so heartily," he whispered, "that we'll look like two he-men and not one straight teenager and one forty-year-old sissy." Billy replies, "I don't care about that. Honest" (*Arizona Kid*, 215).

In the same year, 1988, Barbara Wersba's novel, *Just Be Gorgeous* sympathetically depicted the difficult life of a gay street performer with whom sixteen-year-old Heidi Rosenbloom develops an attachment. Like Koertge, Wersba promotes inclusiveness by embracing a diversity of characters in her humane and humorous fictional world.

At about the same time, in the late 1980s, Francesca Lia Block burst upon the YA scene with her startlingly original novel *Weetzie Bat*. From the first, Block has celebrated love and diversity in her lyrical prose. The passage in which Weetzie's best friend Dirk tells her of his orientation during one of their evenings on the town is characteristic:

> "I'm gay," Dirk said.
> "Who, what, when, where, how—well, not *how*," Weetzie said. "It doesn't matter one bit, honey-honey," she said, giving him a hug.
> Dirk took a swig of his drink. "But you know I'll always love you the best and think you are a beautiful, sexy girl," he said.
> "Now we can Duck hunt together," Weetzie said, taking his hand. (*Weetzie Bat*, 7)

Their "Duck hunting" is so successful that before long, Weetzie finds her Secret Agent Lover Man, and Dirk finds his, well, Duck:

> "I met the best one!" Dirk said. "The perfect Duck. But what is so weird is that this Duck calls himself Duck. Now that is hell of weird!"
> "Lanky lizards!" Weetzie said. (22)

Dirk and Duck are a charming couple. But in the sequel, *Witch Baby*, they had intended to remain cautious around Duck's family, to whom Duck's orientation has never been revealed. However, almost immediately upon their visit to Duck's mother, Darlene, the strange, irrepressible Witch Baby (who had stowed away in Duck's car) blurts out that it's good thing Darlene likes Dirk, "Because Duck likes Dirk a lot too. They love each other more than anyone else in the world. They even sleep in the same bed with their arms around each other!"[21] After being so unexpectedly and dramatically "outed" by the unpredictable

Witch Baby, Duck is compelled to inform his family that he is gay. At first everyone is upset, but finally they realize that all is for the best.

> "And I want to thank you, too," Darlene Drake said shyly, placing a slinkster dog balloon at Witch Baby's feet. "You knew more about love than I knew. You helped me get my son back again."
>
> "Without you, Miss Pancake Dancer Stowawitch, we might never have really known each other," said Duck, stooping to kiss Witch Baby's hand. (*Witch Baby*, 110)

Although most YA literature tackling homosexuality is written for older teens, James Howe's *The Misfits* offers a take on it suitable for middle grade readers. The Misfits of the title are four friends, all seventh-grade outcasts for various reasons, who have formed a "Gang of Five." Bobby is fat; Addie is tall, skinny, and outspoken; Skeezie is scruffy and deficient in his personal hygiene; and Joe "acts more like a girl than a boy much of the time."[22] The harm done by name-calling is the theme of *The Misfits*, and all of the Gang members are called nasty names suited to their respective perceived deficiencies.

> Tuesday morning, we get to school, and what do we find scrawled in big ugly marker on Joe's locker but the word Fagot.
>
> Joe is outraged.
>
> "Don't they teach spelling in this school?" he goes, then yells across the hall to Kevin Hennesey, who is wearing his usual smirk, "There are two 'g's in 'faggot,' you numbskull!" (*Misfits*, 31)

After a series of misunderstandings, Joe and Colin (whose orientation has been a mystery) decide that they like one another and will be, "you know, like boyfriends or something" (*Misfits*, 265). There is a sweet innocence to the initial ventures into dating on the part of these seventh graders.

Howe achieves something special in *The Misfits*. Joe's effeminacy draws the same sort of ridicule as characteristics of his friends, such as Bobby's obesity. Through this association, Howe skillfully depicts nonstandard sexuality as just another among the assortment of individual peculiarities that draw the taunts of small-minded conformists. As the story unfolds, Joe's desire to hold hands or attend a dance with a boy he likes is seen to be no different than the drives of his heterosexual friends. Bobby concludes, "So there will be a whole lot of us going to the dance together, misfits and fits, couples and not" (266).

During 2003, as this book was being completed, a pair of first-rate YA novels with humorous treatment of gay themes were published: Bret Hartinger's *Geography Club* and David Levithan's *Boy Meets Boy*. Hartinger's book takes its title from a ruse devised by a small group of high school students who become known to one another—though not to anyone else—as gays and lesbians. They first meet at a pizza parlor, but soon realize that the best way to ensure privacy is to charter a sponsored school club that sounds so boring no one else will join. One of the funniest episodes in the book unfolds when, to the dismay of the members, a fellow student actually does want to join the Geography Club. They try everything to get rid of her, but she is undeterred.

For starters, the newcomer, Belinda Sherman, is black and all of the others are white or Oriental. Apparently no problem. "Why the Geography Club?" Terese asks. Belinda responds that she thought it might help with her college entrance exams:

> "There is no geography on the SAT," Min said.
> "There isn't?" Belinda said. "Well, it can't hurt, right?"
> "But geography is *boring*," Kevin said, almost indignant.
> "Well, isn't that the point of the club? To make it less boring?" Belinda Sherman wasn't just not gay—she was bubbly. I hated bubbly.[23]

Therese comes up with an inspired lie. "There's a fifty dollar equipment fee!" Terese said. "You know, for maps and atlases and stuff?" (*Geography Club*, 109). Not even this financial disincentive discourages the irrepressible Belinda. Ironically, after Belinda finally does learn that the Geography Club is a cover for gays, she remains a member. Realizing that the Geography Club is really about "some sense of being an outsider, a vagabond, with no place to call home," Russell stops Belinda from leaving the meeting.

> "You want to stay?" I asked Belinda.
> "Belinda looked confused. "But I'm straight."
> "We're an after-school club," Kevin said. "We're not supposed to discriminate."

Belinda cocked her head. "You really don't care?"

"Well," Min said, "don't expect us to spend much time talking about geography."

Belinda giggled. "Damn! I'm a token straight!" (140)

The small community of gays, lesbians, and sympathetic fellow outsiders tenuously created by Russell and his friends in *Geography Club* is imaginatively expanded in David Levithan's *Boy Meets Boy*. Levithan presents an alternative, or perhaps (one might hope) a near-future suburban American town in which transgender and homosexual lifestyles have become accepted by the mainstream. Paul, a high school sophomore, and his friends of both sexes and all persuasions experience the joys and suffering of young love in a "present-day gaytopia" without "gay-bashing, sexual identity crises, and parental rejection."[24]

In what is described by Michael Cart as "a breakthrough book (the first upbeat gay novel for teens),"[25] Levithan depicts an America shifted a bit to the left of the one we know. The novel's humor comes in two flavors. There are the over-the-top, laugh-out-loud antics of the school's Harley-riding cheerleaders and the cross-dressing Infinite Darlene, in a tizzy over her conflicting responsibilities as both homecoming queen and star quarterback:

"Coach Ginsburg is going to have my hat," she declares. "It's the frickin' Homecoming Pride rally this afternoon. He wants me to march with the rest of the team. But as homecoming queen, I'm also supposed to be introducing the team. If I don't do the proper introductions, my tiara might be in doubt."[26]

Meanwhile, Paul's witty narration sustains the entire novel. When he offers his best friend, Joni, advice she doesn't want to hear, he calls it a "Friendian Slip" (*Boy Meets Boy*, 38). He describes a seventh-grade girl as "dressed in a lethal combination of pastels" (4). Encountering Infinite Darlene in the school corridor, Paul is moved to observe:

There are few sights grander at eight in the morning than a six-foot-four football player scuttling through the halls in high heels, a red shock wig, and more-than-passable make-up. If I wasn't so used to it, I might be taken aback. (15)

We can hope that Michael Cart is right, and that the breakthrough achieved by *Boy Meets Boy* will be followed by more such generous, inclusive YA novels. The adolescents in Levithan's warm, large-spirited book are merely trying to attain goals that are important to all of us: they want to love and be loved. Editor Patty Campbell described *Boy Meets Boy* as a novel in which "same sex preference is not the problem."[27]

Funny Ways of Making Up

Making up after a lovers' quarrel is a popular theme of romantic fiction. Several YA novels have offered humorous takes on this situation. Here are some nominations for the all-time funniest making-up scenes.

One of the quirkiest scenes of lovers making-up in a humorous YA novel occurs in Ron Koertge's *Confess-O-Rama*. Tony Candelaria is angry at Jordan, his artistic and unconventional girlfriend, over her use of recordings of his private speech for one of her art projects. Introverted Tony is having trouble coping with Jordan's free-wheeling style. Meanwhile, Jordan is being suspended from high school for wearing one of her characteristically provocative political art costumes. Over her t-shirt she is wearing a bra with a tiny dart board strategically centered on each cup, with three darts in each bulls-eye.

Jordan attracts public attention when she accuses the school administrators of censoring her freedom of expression. While speaking before an assembled crowd, Jordan displays her offending costume and asks for their support. No one dares join her, and school administrators begin to close in to crush Jordan's rebellion. Then Tony steps up, removes his shirt, and reveals the pair of avocados attached to his bare chest with twine and duct tape. The crowd goes wild, and dozens of kids run up on stage, unbuttoning their shirts and blouses. "You did this for me!" Jordan lovingly exclaims to Tony (*Confess-O-Rama*,157). Tony's avocado trick earns him nomination spot number three.

The runner-up for the most extreme making-up scene in humorous YA literature goes to David Levithan's *Boy Meets Boy* for the week of demonstrations by Paul after he has lost Noah's trust. On the first day, Paul stays up without sleeping to create a thousand origami flowers and garlands them throughout the school halls, "centerpiecing it all at his locker" (*Boy Meets Boy*, 159). On the second day, he works at the kitchen table of his friend Tony, whose mother seems to "believe that I will suddenly start ravishing her son on the kitchen table if she doesn't interrupt to get a glass of water every ten minutes" (160). Undeterred by Tony's mother, he prepares a scroll of interesting words and definitions as a gift to Noah. On another day, he arranges a musical concert outside Noah's window, despite "an evil glare" from Noah's sister (162). And on it goes, for a week before the pair reconcile. They celebrate at the I Scream Parlor. Noah "gets a blood-red sundae while I get the sorbet with gummi worms in it" (171).

And finally, the award for the most extreme making-up performance in humorous YA literature goes to Louise Plummer's *The Unlikely Romance of Kate Bjorkman*. Kate's boyfriend, Richard Bradshaw, has been subjected to an all-out seduction campaign by the predatory Ashley Cooper, supposedly Kate's friend. After heroically resisting many of Ashley's advances, Richard finally responds when she literally corners him in a deserted hallway outside a New Year's Eve party. Kate happens to come along at just this unfortunate moment, and she turns violently against Richard, even though she knows he did not initiate the embrace.

Richard's solution to this lover's quarrel is to camp out in the Bjorkman's backyard. Inasmuch as the month is January and the setting Minnesota, this poses a severe challenge. Richard borrows a shovel and sleeping bag and builds himself a snow cave. The temperature dips to $-18°$ that night. The next morning, Kate and her parents look out their kitchen window to the sight of Richard, still alive and in full snow gear, holding up a large sign, "WILL WORK FOR FOOD" (*Unlikely Romance*, 176). That does the trick, and Kate concludes that "laughter, as it turns out, is the best aphrodisiac of all" (183).

Notes

1. Lynn Hall, *Dagmar Schultz and the Powers of Darkness* (New York: Scribner, 1989), 15.

2. Gordon Korman, *No More Dead Dogs* (New York: Hyperion, 2000), 177.

3. Francesca Lia Block, *Weetzie Bat* (New York: HarperCollins, 1989), 37–38.

4. Diana Wynne Jones, *The Lives of Christopher Chant* (New York: Greenwillow, 1988), 58.

5. Hilary McKay, *The Exiles in Love* (New York: Margaret K. McElderry Books, 1998), 50.

6. Gordon Korman, *Son of the Mob* (New York: Hyperion, 2002), 8.

7. Beverly Keller, *The Amazon Papers* (San Diego, Calif. : Browndeer Press, 1996), 47.

8. Meg Cabot, *The Princess Diaries* (New York: Harper Avon, 2000), 222.

9. David Klass, *You Don't Know Me* (New York: Frances Foster Books, 2001), 144.

10. Ron Koertge, *Confess-O-Rama* (New York: Orchard Books, 1996), 75–78.

11. Kate Gilmore, *Enter Three Witches* (Boston: Houghton Mifflin, 1990), 177–78.

12. Susan Juby, *Alice, I Think* (New York: HarperCollins, 2003), 103.

13. David Lubar, *Dunk* (New York: Clarion Books, 2002), 241.

14. Jaclyn Moriarty, *Feeling Sorry for Celia* (New York: St. Martin's, 2001), 139.

15. Ned Vizzini, *Be More Chill* (New York: Hyperion, 2004), 77.

16. Lloyd Alexander, *Gypsy Rizka* (New York: Dutton, 1999), 137.

17. Joan Bauer, *Thwonk!* (New York: Delacorte, 1995), 129.

18. Megan McCafferty, *Sloppy Firsts* (New York: Crown, 2001), 159.

19. Ellen Wittlinger, *Hard Love* (New York: Simon & Schuster, 1999), 109.

20. Ron Koertge, *The Arizona Kid* (Boston: Joy Street Books, 1988), 3.

21. Francesca Lia Block, *Witch Baby* (New York: HarperCollins, 1991), 53.

22. James Howe, *The Misfits* (New York: Atheneum, 2001), 30.

23. Bret Hartinger, *Geography Club* (New York: HarperTempest, 2003), 108.

24. Joanna Lewis, review of *Boy Meets Boy*, by David Levithan, *School Library Journal* 49:9 (September 2003): 216–17.

25. Michael Cart, review of *Boy Meets Boy*, by David Levithan, *Booklist* 99:22 (August 1, 2003).

26. David Levithan, *Boy Meets Boy* (New York: Knopf, 2003), 16.

27. Patty Campbell, review of *Boy Meets Boy*, by David Levithan, www.amazon.com/exec/obidos/tg/detail/-/0375824006/qid=1085930564/sr=1-2/ref=sr_1_2/104-7797624-1539164?v=glance&s=books#product-details (30 March 2004).

~

CHAPTER SEVEN

The Ironic Perspective

Imaginary Worlds: Aliens, Adventure, and Genre Parody

Some of the most entertaining contemporary YA literature is found in fantasy, science fiction, and other genre fiction in which a self-conscious or ironic narrative tone is maintained. While authors of these works usually have tongue firmly planted in cheek, the perspective of the reader is also important. It is often possible to enjoy an ironic work as a straightforward adventure story. Mystery, horror, science fiction, fairy tales, and other speculative genres of fiction have been reworked and parodied, and some of the most popular works are aimed at the younger end of the YA market.

Eoin Colfer's Artemis Fowl series parodies espionage thrillers such as Ian Fleming's James Bond novels. Colfer's distinctive contribution is the humorous pairing of fantasy elements of Irish mythology with more realistic—albeit overblown—elements of the action thriller. Colfer achieves hilarious effects by putting hard-boiled dialogue in the mouths of fairies and pixies.

In *Artemis Fowl: The Arctic Incident*, tough police captain Holly Short finds herself "saddled with Chix Verbil for a pod mate. Like most sprites, Chix believed himself God's green-skinned gift to females." Holly is unimpressed. "Sprites. They were all the same. Give a fairy a pair of wings and he thought he was irresistible."[1] Moments later, Chix is wounded by goblin fire. Holly tucks her "Neutrino 2000 into its holster" and calls out, "Fairy down. Fairy down. We are under fire. E37. Send warlock medics and backup" (*Arctic Incident*, 20). The Artemis Fowl books have been described as "*Die Hard* with fairies," for their depiction of nonstop violent action in a world of ethereal beings.

Colfer plays with the macho language of crime drama, substituting interspecies insults for the ethnic and racial remarks that often characterize gritty human police dramas. Gnomes are associated with many colorful expressions. A luxury transport is described as having "seats softer than a gnome's behind" (109). A control booth is sealed "tighter than a gnome's wallet" (155). In one scene, our heroes run out from their shelter, suddenly realizing that the goblins are about to blow it up. "They nearly made it. Of course *nearly* never won a bucket of squid at gnomish roulette" (124).

The villainous goblins are said to be closely related to lizards, and their reptilian appearance is fodder for comments such as, "Keep your scales on, the pair of you" (127) and "Be careful, friend, or I'll tear that forked tongue right out of your head" (137). Goblin leaders are named Scalene, Sputa, and Phlebum. At one point Sputa becomes unhappy with a subordinate: "Sputa licked his eyeballs furiously. Lieutenant Nyall would be losing his skin before shedding season" (233).

Species insults abound, including frequent remarks about the filthiness of dwarfs: "a clang louder than a dwarf's underpants hitting a wall" (141). "Dwarf toes wriggling are quite a sight. They are nimble as fingers, double-jointed, and the less said about the smell, the better" (179). Most of the dwarf jokes follow from Colfer's notion that the dwarfs are able to tunnel through soil by eating it and passing it directly out the other end. Hence, "Many a dwarf wife was known to scold her husband for venting gas at home and not leaving it in the tunnels" (191). Each of the Artemis Fowl books features episodes detailing gross expulsions of gas and masticated clay from the rear ends of tunneling dwarfs.

Humans are not immune from the barrage of politically incorrect species insults. Other species disparagingly refer to *homo sapiens* as "Mud Men." When Artemis corners the notorious dwarf burglar Mulch Diggums in his DVD-stocked penthouse in Beverly Hills, the dwarf cries out:

"You'll never take me alive, human. Tell Foaly not to send a Mud Man to do a fairy's job."
Oh dear, thought Artemis, rubbing his brow. Hollywood had a lot to answer for. (200)

Foaly, a centaur employed as the fairies' systems expert (much like "Q" in the James Bond books and films), grudgingly admits, "That Fowl is a genius, for a human . . . That's one smart Mud Boy."[2] When Foaly tells Holly Short that he has created a hologram of Artemis so lifelike that he can even arrange for the holo to walk to the bathroom at realistic intervals, Holly replies, "The miracle of modern science. The LEP pours millions into your department, Foaly, and all you can do is send Mud Boys to the toilet" (*Eternity Code*, 234). LEP stands for "Lower Elements Police," the idea being that the fairies and other mythic people now live underground, having been forced below the surface by humans.

Colfer delivers a potent entertainment package for preadolescent boys. Surround a twelve-year-old hero with hi-tech gadgetry and fast vehicles, and immerse him in nonstop action with exotic allies against outrageous villains. Then sprinkle in plenty of macho banter, grossness, silly names and puns, and you've got a winning combination that can't miss with aficionados of superhero comic books and mock-action films. Celtic mythology lends a veneer of historical authenticity, as well as a humorous flavor, to the nonstop action.

Deb Gliori's novels of the eccentric Strega-Borgia family, *Pure Dead Magic* and *Pure Dead Wicked*, are set in nearby Scotland. Titus, the eldest of three children, is twelve, the same age as Artemis Fowl. Like Artemis, Titus is a computer geek with little interest in sports or other strenuous activities. The Strega-Borgias, like the Fowls, reside in an isolated mansion.

In the first novel, Signor Strega-Borgia's evil brother Don Lucifer tries to murder his brother and nephew in order to gain the family fortune. In the second, corrupt builders and real estate developers attempt to drive the family out of their castle to make way for the construction of tacky, overpriced modern subdivisions. In both books the evildoers are foiled by the heroic children, helped by their magic-wielding nanny and the castle's mythical beasts. Gliori's nanny, Mrs. McLachlan, like

Colfer's Butler, is a powerful guardian posing as a mere domestic servant. Like Colfer, Gliori combines wordplay and grossness with comic book superhero fantasy, high-tech James Bond-style espionage, and mythological lore. In the resulting adventures, the young heroes save their clueless parents, aided by Tock, the moat's crocodile, Ffup, a teenage dragon, Knot, a yeti, and Sab, a griffin.

Gliori, too, is fond of puns and wordplay. Funny names in *Pure Dead Magic* include Don Lucifer di S'Embowelli Borgia and Malvolio di S'Enchantedino Borgia. The lake beside Strega-Schloss castle is known as Lochnagargoyle, flanked by the Bengormless mountain range, near the little Highland town of Auchenlochtermuchty. When baby Damp becomes lost in cyberspace, Titus sends his pet spider, Tarantella, to find her, because who better to negotiate the Web? A troublesome computer complains, "<MAY ALL YOUR CRASHES BE FATAL AND YOUR REBOOTS BE DOC MARTENS . . .<"[3]

Pure Dead Wicked introduces local builder Hugh Pylum-Haight, police officers MacBeth and MacDuff, and rat matriarch Multitudina, described as an ILLITERAT, because she cannot read.[4] Computer humor includes the accidental production of "reduced (to 10%) 'draft quality'" clones of Titus and his sister, Pandora. Most of these clones come to a ghastly fate: "the many handfuls that Damp had flushed down the toilet" (*Pure Dead Wicked*, 98), the one "that managed to wedge a tender portion of its anatomy into an electric outlet" (109), and last but not least, "the hapless towel-clad clone that Ffup had mistaken for toilet paper" (157).

Pure Dead Magic is "loaded" with bathroom humor, including frequent references to the smelly, soiled diapers of Damp, the youngest Strega-Borgia. A man dressed in a head-to-toe rabbit costume fails to reach toilet facilities before fouling his costume (*Pure Dead Magic*, 92). Ffup the dragon experiences "the worst case of dragon diarrhea he'd encountered in 600 years" and unloads a "large green projectile" on a thug who had been approaching the castle with criminal intent. "With a tremendous slapping sound, Ffup's digestive overload landed on a human target. There was a scream, a ghastly choking sound, and then silence" (103–4).

There is also mock-horror, as when a gangster strikes a match across the eyeball of what appears to be a stone griffin. Sab then comes to life, "reached downward, and with a brief crunch, neatly removed the hireling's head and spat it across the dungeon. The head landed on the floor beside Latch, its severed nerves and sinews causing it to wink in a horribly lifelike fashion" (116).

Perhaps the best known of recent mock-horror for young readers is *A Series of Unfortunate Events* by Lemony Snicket (pen name of Daniel Handler). The series parodies the horror, crime, and mystery genres as well as Victorian melodramas about orphans and foundlings such as Charles Dickens's *Oliver Twist*. The illustrations by Brett Helquist help create a deliciously spooky atmosphere of Gothic decadence.

Villainous Count Olaf wants to steal the fortune bequeathed to three children by their parents, who are presumed to have died in a fire. Count Olaf, abetted by a variety of grotesque henchmen, pursues the orphans all over the world. Any adult who attempts to help the children soon has a tragic "accident." The children suffer terrible but colorful privations, somehow always managing to barely elude the Count's clutches, thus setting up yet another tale of misery and flight. The series shows no signs of flagging. In fact, the recently published tenth volume, *The Slippery Slope*, is one of the best in the series and showcases many of Snicket's comic techniques.

Snicket takes the persona of an "intrusive narrator" to absurd lengths. He begins by warning readers off on the back cover of each book in the series:

> Unfortunately, I have dedicated my life to researching and recording the sad tale of the Baudelaire Orphans. There is no reason for you to dedicate yourself to such things, and you might instead dedicate yourself to letting this slippery book slip from your hands into a nearby trash receptacle, or deep pit. With all due respect, Lemony Snicket.[5]

The narrator frequently interrupts his tale for asides ranging from definitions of an uncommon word to multipage digressions in the manner of Sterne's *Tristram Shandy*. Mere definitions are teased out to absurd length. A common expression becomes the occasion for a lengthy digression:

> The expression "brace yourself," as I'm sure you know, does not mean to take some metal wiring and rivets and other orthodontic materials and apply them to your own teeth in order to straighten them. (*Slippery Slope*, 207)

If Snicket merely wished to provide helpful definitions of terms that might be unfamiliar to his youngest readers, he could find much simpler ways of doing so. The interruptions of his narrative are so frequent, unnecessarily verbose, and funny that they become an intrinsic part of the story. The narrative persona is that of an earnest pedant, ever ready to abandon narrative continuity for a scholarly aside. At one point, infant Sunny utters the single word, "Set!" A running joke in the series is the contrast of Sunny's meaningful, one-syllable utterances with the garrulous narrator's verbosity. In this instance, Sunny's monosyllable becomes the occasion for a page-and-a-half digression that begins:

> Out of all the words in the English language, the word "set" has the most definitions, and if you open a good dictionary and read the word's long, long entry . . . (216)

Characters' names are often silly. The orphans are named Violet, Klaus, and Sunny, the latter two names being those of a real-life New York couple who were involved in a sensational murder trial in the 1980s. The children's surname, Baudelaire, and that of their banker, Mr. Poe, derive from the two greatest nineteenth-century authors of morbid, Gothic literature. Count Olaf is abetted by Esmé Squalor, whose name alludes to the J. D. Salinger short story, "To Esmé, with Love and Squalor." Another pair of orphans are named Duncan and Isadora, after the great dancer Isadora Duncan.

Puns and wordplay are pervasive. We encounter a "Village of Fowl Devotees" (10) that might signify a community of chicken-worshipers, one populated by detestable (i.e., foul) persons, or perhaps even fans of Artemis Fowl. A girl named Carmelita is described as the "False Spring Queen" (80)—a delightfully ambiguous phrase, since the adjective "false" might apply to either the season or to the queen. Sunny serves up some "False Spring Rolls" (307) again playing on the ambiguity as to which word is modified by "false."

Oxymorons are frequently employed to comic effect. A favorite trick of Snicket's is to present a premise illustrated by a pair of examples, the first commonplace, but the second startling in its unexpected reference to crime or violence as in this pair from *The Slippery Slope*:

Fencing, a sport in which people swordfight for fun rather than for honor or in order to rescue a writer who has been taped to a wall. (74)

If someone asks you how you are, for example, you might automatically say, "Fine, thank you," when in fact you have just failed an examination or been trampled by an ox. (157)

A neat trick to wake up the nodding reader. On occasion, Snicket will reverse the order of elements in an oxymoronic couplet. Instead of beginning with a harmless-sounding premise before unleashing the horrific one, he starts with a dramatic statement, first illustrating it with an apt incident, but then descending into bathos with a ridiculously mundane second anecdote:

In the few moments where I have led a daring life of impulsive passion, it has led to all sorts of trouble, from false accusations of arson to a broken cuff link I can never have repaired. (149)

Logical tricks are used, as when this pair of characters are introduced: "a man with a beard but no hair and a woman with hair and no beard" (122). This exact phrase is repeated each time that these persons are described, with the misleading implication that there is something sinister and horrifying about their appearance.

Snicket makes crime and horror fun. Kidnapping, arson, extortion, and even murder—all of these detestable acts are carried out with such malicious glee by the grotesque villains, and are tut-tutted over so ineffectually by the narrator, that even the youngest reader is aware that A Series of Unfortunate Events is an over-the-top melodrama. In time, one begins to relish the exaggerated evil of the villains, the unbelievably wretched circumstances of the orphans, and the inevitable digressions of the intrusive narrator. The fun is in the journey, not in the resolution of any genuine conflict. While suitable for young children, the series offers allusions, wordplay, and other literary gamesmanship to engage the more sophisticated reader.

Paul Fleischman's A Fate Totally Worse Than Death, like Lemony Snicket's Series of Unfortunate Events, parodies murder mysteries and related genres. Like Snicket, Fleischman makes murder and mayhem fun. Fleischman's little gem is aimed at high schoolers and opens with

Danielle—one of the teens who will suffer "a fate totally worse than death"—reading trashy paperback horror novels. Of course, the genre is popular on the silver screen as well; at one point Danielle's classmate Gavin points out that "*Grievous Bodily Harm Eleven* is playing at the Cliffside Twelve-Screen." Not finding any takers, he assures the gang that it's "nothing at all like *Grievous Bodily Harm Ten*."[6]

Danielle is one of three wealthy, self-absorbed teens, who, as members of Cliffside High School's social elite, had bullied a fellow student, accidentally causing her death the previous year. Worse, they covered up their involvement by forging a suicide note. Danielle, Tiffany, and Brooke now find themselves rapidly aging. They become convinced that the cause of this "punishment worse than death" (*Fate*, 78) must be Helga, a beautiful Norwegian exchange student whom they identify as a reincarnation of Charity Chase, the murdered girl.

Danielle, Tiffany, and Brooke belong to a clique called the Huns, composed of students from the upscale Hundred Palms Estates. Some of the Huns are addicted to "up-talking," in which every sentence is expressed as a question. Here Tiffany tells Brooke about her hundredth reconciliation with Jonathan:

> We made up this morning? Before second period? Then we had this quiet, romantic lunch? In the cafeteria? Which was totally empty because there's no pizza on Tuesdays? We decided we're going to get married the day after graduation? (18)

Jonathan is a slick entrepreneur, and each time she gets back together with him, Tiffany can look forward to "the tears, the euphoria, the reinstating of her special discount on all his merchandise" (101). At one point, Jonathan offers Helga a piece of chocolate cake from a rack in one of his storage lockers:

> This morning, for Community Service, he'd driven the Meals on Wheels van, and had taken the cake from each of the lunches. Pretending puzzlement to his elderly patrons as to why there was no dessert, he'd diverted two pieces into his mouth and the rest to his locker for resale to students. (22)

This petty meanness toward the elderly is routinely practiced by Danielle, Tiffany, and Brooke, as in the book's opening scene, when

Danielle deliberately takes a bus seat designated for seniors, forcing a tottering old lady to stand. The girls are habitually ruthless in their shallow, egocentric pursuits. At one point Danielle wants to get a look at one of the school personnel files. Noting that the office is occupied only by a parent volunteer, she casually tells the woman that her daughter "had just received a knife wound" (45) and gains access to the file as the frantic mother rushes out.

Premature aging is the perfect revenge to be visited upon this trio of self-centered teens. Their horror at discovering ever-increasing signs of geriatric decline is both terrible and funny. After each has privately discovered aging symptoms, they gather at the beach.

> Danielle subtly kept their pace slow, so as not to start wheezing from shortness of breath in front of the whole beach crowd. This suited Tiffany, who wished to hide the gimpy gait caused by her ever more painful hip joints. Though it was near ninety, Brooke was wearing a shirt of her father's over her swimsuit . . . to hide the half dozen spots she sported on each hand. (61)

Tiffany's expedition to a drugstore to buy diapers is priceless. After struggling to find her way to a seedy neighborhood where she won't be recognized, Tiffany pauses to choose between Second Childhood or Sphincter Sentry brands. She feels a need to explain herself to the impassive woman at the register.

> "I'm buying these for my great-grandmother?" she announced unbidden to the clerk. "She just came to live with us? From Kansas? It's the very brand she asked me to get? The same brand she used to use? Back in Kansas?"
> The clerk stared at her. "Where in Kansas?"
> Tiffany swallowed. "Dallas," she answered. (82)

Meanwhile Tiffany suddenly realizes that she is having a little accident. "Floor's a little wet," she remarked offhandedly. "From the rain" (82). Later, Tiffany again finds herself losing bladder control while chatting with her friends, but now she's prepared. "She began to pee in her diaper, an act she'd dreaded performing in public at first, but which she brought off now with perfect aplomb." Tiffany goes right on gossiping with Danielle and Brooke as if nothing had happened (101).

The girls' musical tastes are on a par with their choices in literature and cinema. Their favorite groups include Bleeding Ulcer (11), Pus (96), Wehrmacht, with their hit, "Born to Hate" (59), and Trash, with their "Full Dumpster of Love For Ya" (60). Fleischman takes his readers on a rollicking, satirical tour-de-farce. A *Fate Totally Worse Than Death* is unlike any other YA novel, unique even among Paul Fleischman's own numerous and varied works.

Daniel Pinkwater's *Young Adult Novel* is the definitive satire of the YA problem novel. Originally published in 1982 and reprinted most recently in *5 Novels* (1997), the fifty-eight page novella stands with Fleischman's A *Fate Totally Worse Than Death* as one of the few pure satires in the YA market. Contemporary reviewers agreed Pinkwater's short novel was "a dandy spoof of the modern YA novel,"[7] and "an irreverent parody of motifs found in contemporary young adult problem fiction."[8] Patty Campbell described the book as "an absolutely exquisite put-down."[9]

Five geeky boys, constant companions ignored or scorned by all their classmates, call themselves the Wild Dada Ducks and set about to improve Himmler High School with Dada-inspired installations and events. The boys are known to one another as Charles the Cat, Captain Colossal, Igor, the Indiana Zephyr, and the Honorable Venustiano Carranza (President of Mexico.) Their initial pranks, such as the introduction of a toilet into the school's trophy case, are largely overlooked. But when they accidentally influence a student council election, unexpected consequences ensue. The Ducks had been amusing themselves by inventing stories about a wretched imaginary boy named Kevin Shapiro. *Young Adult Novel* opens with a heart-rending tale that we do not realize is a put-on until, perhaps, the very last sentence.

> So here was Kevin, a thirteen-year-old alcoholic, pusher, and thief. His mother would probably never get well, his father certainly wouldn't, and sister Isobel was turning tricks on State Street. It seemed to Kevin that there wasn't a chance in the world that he would ever get his life straightened out. And he was right. So we hit him over the head and fed him to the pigs.[10]

Like their invented protagonist, Kevin Shapiro, the Wild Dada Ducks themselves never get a break. The Ducks are thrilled to discover that there is a real student in their large high school named Kevin

Shapiro. However, their playful impulse to promote this actual boy who happened to share the name of their fictional hero backfires on the Ducks. Shapiro, unwillingly surrounded by an entourage of supporters known as Fanatical Praetorians, experiences a brief reign as absolute dictator of the school. Virtually his only exercise of power is the arrangement of a public humiliation of the Ducks.

Asked about his satirical intentions in this unusual book, Daniel Pinkwater told a reviewer, "I did finally read a few of the so-called 'problem novels,' and I was disgusted. I thought they were sneaky books; they imposed an adult point of view and morality on kids under the pretext of telling a story."[11] *Young Adult Novel* is not just a satirical sort of novel. It is, from start to finish, a systematic parody of the YA problem novel. That genre is lampooned both in the Kevin Shapiro stories-within-the-story and in the overall saga of the Wild Dada Ducks. Charles the Cat explains the origin of the Kevin Shapiro stories:

> The sad story of Kevin the messed-up thirteen-year-old is one of the pastimes of the Wild Dada Ducks. . . . Sometimes Kevin is an orphan, sometimes a juvenile delinquent, a druggie, a lonely child of feuding parents, a social misfit, a homosexual, a weakling who wants to play sports, and any number of other kinds of hard-luck characters.
>
> Kevin Shapiro, Boy Orphan is different from the novels in the Himmler High School Library in that he never solves his problems. Instead, we usually kill him from time to time. (*Young Adult Novel*, 4–5)

Like the Kevin Shapiro stories, the misadventures of the Wild Dada Ducks form a darkly hilarious panorama of adolescent crises that refuse to be neatly resolved. Pinkwater makes us see that real-life problems are not to be smoothed away by authors attempting social work under the guise of fiction. Pinkwater's ironic novel, like Paul Fleischman's, is most fully appreciated by older teens and adults sufficiently familiar with the ideas and the genres being parodied to appreciate the authors' satirical intent.

A third master of YA black humor, William Sleator, showcases his distinctive comic voice in the science fiction/horror novels, *Interstellar Pig* and its sequel, *Parasite Pig*. In *Interstellar Pig*, sixteen-year-old Barney is invited to join a trio of intriguing neighbors in a role-playing game called Interstellar Pig. Barney gradually discovers that the neighbors are aliens, and that the game is actually an interspecies competition for planetary survival. The object of the game is to capture The Piggy, a small, round, pink token with a hideously leering face, believed to be capable of destroying the home planets of all players but the winner.

Interstellar Pig is packed with quirky bits of humor. The ease with which the aliens manipulate Barney's clueless parents amuses Barney and makes him feel superior, until he discovers that in the Interstellar Pig game, his own "IRSC score" (Interstellar Relative Sapience Code) is far below that of his opponents.

> "But it can't be *that* bad!" I insisted.
> "That's what we're moaning about, Barney," Zena said wearily. "It's just going to drag the game down to have more underdeveloped species like yours . . ."
> "She was trying to protect you, to keep you out; that was what it really amounted to," Manny explained. "Only your IRSC was too pitiful."[12]

The Piggy itself is funny: the notion that such a silly-looking token could cause intergalactic warfare and destroy worlds is preposterous, and, as it turns out, probably false. At one point it appears that The Piggy's powers may be exactly the opposite of what is believed by the players, and that it will destroy its possessor rather than his opponents. Later, Barney begins to suspect that The Piggy can't really destroy anyone; it is merely a sort of emotional voyeur who enjoys the sensations of being coveted and greedily possessed by a rich variety of life forms. During a desperate struggle against terrifying aliens, Barney succeeds in communicating with The Piggy, only to discover that it is interested only in regurgitating phrases it has absorbed while being hidden within a high school yearbook: "*Future Teachers of America, 2,3, President 4; Pep Club, 1,2; Prom Queen Attendant, 4*" (*Interstellar Pig*, 179). At the end, members of a species of lichen which has captured The Piggy ask it many questions:

> "What can we do to keep you happy and satisfied?" "What type of organism do you take the most pleasure in devouring?" "What is the secret of winning the game?"

The Student Council this year has been extremely active in school affairs and in stimulating school spirit among the student body, The Piggy whirred blandly at them.
The lichen were confused. (197)

William Sleator is a prolific author of YA literature, but *Interstellar Pig* stands alone as a science fiction cult classic. Eighteen years after its publication, Sleator brought out a sequel, *Parasite Pig*. Although generally regarded as a weaker novel than *Interstellar Pig*, the sequel is fascinating for the comic horror atmosphere evoked by its lurid immersion into gross, visceral situations. These involve not only several ghastly forms of internal parasitism, but also the elaborate preparation of humans, by a species of giant crabs with gourmet tastes, to be fattened, marinated, and finally grilled alive as the main course in ceremonial feasts. Despite all this, *Parasite Pig* is essentially comic, not only because of its happy ending, but also because of Sleator's skill in infusing his morbid tale with humorous touches.

Retold Fairy Tales and Other Fantastic Wit

The number of YA novels and series playing ironically upon the science fiction and horror genres is relatively small. However, the same could not be said about modern fantasy fiction. In recent years, an enormous number of novels and stories featuring retellings of traditional folktales have been published.

Much of this literature is not humorous, of course. Although many of these works are seasoned with a sprinkling of comic episodes, the dominant tone of fantasy literature continues to be that of romance. Not only romantic feelings between two persons, but romance in the broader sense of heroic quest literature, in which a young person sets out on the adventure of his or her life (represented as a journey) and faces daunting obstacles (often represented as monsters) that must be overcome to fulfill the quest (to become a mature, independent adult). Many of the modernized fairy tales are also infused with feminist and other progressive social themes—usually not promising territory for humor. Nevertheless, a considerable body of humorously retold fairy tales presenting feminist struggles by feisty female protagonists has emerged.

Patricia Wrede's Enchanted Forest Chronicles, a series of four novels plus some later short stories, are among the best humorous YA fantasies. Wrede's signature technique is the mingling of mundane domestic matters with elements of high fantasy. Her protagonist, Cimorene, prefers being a "cook and librarian" to being a princess. She is famous for her cherries jubilee, and she discovers that soapy water with a bit of lemon juice is the best remedy against evil wizards.

Wrede's positive male characters are equally domestic. King Mendanbar charms Cimorene by unplugging her backed-up kitchen sink with his magic sword. At a tournament, a baking contest is equal in importance to the traditional athletic activities. (A barbarian knight wins with his Triple Chocolate After-Battle Cake recipe, included in the story.)[13]

Wrede also plays with the ingredients of fairy tales. In *Searching for Dragons*, Rumpelstiltskin's grandson operates a foster home for the dozens of children he has been compelled to adopt when beneficiaries of his gold-spinning can't guess his name. A weary giant is persuaded by Cimorene to retire from his job fulfilling commissions to pillage and plunder various villages and establish himself as a consultant to other giants wishing to be hired for that purpose.

Gail Carson Levine's *Ella Enchanted* is one of the best-known humorous retellings of a classic folktale. The novel won many awards, including a Newbery honor, for its imaginative expansion of the Cinderella folktale. Most of the book's humor derives from Levine's playfulness with words. Even simple punning is embedded in passages of broader linguistic complexity. When captured by human-eating ogres, Ella disarms them with cheerful jests, as in this passage in which she tries to convince them of the advantages of a vegetarian diet:

> "You might enjoy it," I said. "Perhaps you'd find that you prefer broccoli to flesh and legumes to legs."
> The last suggestion made them laugh.
> The youngest ogre told SEEf in Ogrese, "Maybe we should get to know our meals better. This one makes jokes."[14]

The central conflict of *Ella Enchanted* is the heroine's struggles to resist an enchantment laid upon her at birth. The fairy Lucinda had attended Ella's christening and bestowed upon her the "gift" of obedi-ence. In practice, the gift is a curse and becomes a terrible burden and danger to Ella because of its unlimited nature. Ella is compelled to obey in the most literal sense.[15] For instance, when told to eat cake, she is unable to stop eating until her Mother finally notices she has consumed an outrageous amount and orders her to stop. Although Ella develops clever compensations for her compulsion, her awful stepsisters, Hattie and Olive, learn of and quickly exploit Ella's weakness.

Her curse of obedience gets Ella into numerous quirky predicaments requiring ingenious and often humorous intervention. The logical co-nundrum presented by the requirement of unthinking obedience is well-integrated with other humorous verbal logic in Levine's absorbing narrative.

Jane Yolen's story, "Cinder Elephant" offers other amusing variations on this best-known of all folktales. Yolen's heroine, Elly, is a big girl with size 9½ shoes, a nice reversal of the irritating convention that Cin-derella must be a petite beauty with tiny feet. Yolen focuses upon the bluebirds who assist Cinderella in the Disney film, and extends the mo-tif of birds and birdwatching to startling and hilarious extremes. In her author's afterword, Yolen says, "I hated the Disney Cinderella with a passion. All those mice. All those birds. The birds in 'Cinder Elephant' are a satire on those twittery bluebirds."[16]

Patrice Kindl's *Goose Chase* is liberally adapted from the traditional folk story of the Goose Girl (Andrew Lang, *Blue Fairy Book*). Kindl has fun stretching to absurd lengths (so to speak) the traditional conceit of the heroine's long, beautiful, golden hair. When brushed, genuine gold dust falls from Alexandra's hair, which can grow to any length. The chapter in which the Goose Girl, Alexandra, uses her hair to escape a dungeon is introduced by the epigram, "Hair today, gone tomorrow—paraphrased proverb."[17] When Alexandra and Prince Edmund com-plete their escape in a boat, the tail end of her hair emerges from a doorway of the now-distant castle.

> My hair had been steadily shrinking, at my request, and was now no longer than an eighth of a mile. On it rode a Sergeant with great braided shoulder pads and a high hat, three foot soldiers, four barking dogs, and five dirty children. (*Goose Chase*, 151)

The contrast between the Prince's naïve idealism and the Goose Girl's brisk directness is amusing throughout the story. Alexandra thinks the prince a fool and is often impatient with his courtly manners. She proves herself wonderfully adept at handling the simpleminded Prince, a trio of ogresses, and an evil baroness, not to mention a flock of a dozen geese who accompany her everywhere.

The geese are funny throughout. Though incapable of speech, they frequently nudge Alexandra and Prince Edmund in the right direction to complete the tasks that will return the rightful heirs to their kingdom. Their intelligent and purposeful behavior is a clever take on the behavior of the geese in the fairy tale, "The Goose Girl," who distract the Goose Boy each day just when the Goose Girl wishes for a bit of privacy to attend to her luxurious tresses.

The transformation of the twelve geese into so many princesses is handled nicely. Alexandra guesses "by the size of her lower extremities" which one of the princesses had been known to her as Cassandra Big Foot. "I supposed I would be wise to address her solely as Cassandra from now on" (212). Kindl's handling of a theme of metamorphosis, as in her earlier novels, *Owl in Love* and *Woman in the Wall*, is characteristically witty and entertaining in this highly imaginative postmodern revision of a classic fairy tale.

Nancy Farmer offers another nice retelling of "The Goose Girl" in her short story, "Falada the Goose Girl's Horse." In her author's note, Farmer remarks:

> I was upset by fairy stories (and there are lots of them) where innocent animals were killed so the heroine could live happily after ever. In particular, I thought Falada the horse got a raw deal. How long did her head stay nailed over the gate? who did she talk to? How did she eat?[18]

Farmer comes up with a wonderfully satisfying reversal of the Grimm Brothers tale in which Falada is killed, then decapitated and her head nailed to a gate. As Farmer notes, this grotesque barbarism serves no purpose other than to help the silly princess along. Like most folktales, "The Goose Girl" is narrated in the third person. But in Farmer's clever variation, Falada the horse is the narrator. It is her story throughout, and what happens to her is as important as what happens to any of the human characters. Farmer's Falada avoids her "Grimm" fate, and in a parody of conventional fairy-tale endings, she and her stallion are happily united in the end.

Although not patterned as closely upon any single folk tale, Jean Ferris's *Once upon a Marigold*[19] is a fairy tale romance augmented with ironic modern touches much like Levine's *Ella Enchanted* and Kindl's *Goose Chase*. Ferris had already secured a reputation for humorous, quirky, modern romance with her charming *Love among the Walnuts*. In *Once upon a Marigold* she weaves fairy tale and romance into an appealing story with a happy fairy-tale ending and plenty of laughs along the way.

The book's broadest, silliest humor derives from the mixed metaphors spoken by Ed, the kindly troll who finds Prince Christian lost in the forest and raises him in a cave. Ed is given to malapropisms, many of them fractured proverbs, such as, "it was all spilled milk over the dam" (95), "A closed mind gathers no moss" (104), "I hate to be a wet blanket in the mud" (162), and the insightful, "You know that saying about how it's always darkest just after the lights go out?" (161).

Ferris also makes effective use of the opportunities for comic anachronism that arise for the modern storyteller when writing of a bygone era. Charmingly, Christian begins a romance with Princess Marigold by "p-mail."

> Christian rolled his message into the metal cylinder and attached it to Walter's leg. He didn't know why he hadn't thought of this before. It's what carrier pigeons were meant for—and if the technology existed, he was a fool not to use it. How much harder communication had been before p-mail. (39)

After he has begun this pigeon-mail relationship with Marigold, Christian muses, "Maybe she was shallow and stupid and he'd hate her if they ever met. After all, how much could you really tell about somebody from a couple of p-mails?" (47).

Vivian Vande Velde is one of the finest authors of fairy tales with a humorous twist. In *The Rumpelstiltskin Problem*, Vande Velde opens with an amusing introduction in which she explains that she was struck by a number of outrageously improbable elements in the traditional tale.

Each of Vande Velde's variations on the famous Grimm Brothers tale begins with the oxymoronic pairing of an apt modern element with the time-honored fairy-tale opening.

> Once upon a time, before pizzerias or Taco Bells, there was a troll named Rumpelstiltskin who began to wonder what a human baby would taste like.[20]

> Once upon a time, before eyelash curlers and lip liner, there lived a very plain girl by the name of Rumpelstiltskin. (80)

Each story takes the essential ingredients of the folktale in quite a different direction. In some variations the king is good, in others he is bad or indifferent. Sometimes the miller's daughter is a positive character, but in one very funny tale she is an unbearable girl named Carleen, whose favorite verbal expression fails to endear her to the king.

> "*Duh*," Carleen said in that infuriating way of hers. "Well, it sure isn't straw." She *was* pretty—not the most beautiful girl in the country, but pretty. Except, of course, when she stood with her hand on her hip, rolling her eyes and saying "*Duh*." (104)

A reviewer noted that "The first three stories deal with the motivation of the Rumpelstiltskin character," while the other three "have human characters taking on the role of Rumpelstiltskin."[21] In the latter trio, Rumpelstiltskin appears variously as a woman, as a handsome young elf, and as a captain of the guard. Each of the stories is funny and entertaining in itself, and in addition they have a humorous collective impact as a set of virtuoso performances.

Vande Velde is endlessly creative in her use of fantasy and humor to treat typical concerns of adolescent characters. Her short story "Boy Witch" is illustrative. Thirteen-year-old Clarence, the son of a renowned witch, is alone at home when a pretty girl a few years older than himself comes seeking magic assistance. Emma explains that her younger brother had cut off much of her hair as a prank, at a particularly inopportune time. She is desperate to grow the lost hair back at once.

In a series of follies, Clarence tries one spell after another from a magic book, each time causing things to go from bad to worse. His first spell gives Emma a beard, but when he removes the beard all of her other hair disappears as well. "A Spell for Hayre" causes a rabbit to become attached to her head. Finally, Clarence figures out how to reverse his previous spells, and Emma departs no better but thankfully no worse than she had arrived.

The idea of an enchanter's subordinate overreaching is familiar from traditional tales such as *The Sorcerer's Apprentice*. What is special about Vande Velde's version is her humorous blending of adolescent psychology into the story. Emma's concern over her appearance, and Clarence's desire to show off for the older girl, infuse the narrative with realistic adolescent motivation. In addition to retelling fairy tales, Vande Velde has authored humorous works in several other genres. Her very funny novel, *Never Trust a Dead Man* combines elements of fantasy, murder mystery, and historical fiction.

There are several humorously twisted fairy tales in the excellent Datlow and Windling anthology, *A Wolf at the Door*. We have already mentioned two of them: Jane Yolen's "Cinder Elephant" and Nancy Farmer's "Falada." Yet another story in *A Wolf at the Door*, Kelly Link's "Swans" offers some terrific variations on the classic fairy tale, "The Six Swans," in which a girl must fulfill difficult conditions to restore her six brothers to human form. Narrated by young Emma Bear, Link's story weaves every element of the original folktale into a new pattern. Anachronisms are used to humorous effect, as when Emma's mother "who could spin straw into gold," sews quilts with *Star Wars* and Elvis themes.[22] After her brothers have been transformed into waterfowl, Emma puts them in a bathtub and observes, "It was the first time they ever seemed to enjoy a bath. Even better, they didn't have any teeth to brush." Then she puts them outside "because I wasn't sure if they were house-trained." After a good night's sleep, she goes outside and feeds her brothers. "I'd never had pets before. Now I had six. I tried to decide what I liked better, birds or brothers" ("Swans," 86).

After her wicked stepmother has turned all the teachers and students at Emma's school into swans, Emma decides to read up on enchantments in the school library, while surrounded by honking birds. She laments that her "fairy godfather is never around when you need him. This is why it's important to develop good research skills, and know how to find your way around a library" (90). From her research, Emma determines that in order to break her stepmother's spell, she must "make shirts for all the birds and throw the shirts over their necks." This is ex-actly what happens in the original tale, but modern Emma has a mind of her own. "I think I have a better idea than a bunch of silly shirts that no one is probably going to wear again, anyway" (90). Emma creates an enormous quilt, large enough to cover "all the swans I can find." How-ever, she seems more interested in her quilting than in transforming the swans—her teachers, classmates, father, and brothers—back into hu-man form (91).

Emma's obsessive quilting is a nicely ironic turn on the traditional expectation that women should spend most of their time on domestic chores. Indeed, Emma's droll narration reveals an enormously confi-dent and composed young woman who, far from frantically trying to rescue her brothers, is quite relaxed, even humorously detached, about the fantastic events that have befallen her family.

Several varieties of nonrealistic YA literature have been considered here: the straightforward, the satirical, and the postmodern. Most con-temporary humorous fiction, particularly that of a speculative or fantas-tical nature, includes satirical and postmodern elements. Indeed, one of the most basic ingredients of humor—surprise at an incongruity—is also a common element of ironic and postmodern perspectives. If a humor-ous incongruity happens to puncture a pretension, then we have satire as well as comedy. If the incongruity is best shown by use of a nontradi-tional perspective, perhaps feminist or nonlinear, the result is fiction with postmodern as well as humorous and ironic tones.

Even works targeted primarily to middle school readers, such as the series by Colfer, Gliori, and Snicket, contain nods to earlier texts ("in-tertextuality") and such postmodern literary features as nonlinear nar-ration and fragmentation of subject. Works written for older teens, such as the parodies by Fleischman and Pinkwater, offer sophisticated irony, including a healthy skepticism about modern culture, technology, and authority structures. The retold fairy tales add feminist and multicul-tural viewpoints, psychological insights, and deeper explorations of postmodern themes of marginalization and alienation. The author who is able to wield such heavy implements and yet can serve up, in the end, a light confection that is devoured eagerly by young readers, has pulled off a rare and valuable literary accomplishment.

Two Masters of Modern Fantasy

This review of nonrealistic, humorous YA literature would not be complete with a consideration of recent works by two of the finest contemporary authors of humorous YA fantasy, Terry Pratchett and Diana Wynne Jones. Both British writers have recently gained much greater attention on this side of the Atlantic. Within the works of Pratchett and Jones a reader can find wordplay to match Lemony Snicket's, social satire as sharp as that of Paul Fleischman or Daniel Pinkwater, and powerfully transformed folktales as strangely humorous and romantic as those of Patrice Kindl.

Terry Pratchett has published more than forty works of fiction, most of them in his Discworld series. The Discworld novels generally fall into one of four subseries: Ankh-Morpork with its City Watch; the Unseen University and its wizards; the witches of Lancre, and Death. Some of Pratchett's novels cut across multiple Discworld settings, and others are only loosely associated with Discworld. Among the latter are Pratchett's three recent books marketed specifically to youth audiences, *The Amazing Maurice and His Educated Rodents*, *The Wee Free Men*, and *A Hat Full of Sky*. All are connected to the Discworld series so loosely that familiarity with the adult-marketed Discworld books is not important to their appreciation.

The Amazing Maurice and His Educated Rodents is a superb novel, highly praised by reviewers and critics, and winner of the Carnegie medal, an ALA Best Book for Young Adults, and numerous other awards.

> Pratchett hasn't blunted his wickedly funny pen for younger readers; the only apparent concessions to a teen audience are the adolescent humans abetting the rats, and the story's relative brevity. He retains the lethal combination of laugh-out-loud farce, razor-sharp satire, and the underlying passionate idealism unique to the confirmed cynic that make his adult Discworld series so popular.[23]

A scheming cat, Maurice, and a group of rats have accidentally gained intelligence and speech by dining at a rubbish heap behind the wizards' university. Maurice persuades the rats and a "stupid-looking kid," Keith, to join him in a Pied Piper scam. At each village, the rats stage bold appearances to convince the citizens that a rodent plague has developed. Keith then shows up with his flute, the rats pretend to be piped out of town, and then the whole gang rendezvous to share the reward paid the piper by the grateful villagers.

Humor in *The Amazing Maurice* is pervasive and varied. The rats have taken names such as Big Savings, Dangerous Beans, HamnPork, and Sardines, from labels found in the rubbish heap. Despite enhanced abilities, the nonhuman characters are absolutely faithful to their species identity, like the rabbits in Richard Adams's *Watership Down*. The rats tell one another, "Smell you later!"[24] At one point, someone uses the expression "I smell a rat" figuratively, and Sardines apologizes. "Sorry," said Sardines. "I think that was me. I'm a bit nervous" (*Amazing Maurice*, 63).

Maurice is a vivid character, a swaggering, lop-eared tomcat whose self-centered instincts are not at all moderated by his powers of intelligence and speech. Maurice can be wonderfully sarcastic. At one point the startled mayor of Bad Blintz exclaims, "But cats can't talk!"

> "Well, I can't promise that I could give a, you know, full-length after-dinner speech, and don't ask me to do a comic monologue," said Maurice. "And I can't pronounce difficult words like 'marmalade' and 'lumbago.' But I'm pretty happy with basic repartee and simple wholesome conversation." (219–20)

Maurice is the ringleader of the gang and has scant respect for its only human member, the young piper, Keith. At one point, they are told that the only food available is "some milk that's not gone hard yet and a couple of fish heads." Maurice, who "was a street cat and would drink milk so rotten that it would try to crawl away" (51) is game.

> "Sounds good to me," said Maurice.
> "What about your human?
> "Him? He'll eat any old scraps." (50)

Maurice and Keith meet Malicia Grim, daughter of the mayor, who describes herself as a descendent of "the Sisters Grim . . . Agonista and Eviscera Grim" (62). Malicia is addicted to stories, and she is convinced that life should unfold as in formulaic folktales. She tells Maurice, "I don't think you're a proper talking cat anyway . . . I mean you don't wear boots and a sword and have a big hat with a feather in it." Maurice's reaction is predictable. He gives her a long stare. "Boots?" he said at last. "On *these* paws?" (80). When she learns that Keith is an orphan, Malicia gets carried away with speculation.

> You were stolen away at birth, I expect. You probably are the rightful king of some country, but they found someone who looked like you and did a swap. In that case you'll have a magic sword, only it won't look magic, you see, until it's time for you to manifest your destiny. (52)

The Amazing Maurice is altogether an amazing book. It's a superb animal story, full of danger, adventure, and authentic species behavior, in the tradition of *Watership Down* and *Mrs. Frisby and the Rats of NIMH*. As in all of Pratchett's books, there is humor on nearly every page. Meanwhile, serious philosophical issues are raised concerning man's treatment of animals and the significance of stories in our constructions of reality. As one reviewer noted:

> This book is pure, unadulterated fun as Dangerous Beans and the gang struggle with unusual quandaries that only educated rats encounter, such as the true meaning of life and whether it is okay to eat a dead friend. The action is fast paced, the dialogue witty, and the characters endearing and unforgettable.[25]

Pratchett's second Discworld novel marketed to youth, *The Wee Free Men*, might appear to be aimed at children, not young adults, since protagonist Tiffany Aching is only nine years old. However, the book's length (262 pages) and the sophistication of its language and content are well-suited to adolescent and adult readers. Moreover, Tiffany doesn't act or think like a nine-year-old. She's a bit like Lewis Carroll's Alice.

> Tiffany is (unrealistically) said to be only nine years old, but this should not deter older readers in any way: the satiric sense of humor is perfect for anyone who enjoys *The Princess Bride* and the works of Douglas Adams. A wonderfully funny fantasy for all ages.[26]

Precisely because of Tiffany's unusual emotional maturity, the occasions on which her preadolescent status suddenly comes to the fore are quite funny. On one occasion, she recalls that one of her uncles liked to tilt a tobacco wrapper in just a certain way so that it suggested to him the image of a naked woman. Tiffany can't make it out, "and couldn't see what the point would be in any case."[27] On another occasion, Tiffany cleverly dodges a situation calling for her immediate betrothal to one of the tiny warriors she has enlisted (*Wee Free Men*, 134).

As in *The Amazing Maurice*, Pratchett transforms elements of folk tales into a sophisticated postmodern fantasy. Aided by the Nac Mac Feegle—a race of six-inch-tall, red-headed, blue-tattooed warriors in kilts—Tiffany finds and enters the Fairy Queen's nightmare realm and rescues both her baby brother and the son of the local baron, both of whom have been stolen by the Queen. At the end, Tiffany is briefly visited by a pair of Pratchett's famous Discworld witches and confirmed as Granny Aching's spiritual heir.

The Nac Mac Feegle, first introduced in Pratchett's *Carpe Jugulum*, steal the show—along with everything else that isn't nailed down. Their archaic Gaelic accents are deliciously funny, as in these war cries:

They can tak' oour lives but they canna tak' oour troousers!
Ye'll tak' the high road an' I'll tak' yer wallet! (135)

The novel is filled with Pratchett's witty wordplay. When Tiffany encounters a talking toad sitting in a witch's hat, she describes it as the witch's familiar. "I'm not familiar," said a voice from among the paper flowers. "I'm just slightly presumptuous" (27). The Feegle never tire of boasting about their bravery. While rowing a boat one of them yells, "It's ne'er be said that the Nac Mac Feegle turned their back on a foe!" Tiffany points out, "But you're rowing *facing* backward!" (215).

The Wee Free Men, following *The Amazing Maurice*, is another example of Pratchett's skill in adapting his adult-marketed *Discworld* series to wider and younger audiences. Pratchett has said that he invented Discworld to parody a wave of mediocre Tolkien imitations. "Discworld started as an antidote to bad fantasy, because there was a big explosion of fantasy in the late '70s, an awful lot of it was highly derivative, and people weren't bringing new things to it."[28] However, "as the series progressed Pratchett moved away from parodying fantasy novels and began to satirize daily existence in the real world."[29]

Although filled with parodies, ironic allusions, and satirical observations, the flow of Pratchett's narration is rarely impeded. Pratchett's characters are not flat, stock objects of pure satire, like Pinkwater's Dada Ducks or Fleischman's Cliffside High Huns. We care about Maurice and Dangerous Beans and Tiffany Aching because as funny as they are, they are also warm, lovable characters with believable motivations. Perhaps the most succinct explanation of Terry Pratchett's achievement is that, "His fiction is both a hilarious parody of the fantasy genre, as represented by Tolkien and 'sword and sorcery' novels, and a genuine contribution to it."[30]

That other marvelous British fantasy writer, Diana Wynne Jones, has been producing outstanding fantasy and science fiction for more than three decades. Her Chrestomanci Chronicles, four novels and several short stories, beginning with *Charmed Life*, have a timeless appeal and are selling quite well in American paperback editions. Her 2003 novel, *The Merlin Conspiracy*, is marketed in the children's, young adult, and fantasy sections in large bookstores.

Jones's works are not as consistently comic as those of Pratchett. *The Merlin Conspiracy* is not a humorous work, nor is her *Dalemark Quartet* (1975–1993), nor some of her best-known novels, among them *The Homeward Bounders* and *Fire and Hemlock*. It might be fair to say that while Pratchett is essentially a humorist and satirist who happens to write fantasy, Jones is first and foremost an author of speculative fiction, much of which happens to contain humor. Jones has said that she can't deliberately plan the humor in her books because it must "come out through the story in a natural way." She went on to say, "There's no reason why one can't make a serious point and be funny too, actually, and I always like to have something humorous in my books—but it's the book itself that dictates what kind of humour you're going to have."[31]

Among Jones's recent publications, those of greatest appeal to young adult readers are *Dark Lord of Derkholm* and its sequel, *Year of the Griffin*. "How would you like it if your entire planet was treated as a theme park for off-world tourists?" asks reviewer Paula Rohrlick in her review of *Dark Lord of Derkholm*.[32] That's it in a nutshell. Mr. Chesney, a wealthy and powerful businessman from an unnamed planet that sounds like our own, has managed to corrupt what had been a functioning world, with its own economies and ecosystems, into an amusement park for wealthy, offworld tourists. The planet has been destabilized and rendered nearly uninhabitable for its natives, who are now totally dependent upon the tourist trade on which Mr. Chesney holds a monopoly. When Derk, a most unconventional wizard, and his adolescent son, Blade, are placed in charge of the annual Pilgrim Party, aided by Derk's six other children (five of whom are griffins), the most amazing events unfold.

The novel, characteristically for Jones, partakes of both science fiction and fantasy traditions: on one hand, the story is set on another planet and involves faster-than-light travel, genetic engineering, and other hi-tech scientific concepts. Yet, the planet Derkholm is inhabited by elves, dwarfs, griffins, and magic-using wizards and dragons. As with much of Jones's work, it is difficult to identify a particular age audience for the novel. Discussing both *Dark Lord* and its sequel, a critic asked:

> But where does one place *Dark Lord of Derkholm* and *Year of the Griffin?*
> Their thematic concerns—the destruction of landscape, economy, polit-
> ical stability and culture because of overaggressive tourism in the first
> case and the continuing ramifications of that tourism after its end, par-
> ticularly on the intellectual endeavors and training of new generation,
> in the second—are certainly not common in children's and young adult's
> literature. Yet the manner in which the stories are told makes them en-
> tertaining and approachable in a way that simply stating the theme does
> not suggest is possible.[33]

Dark Lord of Derkholm is filled with quirky humor, most of it situational rather than deriving from the sorts of puns and one-liners for which Terry Pratchett is famed. Jones often brings wildly disparate characters together in ways that humorously set off their divergent personalities and motivations. Timing is also crucial to Jones's humor, and in *Dark Lord* the formal meetings of assembled dignitaries at the beginning and end of the annual pilgrim tour are both riotously disrupted by joyous stampedes of Derk's flying pigs, friendly cows, winged horses, and intelligent geese. In the second instance, the stampede is a diversion that allows a professional thief to pick Mr. Chesney's pocket. Many of Jones's works wind up like the final scene of a Shakespearian comedy, with all the wildly disparate characters and the many loose plot threads miraculously conjured together against all expectation. Jones told an interviewer:

I do love ending up with very logical situations in which everything is totally absurd. And when the situation finally peaks, I tend to burst out laughing and fall off the seat I'm sitting on. Members of my family put their heads anxiously round the door and ask, "Are you all right?"[34]

Katrina Hill described *Dark Lord* as "a Tolkien parody."[35] That is an oversimplification.[36] *Dark Lord* does seem to parody certain characters and situations from *The Lord of the Rings*. These include a dwarf named Galadriel (after Tolkien's elf queen); a mannish equestrienne named Wendela Horselady who will remind some of Tolkien's Eowyn of Rohan; and the costuming of Blade and his griffin brother, Kit, to create a scary appearance rather like that of the lord of the Nazgul upon his winged beast. Another Tolkienesque touch is the requirement—as spelled out in Mr. Chesney's contract—that Derk convert his cozy home into "a black castle with a labyrinthine interior lit by baleful fires," which sounds a bit like Sauron's fortress. Mr. Chesney continues, "and it would be helpful if you could introduce emaciated prisoners and some grim servitors."[37]

Like Terry Pratchett, Jones admires the work of J. R. R. Tolkien (she attended lectures by both Tolkien and C. S. Lewis at Oxford in the 1950s) and she also affectionately parodies elements of *The Lord of the Rings*. However, the real target of her satire is not Tolkien himself, but rather the whole post-Tolkien fantasy boom. Jones's satirical intent is made more clear in her *Tough Guide to Fantasyland* (1996). Teya Rosenberg explains that *Dark Lord* and *Year of the Griffin* are essentially exercises to give flesh to ideas Jones first published in *The Tough Guide*:

> In her most recent books, the focus is on skewering high fantasy conventions that have been used to the point of cliché. Beginning with *The Tough Guide to Fantasyland* (1996), a spoof encyclopedia that parodies elements of those heroic fantasy quest stories that usually appear in five or more volumes, Jones has taken to calling into question the heroic nature of such books or series. Having posited that those stories are basically similar to "three countries in three days" bus tours, Jones uses the tourism element to consider the effects such quests might have on a countryside and culture in *Dark Lord of Derkholm* (1998) and their continuing ramifications in *Year of the Griffin* (2000).[38]

Terry Pratchett called Jones's *The Tough Guide* "An indispensable guide for anyone stuck in realms of fantasy without a magic sword to call their own."[39] In fact, the entry for "Sword" happens to be one of the longest in this tongue-in-cheek guide. Advice is given the tourist on many different types of swords, most magical, including those "Broken into two or more pieces."

> Get rid of it at once. Before the Tour has lasted much longer, you will be required to re-forge the bugger for a special purpose of a dangerous and frightening nature. First you will have to spend nearly a year learning metalwork and forging and then you will have to do the unpleasant thing the sword has set you up for. It is not worth it.[40]

Jones also shares with Terry Pratchett a cleverness in linking characters and settings of her various books. Both authors avoid the pitfalls of series fiction by reusing characters and situations from their earlier books in creative and carefully limited ways. We noted that Pratchett's *Wee Free Men* includes cameo appearances by characters from some of his other novels. Jones uses such loose connections frequently and with great effect, as when the main characters of *Howl's Moving Castle* inhabit the sequel, *Castle in the Air*, in such unexpected disguises (one as a genie in a bottle, the second as a flying carpet, and the third as a black cat) that we don't realize until near the end of that novel that they have been present all along. *Year of the Griffin*, Jones's sequel to *Dark Lord of Derkholm*, focuses upon a single one of Derk's five Griffin offspring, while Derk and other major characters of the earlier book are limited to minor roles in the sequel.[41]

Year of the Griffin follows a school year of Elda, one of the five griffins who were introduced in *Dark Lord of Derkholm*. Mr. Chesney has been defeated, but the Wizard's University of Derkholm, like all of the planet's institutions, is still in shambles following decades of the disastrous pilgrim tours. Like that earlier novel, *Year of the Griffin* is bursting with a huge cast of exuberant characters. None are funnier than Elda, the great golden griffin who must drink her coffee with a straw, whose handbag is decorated with feathers from her last molt, and who uses expressions such as "I think we should stand on our own four feet."[43] Jones is ever-attentive to nonhuman points of view; another griffin in the novel speaks of "killing two humans with one stone" (*Year of the Griffin*, 219).

Year of the Griffin has been favorably compared to the Harry Potter series as a sharper, funnier school narrative. The novel parodies many features of higher education. Administration and faculty are mercilessly lampooned, the former for pursuing money rather than educational values, the latter for failing to inspire and stimulate students. Wizard/professor Corkoran gives poor grades to the most creatively written student papers on the grounds that they are impractical, meanwhile he is spending most of his time and a lion's share of the university's resources on an absurd project to reach the moon. The university library's cataloging system is designed to make materials difficult to find, and when Elda and her friends aren't easily discouraged, the librarian sends Wizard Corkoran a memo via a "stickit spell" (*Year of the Griffin*, 52).

Dark Lord of Derkholm and *Year of the Griffin* fully establish Jones as one of the leading authors of humorous fantasy fiction for young adults. Among her previous works in this vein, the Chrestomanci novels (1977–1988) and associated short stories include wonderful humor amidst a Gothic horror background a bit like that of Lemony Snicket's Series of Unfortunate Events, but far richer and much more fully formed. In two of the Chrestomanci novels Jones created immortal tomcat personalities—Throgmorten of *The Lives of Christopher Chant*, and Benvenuto of *The Magicians of Caprona*—as vivid and funny and unforgettable as Terry Pratchett's swaggering Maurice. In *Howl's Moving Castle* and its sequel, *Castle in the Air*, Jones combines elements of folk-tales and *The Arabian Nights* with her own marvelous inventiveness to create charming light and humorous romances.

Particular attention has been given the humorous YA fantasies of Terry Pratchett and Diana Wynne Jones because their respective works exemplify the qualities we have tried to identify and praise in this chapter. The stories of Pratchett and Jones are first and foremost wonderfully readable: filled with high adventure, memorable characters (of numerous species!) and seasoned with plenty of humor. In addition, the fiction of both authors is richly intertextual, presenting several layers of reference—usually humorous—to previous fictions. These include nods to their own previous works; imaginative reworkings of traditional folktales; affectionate salutes to the works of great modern fantasists such as J. R. R. Tolkien; and parodies of the banal, cliché-ridden scribblings of the host of Tolkien imitators. Both authors have harnessed their formidable talents to themes of adolescent questing and self-discovery, and YA literature has been enormously enriched by those contributions.

Notes

1. Eoin Colfer, *Artemis Fowl: The Arctic Incident* (New York: Talk Miramax/Hyperion, 2002), 17.

2. Eoin Colfer, *Artemis Fowl: The Eternity Code* (New York: Miramax/Hyperion, 2003), 73.

3. Deb Gliori, *Pure Dead Magic* (New York: Knopf, 2001), 77.

4. Deb Gliori, *Pure Dead Wicked* (New York: Knopf, 2002), 133.

5. Lemony Snicket, *The Slippery Slope* (New York: HarperCollins, 2003), back cover.

6. Paul Fleischman, *A Fate Totally Worse Than Death* (Cambridge, Mass.: Candlewick, 1995).

7. Robert Unsworth, review of *Young Adult Novel* by Daniel Pinkwater, *School Library Journal* 28:5 (May 1982): 74.

8. Unsigned review of *Young Adult Novel* by Daniel Pinkwater, *Horn Book* 58 (June 1982): 301.

9. Patty Campbell, "Young Adult Perplex," *Wilson Library Bulletin* 56:7 (March 1982): 533.

10. Daniel Pinkwater, *Young Adult Novel* (New York: Crowell, 1982), 3.

11. Joann Davis, "Spring Is a Season of Plenty for Children's Author Daniel Pinkwater," *Publisher's Weekly* (7 May 1982): 53–54.

12. William Sleator, *Interstellar Pig* (New York: Dutton, 1984), 141.

13. Patricia C. Wrede, "Utensile Strength," in Patricia C. Wrede, *Book of Enchantments* (San Diego: Harcourt Brace, 1996), 204–23.

14. Gail Carson Levine, *Ella Enchanted* (New York: HarperCollins, 1997), 89.

15. Such "compulsion stories" can be a lot of fun. Another good one is Bruce Coville's *Skull of Truth*, in which a habitually lying boy becomes the owner of a skull that forces anyone in its vicinity to tell the truth.

16. Jane Yolen, "Cinder Elephant," in *Wolf at the Door: and Other Retold Fairy Tales*, ed. Ellen Datlow and Terri Windling (New York: Simon & Schuster, 2000), 29.

17. Patrice Kindl, *Goose Chase* (Boston: Houghton Mifflin, 2001), 145.

18. Nancy Farmer, "Falada the Goose Girl's Horse" in *Wolf at the Door: and Other Retold Fairy Tales*, ed. Ellen Datlow and Terri Windling (New York: Simon & Schuster, 2000), 54.

19. Jean Ferris, *Once Upon a Marigold* (San Diego: Harcourt, 2000).

20. Vivian Vande Velde, *The Rumpelstiltskin Problem* (Boston: Houghton Mifflin, 2000), 1.

21. Unsigned review of *The Rumpelstiltskin Problem*, by Vivian Vande Velde. *Kirkus Reviews* 68:19 (October 1, 2000).

22. Kelly Link, "Swans," in *Wolf at the Door: and Other Retold Fairy Tales*, ed. Ellen Datlow and Terri Windling (New York: Simon & Schuster, 2000), 77.

23. Unsigned review of *The Amazing Maurice and His Educated Rodents*, by Terry Pratchett. *Kirkus Reviews* 70:20 (October 15, 2001).

24. Terry Pratchett, *The Amazing Maurice and His Educated Rodents* (New York: HarperCollins, 2001), 42.

25. Nancy K. Wallace, review of *The Amazing Maurice and His Educated Rodents*, by Terry Pratchett. *VOYA* 24:6 (February 2002).

26. Paula Rohrlick, review of *The Wee Free Men*, by Terry Pratchett. *KLIATT Review* 37:3 (May, 2003).

27. Terry Pratchett, *The Wee Free Men* (New York: HarperCollins, 2003), 87.

28. *The L-Space Web: A Terry Pratchett/Discworld Web Site.* http://www.ie .lspace.org/books/analysis/stacie-hanes–2.html (2 February 2004).

29. Steven H. Silver, "A Conversation with Terry Pratchett—Part 1." April, 2000 http://www.sfsite.com/04b/tp79.htm (11 December 2003).

30. Nicholas Tredell, "Terry Pratchett," in *Contemporary Novelists* (Farmington Hills, Mich.: St. James Press, 2001), 816.

31. Charles Butler, "Interview with Diana Wynne Jones," in *Diana Wynne Jones: An Exciting and Exacting Wisdom*, ed. Teya Rosenberg et al. (New York: Peter Lang, 2002), 169.

32. Paula Rohrlick, review of *Dark Lord of Derkholm*, by Diana Wynne Jones. *KLIATT Review* 32:6 (November 1998).

33. Teya Rosenberg, *Introduction* in *Diana Wynne Jones: An Exciting and Exacting Wisdom*, ed. Teya Rosenberg et al. (New York: Peter Lang, 2002), 7.

34. Butler, "Interview with Diana Wynne Jones," 169.

35. Karina Hill, "Dragons and Quantum Foam: Mythic Archetypes and Modern Physics in Selected Works by Diana Wynne Jones," in *Diana Wynne Jones: An Exciting and Exacting Wisdom*, ed. Teya Rosenberg et al. (New York: Peter Lang, 2002), 41.

36. There has been at least one all-out, book-length parody of *The Lord of the Rings*, the side-splitting *Bored of the Rings* by members of the Harvard Lampoon staff: Henry N. Beard and Douglas C. Kenney, *Bored of the Rings: A Parody of J. R. R. Tolkien's Lord of the Rings* (New York: New American Library, 1969).

37. Diana Wynne Jones, *Dark Lord of Derkholm* (New York: Greenwillow, 1998), 27.

38. Rosenberg, *Introduction* in *Diana Wynne Jones: An Exciting and Exacting Wisdom*, 5.

39. Terry Pratchett, quoted on the back cover of the British paper ed. (London: Vista, 1996).

40. Diana Wynne Jones, *The Tough Guide to Fantasyland* (London: Vista, 1996), 183.

41. Terry Pratchett recently alluded to this technique, which he and Diana Wynne Jones have each used to such great effect: "I enjoy introducing former lead characters as background characters. They come with their baggage, which is not mentioned but simply *there*, and changes the perception of the character." Terry Pratchett, "Terry Pratchett: 21 Years of Discworld" *Locus* (May 2004): 59.

42. Diana Wynne Jones, *Year of the Griffin* (New York: Greenwillow, 2000), 36.

CHAPTER EIGHT

~

Coming of Age:
Who Am I, and What
Am I Going to Do about It?

Can Coming of Age Be Fun?

Bildungsroman, a German compound that has become the standard literary term for coming-of-age fiction, has been defined as "literally, novel of formation . . . A class of novel in German literature that deals with the formative years of the main character;"[1] and, "A novel that has as its main theme the formative years or spiritual education of one person (a type of novel traditional in German literature)."[2]

Whatever definition we use, the themes of humor and coming of age are not commonly found together. Most coming-of-age fiction, even when presented with humor, tends toward the bittersweet, as in the young adult novels of Joan Bauer, Ron Koertge, and Randy Powell. In these stories, humor is often used in the face of adversity, to make genuinely painful situations more tolerable.

Light comedy, as in the works of Meg Cabot, Ellen Conford, and Gordon Korman, generally does not provide the in-depth character development necessary to the coming-of-age process. For example, Meg Cabot's *All-American Girl* presents some excellent growing-up scenes and situations as fifteen-year-old Samantha Madison learns from her wise art teacher how to see and to listen. However, the novel's frothy tone and outrageously improbable premise prevent us from taking it all very seriously.

The typical light comedy protagonist learns a lesson or two and gains some wisdom, but the reader will not vividly experience the character's growth in maturity. An overall comic tone encourages a degree of separation and detachment that limits our empathy with the characters. If the protagonist (and vicariously, the reader) do not feel some fairly unpleasant growing pains, character formation and the maturation process seem incomplete.

All that having been said, we may be able to identify a few YA novels in which a coming-of-age process is presented rather cheerfully. Stephanie Tolan's *Surviving the Applewhites* presents character development in an upbeat manner. In Tolan's novel, teen angst is somewhat dissipated by the presence of two protagonists. Jake Semple is a delinquent, expelled from several schools, whose final chance at an education without barred windows is being offered at the Applewhite's unconventional homeschool. Jake cultivates a hostile and scary demeanor, complete with spiked hair, body piercings, and a perpetual scowl. E. D. Applewhite, who like Jake, is thirteen years old, feels out of step with the rest of the Applewhite clan. An orderly, highly organized personality in a family of noisy, eccentric, and unpredictable artists, E. D. feels that her strengths are unappreciated amidst her family's chaos of creative impulses. The novel is narrated in the third person, with insights into the growing pains of both Jake and E.D. as these two very dissimilar teens each work at "surviving the Applewhites."

Jake is supposed to be a tough guy, but his rebelliousness doesn't run deep. We sense that the story will be comic from the start, and we are confident that Jake will come around. The extended Applewhite clan, and Wit's End, their suitably eccentric pastoral homestead, are as much the subjects of Tolan's novel as either of the protagonists.

Stories about a teen's coming of age are sometimes made less serious (and funnier) by the use of cute, whimsical passages throughout a story. The technique is most often employed in epistolary (diary or correspondence) novels. In Jaclyn Moriarty's *Feeling Sorry for Celia*, Elizabeth Clarry experiences some genuine adversity. Her dog is killed by a car, her supposed friend, Celia, runs away with the boy Elizabeth likes, and her father is distracted by divorce and remarriage. Despite the character-forming adversity Elizabeth encounters, the funny notes and memos sprinkled throughout the novel sustain an upbeat tone. A typical note from her mother:

!!!IMPORTANT!!!!! LOOK AT THIS NOTE!!!!
!!!ELIZABETH!!!! OVER HERE!!!! ON THE FRIDGE!!!!!
LIBBY,
    I HOPE YOU SAW THIS NOTE.

    GOOD MORNING.
    EAT THE OATMEAL IN *THE BIG, SILVER SAUCEPAN ON
    THE STOVE.* PUT SOME ALOE ON YOUR FACE.
    *DON'T BURN YOUR FACE LIKE THAT AGAIN. YOUR SKIN
    WILL ALL PEEL AWAY AND THERE WILL BE NOTHING LEFT
    BUT BONES AND BRAIN AND EYEBALLS.*
    IT IS VERY AND EXTREMELY COLD TODAY. WEAR SEVEN
    PAIRS OF STOCKINGS.
    HAVE A NICE FIRST DAY BACK AT SCHOOL.
                    LOVE FROM YOUR THOUGHTFUL AND
                    CONSIDERATE MOTHER.[3]

Similar refrigerator notes throughout the story keep the reader smiling, despite Elizabeth's sometimes painful and often awkward coming of age.

Karen Cushman's first book, *Catherine, Called Birdy*, is an equally clever epistolary coming-of-age novel, set in the year 1290. Catherine faces some stern challenges: her mother nearly dies, and her father plans to marry her off to the first wealthy suitor who comes along, regardless of her own preferences. But Catherine's high spirits rarely falter. The journal of her fourteenth year is filled with humorous oaths and lively accounts of her efforts to fend off unsuitable suitors. "Corpus bones! He comes to dine with us in two days' time. I plan to cross my eyes and drool in my meat."[4]

Although Cushman's several historical novels are generally similar, *Catherine, Called Birdy* is perhaps a bit lighter in tone than her later works. Along with Catherine's exuberant personality, much of the humor in this story can be attributed to clever epistolary devices used in Catherine's journal. Many of the entries are—quite appropriately for a medieval diary—headed by a note on the martyr whose feast day is being celebrated. Some of these devout annotations are immediately followed by a comment from Catherine: "19TH DAY OF OCTOBER, *Feast of Saint Frileswide, virgin, though why that should make someone a saint I do not know*" (*Catherine, Called Birdy*, 33). "26TH DAY OF OCTOBER, *Feasts of Saints Eata and Bean, which I think is very funny*" (38).

Catherine sometimes adds a comment about her own life when discussing the plight of a martyr. When she is angry at her father: "11TH DAY OF MAY, *Feast of Saint Credan, who killed his father and in remorse became a hogherd and a saint.* I wonder how he did it" (149). And when she is hoping to escape an arranged marriage: "13TH DAY OF JULY. *Feast of Saint Mildren, who became a nun to escape the attentions of an unwelcome suitor.* There must be a better way" (174).

Even when Catherine's prospects seem grim, we are swept along by her energy and by the funny passages heading each daily entry in her journal. We sense that such a lively and lovable protagonist will somehow succeed against formidable odds in maintaining some control of her life. Indeed, an unexpected and fortuitous event—the demise of her intended in a tavern brawl—occurs just in time to save her from marriage to that uncouth, violent, and much older man. Although that chance occurrence makes possible the book's upbeat ending, Catherine's journal shows that she has grown in character and in emotional depth during the year chronicled in her journal.

Having probed the outer limits of cheerfulness possible in a true coming-of-age novel, there is one other boundary we might explore. At the opposite extreme from the feel-good success story, perhaps there's a kind of "but don't take it so hard" failure story. Can a novel be humorous if its protagonist does *not* successfully come of age?

Stunted Growth: Can Failure Be Funny?

Surely, the failure of a teen to grow into an emotionally healthy and mature adult should be no laughing matter. And yet, some authors have managed to generate humor from situations in which a protagonist experiences a major setback in some rite of passage. In the life of a younger teen protagonist, such a misstep may not be irrevocable, and we can hope that he may have future opportunities to redeem himself. But within the confines of the novel, in some crucial way, the protagonist has failed to surmount a challenge that forms the central conflict of the novel and of the character's progress toward adulthood. Yet the book is still funny. How can that be?

In *Extreme Elvin*, Chris Lynch paints an unforgettable portrait of a young man who is emotionally unprepared for the social trials of adolescence. Elvin is eager to date girls, but when he gets his chance with Barbara, a girl he likes very much, his impulsive, panicky behavior betrays his immaturity and lack of confidence. "I know that you're really sweet," Barbara tells him. "But I also don't think you're ready for this. You don't know how to act. You make me nervous. Your reactions to everything are so *extreme*."[5] Elvin is crushed by his failure with Barbara and the novel ends on a low note, relieved a bit by wisecracking support from his best friend, Mike:

> "Well, am I coming in, or what, El?"
> "Okay, but you have to promise not to make fun of me."
> A loud sigh.
> "Don't be stupid, Elvin. What else would I want to come in there *for*? Open the door, butt-boy." (*Extreme Elvin*, 234)

Lynch concludes this poignant, often painful, and yet very funny novel with his hero's problems completely unresolved. Despite a lack of self-confidence, Elvin has bravely ventured forth and engaged in the rituals of young adulthood. Unfortunately, he has failed to negotiate some initial rites of passage.

Other funny YA novels that end on a similar downturn include Megan McCafferty's *Sloppy Firsts* and M. T. Anderson's *Burger Wuss*. Like Lynch's Elvin Bishop, the protagonists in each of these novels are introverted teens whose efforts to attain a happier social life seem doomed by their own neurotic and self-defeating tendencies. Anderson's Anthony and McCafferty's Jess Darling are witty, cynical observers, outsiders in the mold of J. D. Salinger's famous antihero, Holden Caulfield. Although neither achieves love or happiness during the time we share with them, their sardonic observations on classmates, adults, and popular culture are witty and entertaining.

In Anthony of *Burger Wuss*, we also see tendencies toward a kind of creepy furtiveness that has been appearing with some regularity in satirical coming-of-age novels narrated by teenage boys. Throughout *Burger Wuss*, Anthony schemes to get even with Turner, the macho bully who stole his girlfriend at a party and has humiliated him in numerous other ways. Anthony doesn't have the courage to stand up to Turner, so he makes elaborate plans to anonymously exact revenge upon his enemy. Anthony's obsessive secrecy, and his chicken-hearted use of skulking and evasive tactics against an adversary who has humiliated him openly and publicly are funny but also disturbing. This sort of maladjusted narrator has been featured in a number of other recent YA novels.

Josh Swenson of Janet Tashjian's *The Gospel According to Larry* is the anonymous creator of an Internet personality, "Larry," who attains the status of an international cult hero. As a result, Josh's own life becomes a lie: in order to continue as the mysterious Larry he must deceive everyone who is close to him. Josh's longtime friend, Beth, would like to take their relationship to a romantic level, but Josh is so compromised by his double identity that he cannot behave according to his feelings.

The sardonic humor of *The Gospel According to Larry* is derived both from Josh's satirical jabs at consumerism and from his equally perceptive observations on the wreck he has made of his personal life. Josh eventually fakes his own suicide—his "pseudocide,"[6]—and goes underground, continuing to deny his own identity. Instead of completing high school and going on to the Ivy League college that has accepted his application, Josh seems to have completely erased himself. His fate almost defines the concept of a failure to grow up.[7]

Ned Vizzini's *Be More Chill* explores the autoerotic lure of computers in the bedrooms of teenage boys. Jeremy Heere explains, "I use the Internet like most teenage boys do: exclusively for sex. In the last ten years teen pregnancy is way down in America and I think I know why."[8] Jeremy is addicted to viewing pornographic photos and videos and engaging in live sex chats with persons he presumes are young, heterosexual women.

Taking his dependence upon computers a step further, Jeremy obtains a squip, an illegal pill containing a tiny computer chip that is programmed to train its host to be "cool." The squip, which silently communicates with Jeremy's brain in the voice of Keanu Reeves, is unintentionally funny. All of its powerful computational abilities are focused upon transforming dorky Jeremy into a stud.

YOU MUST ALWAYS WALK THIS WAY, JEREMY. I WILL STIMU-LATE YOUR SPINE TO REMIND YOU. YO U ARE TALL; IF YOU DON'T USE YOUR HEIGHT TO THE FULLEST, TARGET FE-MALES WILL ASSUME YOU ARE A LOSER AND A MASTUR-BATOR.
But I *am* a masturbator.
WE'LL FIX THAT. (*Be More Chill*, 115)

Jeremy has some successes with the squip, but in the end, the device fails him spectacularly, and then commits a sort of ritual suicide by instructing Jeremy to eliminate it with a special formula:

THEN YOU SHOULD FLUSH ME. YOU KNOW MOUNTAIN DEW
CODE RED?
Yeah.
IT'S A FAILSAFE. IF YOU DRINK A BOTTLE, I DISSOLVE. (289)

Jeremy's attempt to shortcut the lengthy, awkward, painful process of adolescence by means of a pill is doomed to failure. Since Vizzini's novel is a satire much like *Burger Wuss*, empathy with the narrator is beside the point, and the fact that Jeremy may have learned a lesson is inconsequential.

The use of an unsympathetic—and unreliable—narrator is taken to extremes by Daniel Handler in his wicked satire, *The Basic Eight*. Narrator Flannery Culp describes her interactions with a beautiful, charismatic best friend, Natasha, whom we, and Flannery, finally discover to be, shall we say, insubstantial. Handler ridicules the tedious moralizing so prevalent in media and popular culture. In the aftermath of Flannery's crimes, pop psychologists are lionized by the media as they offer their sensationalistic interpretations of a supposed satanic cult, the "Basic Eight" at Flannery's private school. The unreliable narrator and her imaginary friend provide Handler a clever means of spoofing this unholy alliance of an insatiable media with a mutual admiration society of quack social scientists who pose as guardians of morality. In the end we find Flannery editing her journal from prison, but we do not mourn her personal tragedy because she is clearly an instrument of satire.

C. D. Payne's cult classic, *Youth in Revolt: The Journals of Nick Twisp* is another ironic novel in which the narrator is not meant to be taken seriously. Like Handler's Flannery Culp, Nick is a caricature whose outrageous behavior allows Payne to give full play to his merciless satire of both adolescence and contemporary American society. Teenage Nick is a bundle of raw nerves, adolescent angst, raging hormones, complete self-absorption, and total disrespect for authority—just the opposite of the shy, fumbling male protagonists mentioned earlier in this chapter. Nick's failure to progress toward mature, responsible adulthood is merely a by-product of Payne's satiric purpose. At the end of *Youth in Revolt*, fourteen-year-old Nick, unlike Flannery Culp, is still at liberty. However, he is wanted for multiple felonies and is obliged to remain disguised as a woman indefinitely to avoid incarceration. In his Carlotta disguise, he complains to his beautiful, brainy girlfriend, Sheeni:

> "Sheeni, do you realize I may have to live out the balance of my teen years as a woman? Do you comprehend what that entails?"
>
> "Certainly, Nick. After all, it is a fate we share."
>
> "Yes, but it's easier for you. You are emotionally and physically adapted for the role. I find it a daunting burden."
>
> "We all have to accept some measure of compromise in our lives, Carlotta," she replied. "Try to show a little more pragmatism. Look what I've had to settle for."
>
> "What do you mean, Sheeni?"
>
> "Life in dreary Ukiah. And a computer-obsessed boyfriend who snores, eschews veracity, and wears a padded bra under his unfashionable dress."[9]

If Flannery Culp and Nick Twisp seem outrageous examples of teens who fail to grow up normally, what should we make of adolescents who turn into animals rather than becoming human adults? Two such notable characters are Eva, the title character of Peter Dickinson's extraordinary science fiction dystopia, and Sandra Francy, the protagonist of Melvin Burgess's *Lady: My Life as a Bitch*. Both novels are more satirical than humorous, but we might say of each that its basic premise is so startling that humorous incongruities cannot help but follow.

Peter Dickinson's Eva awakens to find that her brain has been transferred into the skull of a chimpanzee whose own brain has been sacrificed for the purpose. After Eva's human body was nearly destroyed in a car accident, scientists undertook the daring transplant as the only chance of saving her life. Over the years, Eva comes to prefer the company of her new species to that of humans. Eva matures, but as a chimpanzee, not a human. As the revered matriarch of the last clan of wild primates on a Earth, Eva has a unique perspective on the decline of a self-destructive *homo sapiens*.

In Burgess's novel, Sandra, a wild seventeen-year-old who has dumped her affectionate boyfriend in favor of tawdry one-night stands with a shocking number of boys she barely knows, ironically turns into a literal "bitch," the very creature she has personified. The initial transformation is performed without her consent, but when she is ultimately faced with a choice whether to cast her fate with humans or dogs, she responds to the call of her pack. Like Eva, Sandra retains her human brain and memory, and her comparisons of human with canine experiences, mainly to the advantage of the latter, are vivid and startling.

M. T. Anderson's vampire novel, *Thirsty*, also develops the theme of a human adolescent turning into another kind of creature. However, unlike Eva and Sandra, Anderson's protagonist, Chris, refuses to accept the inhuman fate that has been imposed upon him. Although the only alternative is death, Chris is unable to embrace the vampirism with which he has been cursed. Chris's horrific destiny seems an unlikely topic for humor, but *Thirsty* is quite a funny novel, once one realizes that the pathetic Chris is more a stooge than a sympathetic protagonist.

In his satirical novels, Anderson has a penchant for presenting characters who fail to grow up. In *Feed*, he describes a bleak world of the near future in which an entire nation has been seduced into a sort of permanent immaturity.

> . . . an utterly hedonistic world of trend and acquisition, a world only momentarily disturbed by the news reports of environmental waste and a global alliance of have-not nations against the obliviously consuming U.S.[10]

The Feed is a communications chip usually implanted at birth, which broadcasts a constant barrage of stimuli, including instant chat, pop culture trivia, relentless advertising, and personalized buying guides. This future society is horrifyingly funny, and language has been degraded to barely articulate slang: "'Oh, unit,' I was like, 'is this malfunction?'"[11] Vocabulary beyond this must be supplied by the Feed: "Her spine was, I didn't know the word. Her spine was like . . .? The Feed suggested 'supple'" (*Feed*, 11).

Titus, the narrator, becomes involved with Violet, a beautiful young woman who is one of the few remaining persons not completely tranquilized by the Feed. Through Violet, he begins to see the environmental devastation and degraded culture surrounding him. Titus matures, but too late to help Violet, just as in the larger world of Anderson's dystopia it seems to be too late for the arrogant, self-absorbed consumer nation to learn to coexist with an angry outside world.

Most humorous coming-of-age novels are not so extreme; neither so cheerful as to barely contain any character development, nor so satirical that the protagonist's successes or failures are largely irrelevant to the book's main thrust. In the more typical *bildungsroman*, humorous or not, we empathize with a protagonist who faces tough challenges that strengthen his character. To get a firm fix on the genre, let's examine the structure of a few classic coming-of-age novels containing a good deal of humor.

Boys and Girls Coming of Age: Four Classics

Terry Davis's *If Rock and Roll Were a Machine* and Rob Thomas's *Rats Saw God* are two of the best-known, male, coming-of-age novels. Adult male mentors are of central importance to both stories, and each novel employs a school writing assignment to bring out past traumas. The autobiographical assignment brings the traumatized teen to the attention of a helpful adult mentor and provides the boy a means of confronting his past and beginning to heal. The device provides the author an effective way to convey to the reader key events from the past that caused the protagonist's trauma.

If Rock and Roll Were a Machine introduces us to Bert Bowden and the important adults in his life: Gary Lawler, a teacher who destroyed Bert's confidence in the fifth grade; high school teacher Gene Tanneran, and motorcycle shop owner Scotty Shepard, two mentors who help Bert recover his self-esteem.

Bert first appears as a depressed loner. His gradual emergence and recovery are measured by his progress in several arenas: writing, motorcycles, and racquetball, and there are flashes of humor in each of these endeavors. As a writer, Bert is able to tap a vein of humor that he is too shy to articulate verbally. His writing talents also bring him to the attention Darby Granger, the attractive editor of the school newspaper.

"You know why I call you Egg, Bert?"

Bert squinched his face. "Because I remind you of something shot out of a chicken's ass?"

Darby smiled. "Besides that," she said. "I call you Egg because you have a shell."

It didn't hurt Bert's feelings. He knew it was true.[12]

Bert's immersion in the world of motorcycle operation and maintenance is filled with good-natured macho banter of the guys at Shepard's cycle shop. They affectionately address Bert as a "young shitball" (*If Rock and Roll*, 64) and remind him to "stay off his head" (66). Hearing Bert shout an obscenity at a car that cut him off, Scotty Shepard tells him, "You've had that bike what—twenty-four hours? And already you're talking like a biker. Who says the American teenager ain't a fast learner?" (63).

On the day of his motorcycle road test, Scotty and Steve Shepard enjoy pulling Bert's leg. "There's one person a Harley guy can run into who transcends a Washington State Trooper in terms of pure malevolence. That is a female trooper on any duty whatsoever . . . they're tough as badgers," Scotty tells him. Steve adds, "They pride themselves on their knowledge of primitive circumcision techniques, Bootsie. . . . We're talking blunt rock and mussel shell" (78–79). Naturally, the test is administered by a female officer, as the Shepards had known all along.

If Rock and Roll Were a Machine is far from a perfect novel. Some characters and themes are unevenly developed, The novel is a bit dated by its fixation on rock music of the 1970s, and there are sexist overtones. Despite those flaws, it is a classic coming-of-age novel for teenage boys, featuring a vulnerable, sympathetic protagonist and some strong, well-rounded, adult male role models and mentors. Bert's recovery and increasing self-confidence in the varied settings of journalism, athletics, and motorcycle maintenance give the narrative a distinct three-dimensional authenticity. The novel's humor, mainly of the rough male variety, but occasionally seasoned with some nice female repartee, is unforced and contributes to the novel's appeal.

Another classic coming-of-age story, Rob Thomas's *Rats Saw God*, is widely regarded as one of the all-time top YA novels. In addition to its popularity with a broad spectrum of readers both male and female, the novel also has a cult following for its humorous description of the countercultural activities of a high school Dadaist club.[13]

As in Terry Davis's *If Rock and Roll Were a Machine*, *Rats Saw God* gives the reader a crucial window on the protagonist's unhappy past via a high school writing assignment. However, in Thomas's novel the autobiographical essay isn't presented only at the beginning of the book. Protagonist Steve York is one English credit short, and his counselor, Mr. DeMouy offers him a chance to pick up the credit so he can graduate on time. Steve must turn in a 100-page essay on any topic, a few pages at a time. He chooses to write about his own recent past, and those submissions function in the novel as flashback chapters alternating with Steve's first-person narration in present time.

Steve confronts two painful issues in his essays: first, a lifelong rebellion against his famous father, an astronaut and all-around American hero. Then, more recently, the heartbreaking loss of his first love, whom he finds to be sleeping with their English teacher. As in Davis's novel, a good educator, here counselor DeMouy, is able to counter the harm done by a bad one, in this case the hip young teacher who can't keep his hands off his female students.

Rats Saw God is a wonderfully funny novel, with sharp dialogue and narration by an exceptionally bright, witty, and sarcastic narrator. On his first sexual experience:

> I realized five or six seconds after the actual event . . . that I was no longer a virgin, that I would finally be allowed to hunt buffalo with the village elders. I could almost feel my complexion clearing up.[14]

Steve's girlfriend, Dub, asks him why he doesn't get along with his father as she puts ice cream in his mouth.

> The ice cream gave me time to frame my answer eruditely.
> "He's a dick."
> "Thank you for that contemplative and comprehensive assessment."

When Dub continues to press the subject, Steve elaborates.

> "I can't stand the fact that he's in better shape than me. I hate it that he buys American. He watches CNN nonstop. He drinks bottled water. He reads the entire newspaper, section by section, and he folds it back the way it was delivered. He thinks its normal to work sixteen hours a day.

He never air-guitared the Rolling Stones. Hell, I don't think he knows who they are."

"Well, I can see what you mean. I don't see how you put up with it." (*Rats Saw God*, 121)

Steve has the burden of following the nearly impossible standards set by his father, and he is unable to develop his own independent adult personality until he can come to terms with that problem. Steve's gradual reconciliation with his father is authentic, funny, and very moving, like all of the themes in this exceptional coming-of-age novel.

Let's also consider two outstanding humorous coming-of-age stories with female protagonists. Among Joan Bauer's numerous YA novels, *Backwater* offers a particularly nice blend of coming-of-age themes. Ivy Breedlove is an enthusiastic amateur historian amidst a family of lawyers, and her stern father is determined that she should follow the family tradition. While taking up a family history project that her great aunt was unable to continue, Ivy becomes fascinated by one of the "backwater" Breedloves, her reclusive Aunt Josephine.

Despite her father's lack of enthusiasm for the undertaking, Ivy discovers the location of Aunt Jo's mountain hideaway and hires a wilderness guide to take her to meet her aunt. Although Aunt Jo initially comes off as a disturbingly eccentric hermit, Ivy soon comes to admire her aunt and begins to appreciate the values of peace and solitude that Jo favors over the noisy, aggressive competitiveness that characterizes the rest of the overachieving Breedlove clan.

Like Steve York, Ivy Breedlove needs to come to terms with a stiff, demanding father whose own near-perfection has set an impossible standard. Bauer skillfully weaves together the discovery of Aunt Jo and her way of life with the theme of Ivy's struggle to establish the value of her own identity as a historian. Ivy's father had been equally wary of his reclusive sister and of Ivy's interest in a field of knowledge outside the practice of law. By bringing Aunt Jo back into the family circle, Ivy convincingly demonstrates the utility of her family history project, of her intended profession, and of her more general contention that the world needs all sorts of people, historians and hermit sculptors as well as lawyers. As Ivy puts it, "I went off in search of my aunt, and when I found her, I discovered a missing piece of myself in the process."[15]

Like all Joan Bauer's novels, *Backwater* has a full share of humorous episodes and observations. Ivy's hearty wilderness guide, Mountain Mama, is a colorful character who expresses affection with hearty slaps on the back. As Ivy stands gazing at the mountain toward which they are hiking,

> Mountain Mama slapped my back and sent me sailing into a snow drift.
> I got up, brushed myself off, focused on the snowy peak in the distance.
> She slapped me again, but this time I held on to a tree. (*Backwater*, 66)

During her quest, Ivy meets hunky Jack, a handsome ranger, and she later confides in her friend Octavia that it is hard having a boyfriend who lived five hours away.

> Octavia said Jack was "pitifully G.U." (geographically undesirable), but she changed her tune fast when I showed her his picture, standing in front of a mountain with a frame pack on his back looking like something out of Outside magazine.
> Octavia held the photo to the light and whispered, "Five hours is nothing, Ivy." (171)

When handsome, smiling Jack steps into the house, Ivy reflects, "The blessings of those who pursue history are many" (181).

In contrast with *Rats Saw God* and *Backwater*, whose protagonists struggle against a paternal agenda, Carolyn Mackler's *The Earth, My Butt, and Other Big Round Things*, features a teenaged girl who must struggle for autonomy against a powerful matriarch. The Shreves family is dominated by Dr. Phyllis Shreves, a noted adolescent psychologist. Mr. Shreves is an amiable husband and father whose only noticeable fault is his blatant preference for slender females, which his daughter Virginia begins to find annoying.

Fifteen-year-old Virginia is the ugly duckling in the patrician Shreves family. Her parents and older siblings are slender, dark, and handsome, while she is chubby, blonde, and rather plain. Virginia has grown accustomed to being a wallflower, despite her mother's ceaseless efforts to remake her unfashionable younger daughter.

Things begins to change when Virginia's brother is charged with date rape and expelled from college. This huge crack in the family's carefully polished veneer emboldens Virginia to rebel against her mother's script. In fact, many of Virginia's initial acts of rebellion are too obviously a simple antiscript—reflexively doing the exact opposite of what her mother wants—but they're nonetheless quite funny. She begins by buying the "wrong" clothes at thrift shops.

> I buy a polyester orange shirt with horizontal green stripes. Mom's always telling me I should stick to neutral colors. And definitely no horizontal stripes, since they reveal extra poundage.[16]

Later she buys a purple dress for a holiday party and her mother responds, "Purple doesn't go with your hair. Blonds should wear yellow or beige, something that isn't so domineering" (*Earth, My Butt*, 211). Virginia immediately dyes her hair "Pimpin' Purple" to match the dress. When her mother gets over the shock, she remarks, "Well, at least you didn't dye it green." Virginia ruefully notes, "Special Effects had a particularly offensive shade called 'Iguana Green.' I kick myself for not going that route" (212–13).

Virginia's well-meaning but overbearing mother is at the center of a bundle of coming-of-age challenges for her daughter. Virginia must combat her family's elitism, smug self-assurance, sexist assumptions, and the disproportionate value they place on physical beauty. Her initial acts of self-assertion are merely reflexive anti-Mom statements, but as she gains self-confidence, Virginia becomes an active, outgoing young woman who joins a kickboxing class and starts a school club and webzine.

Surviving a Loss

The central conflict of many YA novels is an adolescent's need to come to terms with the loss of a loved one. Sometimes the traumatic loss involves a sibling, a more distant relation, or a close friend. But loss of a parent seems to be the most frequent cause of unresolved grief in YA literature. Premature death of a parent, or loss of contact with a parent following divorce, is such a common situation in YA novels that it could almost be considered a cliché. The phenomenon has been noted by a number of critics, particularly by Nancy Werlin in her fine essay, "Get Rid of the Parents."[17] YA novels in which this theme is central to a protagonist's coming of age are numerous, but less common are those in which the resolution of such grief is handled with humor.

Grady Grennan of Randy Powell's *Tribute to Another Dead Rock Star*, already fatherless, has recently lost his mother as well, and is now dependent upon stepparents and other relatives. Fifteen-year-old Grady seems to be handling the death of his rock-star mother quite well, but now confronted with a variety of possible parental figures, he's not sure where he should live. He'd like to join the household of Mitch, a sort of unofficial stepfather who had been his late mother's companion for several years. Mitch is also the father of Louie, the retarded half-brother of whom Grady is very fond. However, Mitch's strict, born-again wife, Vickie, detests the grunge-rock culture in which Grady was raised and thinks that he's a bad influence on Louie and her own children. Grady constantly annoys Vickie by introducing Louie and Vickie's children to popular culture entertainments she deems too worldly.

> Vickie has banned the Sinbad movies, because she thinks they're too full of occultism and Eastern mysticism. She has yet to ban Tarzan, Robin Hood, or Prince Valiant, but it's probably just a matter of time before she decides they're too New Age or something.[18]

Grady is a wonderfully authentic narrator, with a skeptical outlook and a low-key, ironic sense of humor. The accommodation he gradually negotiates with Vickie, against the background of his mother's tragic, but all-too typical rock-star demise, is both funny and poignant.

Julie Johnston's *In Spite of Killer Bees* uses quiet humor in its portrayal of a trio of parentless teens attempting to make a home for themselves. The three Quade sisters are left alone following the death of their father and abandonment by their mother, who simply disappears when the responsibilities of motherhood become too much for her. The title refers to an episode in which fourteen-year-old Aggie Quade is followed through town by a swarm of bees attracted by a loaf of sweet bread she is carrying. "In spite of" the bees and other obstacles, Aggie and her sisters are able to bring closure to their parents' failures and begin anew.

The almost continuous bickering at home between the three parentless sisters whose lives are so intimately bound together serves as a humorous counterpoint to the brave, united front they present to outsiders.

A imaginative twist on the dead father theme plays out in Arthur Slade's *Tribes*. In the novel's very first sentence, Percy Montmount tells us, "My father, Percival Montmount, died in the Congo after lunch on a Sunday three years ago."[19] Throughout his story, Percy talks about and dreams of his absent father. So, near the very end of the novel, when Percy claims to see the man, we suppose it must be yet another of Percy's hallucinations. However, the simple, declarative sentence with which the book began takes on a new meaning. Not until he understands the sense in which his father "died," and the sense in which he is still living, is Percy able to reclaim his own life. Percy's pedantic language and behavior, as he embodies the field anthropologist persona of his father in a mundane, suburban high school setting, are laugh-out-loud funny despite the seriousness of his maladjustment.

An equivocal, unresolved parental absence is taken in another direction in Susan Heyboer O'Keefe's quirky novel, *My Life and Death, by Alexandra Canarsie*. Allie, fifteen, lives with her mother and has had no contact with her father in years: "My dad disappeared after the divorce and was a forbidden topic."[20] Allie and her mother have moved ten times in the six years since the divorce and, since it is hard for her to keep making new friends, Allie takes up a solitary hobby of haunting the local cemetery and attending funerals of strangers. Not content with that minor eccentricity, Allie decides on the basis of very slim evidence that a boy who recently drowned must have been murdered, and she creates havoc throughout her school and town with her obsessive, reckless investigation of his death.

Allie has a smart mouth and she's an entertaining narrator. Describing a teacher, she muses, "Mr. Penn explored, and sometimes crossed, the very fine line between boring and dead" (*My Life and Death*, 54). Of a new friend, "who just happened to be my best suspect for murder," Allie ponders:

> If Dennis really was the murderer—there, I'd said it—and I ignored the facts, I might be starting my own life of crime. I could see it so plainly: I'd end up as his moll and we'd spend our lives fleeing from place to place

as desperately hunted fugitives. . . . It would be an endless series of dirty motel rooms and fast food restaurants. We could trust no one but each other, and some days not even that.

I had to admit, it was appealing. (113)

In the end, Allie is given her father's phone number. His whereabouts had been withheld because her parents had fought bitterly during their breakup, and this eventually led to her father once striking his wife. Mrs. Canarsie sometimes imagined she saw her ex-husband and, in a panic, moved whenever she thought he was near. Like Percy Montmount, Allie needed to know the truth about her absent father before she could move on with her life.

Finding the Father

In some YA novels a search for one's father takes the form of a quest. This is quite explicit in Sharon Creech's *Absolutely Normal Chaos*. The story is presented as Mary Lou Finney's summer journal, a requirement for her English class. Mary Lou begins, "How was I to know Carl Ray would come to town and turn everything into an odyssey?"[21] Carl Ray is the Finney's hillbilly cousin, an odd-looking seventeen-year-old scarecrow. In addition to his rural West Virginia origins and goofy appearance, Carl Ray is a young man of few words. So, Mary Lou is stunned to find that he knows all about Homer's *Odyssey*.

I just threw the book down and said, "Telemachus! Who the heck is Telemachus?"

And do you know what Carl Ray did? He said, without even looking away from the TV, "The son of Odysseus."

You could have knocked me over with a feather. "And how do *you* know *that?*" I asked.

"Simple," he said, and he kept right on watching *The Dating Game*.

I didn't think Carl Ray even knew how to *read*. (*Absolutely Normal Chaos*, 63)

In fact, Carl Ray is engaged in a search for his father, much like that of Telemachus in the *Odyssey*. Mary Lou and Carl discuss the *Odyssey* throughout the summer, as each undergoes rites of passage. Mary Lou experiences her first romance as well as other important firsts, and Carl Ray finds his biological father.

When I mentioned about Circe and the pigs, he said, "Oh yeah. Book Ten." This surprised the heck out of me. And when I said I thought it was a little far-fetched about the men turning into pigs, he said, "Well, it's a metaphor." (Can you imagine Carl Ray even knowing what a metaphor is?) And I said, "How so?" and he said, "Women turn men into pigs all the time."

And then he went into the kitchen to make himself about four sandwiches. (131)

Wylie Jackson of Ric Lynden Hardman's, *Sunshine Rider: The First Vegetarian Western*, doesn't realize that he's on a quest to find his father. In this entertaining, picaresque novel, seventeen-year-old Wylie joins a cattle drive, gets into a bit of trouble and gallops off on the drive boss's prize horse, and then has a harrowing series of adventures with a rich variety of eccentric frontier characters. In the end, Wylie discovers that the wealthy cattleman whose horse he had stolen is his own father, who had since been pursuing the boy to reestablish their relationship, not to punish him. By the time father and son are reunited, Wylie has matured from a callow youth into a promising medical student whose tutors have included an Indian medicine man and a prairie doctor who navigates the windswept prairie flatlands by hoisting a sail over his buggy.

The vegetarianism of the book's subtitle is an essential part of Wylie's coming of age. Traumatized by the experience of shooting a newborn calf in front of its mother, the boy vows to eliminate meat from his diet, as well as embracing the healing arts. Each chapter of *Sunshine Rider* begins with a trail recipe or two, many of them sufficiently gory and visceral to persuade some readers to join Wiley in his vegetarianism. The recipes include helpful annotations, such as these on Chauncey Potter's Son of a Bitch Stew: "This fare is designed to use fresh beef on the trail before the maggots get it," and "Serves fifteen men three days unless they rebel."[22]

One of the strangest and funniest father quests in recent YA literature takes place in Alison Goodman's science fiction novel, *Singing the Dogstar Blues*. Eighteen-year-old Joss Aaronson had never worried much about who her father might have been, since his only parental contribution was a donation to a sperm bank. Under privacy regulations, he would not even have known if his donation resulted in any live births. However, Joss is put in the unique situation of being pressured to identify her biological father, by an alien friend to whom it matters very much.

Mavkel, a visitor from the planet Choria, is the survivor of a pair, in a species to whom intense pair bonding is vital. Joss is selected to be his school partner when it is discovered that she possesses a special harmonic resonance with Mavkel. The Chorian persuades Joss to time-travel nearly twenty years back to the laboratory in which she began life as a test-tube baby. He finds the petri dish labeled "Aaronson," and, to Joss's horror, accidentally sneezes into it!

> "I can't believe you snotted in my dish," I wailed.
> Mav held up his hand.
> "No. Be still." His voice was professional. "Yes. Yes. It is happening."
> "What? What's happening?"
> Mav passed the goggles to me. I held them up to my eyes.
> "Do you see?" he sang happily . . . "It is your resonance," Mav sang. "You are of the Mav line. You are of me!"[23]

In short, Mavkel's timely sneeze introduces into Joss's petri dish a bit of alien genetic material that causes her, nineteen years later, to resonate like a Chorian so that she is paired with Mavkel, so that they can travel together back in time, so that he can sneeze in her dish . . . Such is the time-travel paradox. Joss and Mavkel go on to search the records to discover the identity of Joss's father, but it's almost anticlimactic after finding that Mavkel, an alien from the planet Choria, is in effect one of Joss's parents.

Of course, a long-lost father might turn out to be a bit of a disappointment. Kathleen Karr's *The Great Turkey Walk*, a Western frontier epic like *Sunshine Rider*, features a no-good father in the mold of Mark Twain's Pap Finn. While driving one thousand turkeys from Missouri to Denver, Simon Green is surprised to come across his father running a crooked shell game at a circus in Jefferson City.

Samson Green affects to be deeply moved at being reunited with his son, ten years after he had casually abandoned the boy upon the death of the mother. However, as soon as Samson learns of the valuable turkey flock, he undertakes the first of his three attempts to steal the birds from his son. As Simon tells his muleskinner Bidwell Peece, "It's kind of hard to find and lose your pa all in the same day, Mr. Peece."[24] Simon's epic coming-of-age journey is thus punctuated by this trio of renunciations of an unworthy father.

One of the most pleasing features of many coming-of-age stories is the recognition that, despite some hard knocks, a distinctive young character has come through still recognizably himself, retaining his identity, high spirits, and sense of humor. Simon Green of *The Great Turkey Walk* is still a simple-minded, big-hearted fellow when he reaches Denver and becomes a wealthy man. Joss Aaronson of *Singing the Dogstar Blues* remains a smart-mouthed rebel after all of her adventures. These characters become stronger as they mature, yet they retain the essential core of personality that grabbed our interest and made us want to read what happens to them.

Other Quests

In the quest-romance, a hero takes an epic journey, battles powerful foes, and may even win fame and riches, but what he really finds is himself. The quest is a particularly potent metaphor for a young person's coming of age, and the quest for one's father, or for one's origins, is often an essential element of the process.

However, not all quests place a special emphasis on paternal origins. In particular, folktales told from a feminist perspective often emphasize the development of the heroine's own strengths and identity rather than her connection to any patriarch. A common scenario in traditional fantasies and fairy tales is the delivery of a princess to a happy ending that has not been merited by any test of her character. The fairy tale princess is all too often depicted as a prize passively waiting to be rescued by her knight in shining armor. Deviations from that script in feminist retellings of fairy tales are especially satisfying when they present an active young heroine whose wit and courage carry her through.

In Gail Carson Levine's acclaimed revision of the Cinderella folktale, *Ella Enchanted*, Ella's salvation is achieved entirely through her own efforts to break the "gift" of obedience wished upon her by a misguided fairy. Ella's chief adversaries—man-eating ogres and wicked step relations—are so comically and one-dimensionally malevolent that readers feel confident that these grotesque villains will not prevail. The novel's tone is consistently comic, and yet Ella endures considerable unhappiness and comes through character-building trials that create a sense she has genuinely come of age. At the climactic moment of the story, when she is finally able to profess her love for Prince Char, Ella jests about her maturity:

> "When you asked for my hand a few minutes ago, I was still too young to marry." I looked up at him and saw a smile start. "I'm older now, so much older that not only can I marry, but I can beg you to marry me."[25]

This is an inside joke between the pair, and yet it is precisely true: until she finally broke the curse of obedience, Ella had not come of age, she was "too young" to marry; still a child, not a woman.

Fulfillment of a prophecy may be intertwined with a hero's coming of age, even if that hero—or heroine—is ignorant of the prophecy. Alexandria Aurora Fortunato, the plucky protagonist of Patrice Kindl's *Goose Chase*, is completely unaware that she's fulfilling the requirements of a benevolent witch's prophecy that the daughters of the House of Fortunato must remain geese until one of them again wears the crown jewels of Gilboa.

By the time the geese are transformed into princesses, Alexandria has already proved her courage in many dangerous adventures. Formal satisfaction of the prophecy is merely a ceremonial recognition of worthiness already demonstrated. The witch is comically impatient with what is for her, an anticlimactic windup of a long story. She rolls her eyes, mutters in exasperation, and lispingly orders Alexandria, "jusst you hand over the (crown) jewels" because "She's your sssissster, Dadgummit!"[26] Kindl's imaginative reworking of *The Goose Girl* is filled with comic situations and dialogue that overlay traditional elements of courtly romance.

Louis Sachar's renowned novel, *Holes*, enacts a fantasy quest in a modern setting. When Stanley Yelnats befriends Hector (Zero) Zeroni at Camp Green Lake, teaches him to read, and carries him up the rise known as God's thumb, neither of them has any idea that together they are fulfilling a promise made by Stanley's great-great-grandfather to Madame Zeroni, Hector's great-great-grandmother. In realistic terms,

Stanley develops strength through the ordeal. But Sachar downplays the importance of such a straightforward reading in this teasing narrative intrusion: "The reader probably cares more about the change in Stanley's character and self-confidence. But those changes are subtle and hard to measure. There is no simple answer."[27]

Sachar wants his reader to be equally attentive to the mythic layer also at work in *Holes*. All of the wonderful things that happen at the end of the novel—the recovery of the treasure, the boys' escape from Camp Green Lake, and the successful search for Hector's mother—flow not just from Stanley's general courage and resolution, but specifically from his repayment of exactly that debt a Yelnats had failed to pay to a Zeroni generations earlier in Latvia.

Conclusion

The very notion of a humorous coming-of-age novel, if not an oxymoron, is at least somewhat paradoxical. Since growing to maturity and adulthood is such a fundamentally serious and essential business for the individual, his family, and his community, how can it be funny?

It must be understood that finding humor in the absurdities of life does not signify a superficial attitude. There is sometimes a sense that comedy is inherently frivolous, that it lacks the gravitas we associate with other forms of literature. But serious purpose is not incompatible with humor. In a recent interview, YA author M. T. Anderson put it this way:

> Humor gets a bad rap. People assume somehow that humor is lightness, is evasion, is a sign that you are "not dealing with something"—when in fact, humor may be a perfectly legitimate response to a world that is fundamentally absurd. Humor is not about trivialities. We should remember that comedy was, for Shakespeare, about concealment, betrayal, and reunification; for Beckett, it embodied the senselessness of life itself; and for Dante, it held forth the promise of heaven.[28]

The importance and solemnity of a subject or situation can actually enhance rather than detract from its comic potential. The vital processes and stages of life, including the most serious rites of passage, have always been subject to comic interpretation. Adolescence is often funny because of its awkwardness. The maturation process is rarely a smooth incline from childhood to adulthood. The ups and downs teenagers inevitably experience can be a source for comedy, as the adolescent lurches unpredictably from childish to surprisingly mature behavior. Embarrassing situations abound as young people wonder how to deal with out-of-control growth spurts, how to behave on a date, how to explain an eccentric parent to a friend, and so on. The pressures on teens to measure up to the often-conflicting expectations of both parents and peers can result in extreme behaviors, extreme emotional states, and very funny situations.

Humor provides a safety valve for this high-pressure condition of adolescence. Humor can provide a teen a way of taking himself a bit less seriously, of gaining some degree of perspective on problems that at times seem overwhelming. Thus, counterintuitively, a humorous perspective contributes to the process of growing to healthy adulthood. A funny story can help one attain a degree of acceptance of those things one can't change: physical limitations, ethnicity, the loss of a parent, the problems of the world. Humorous fiction can also suggest creative ways of perceiving and handling obstacles that need to be faced. And finally, it can simply lighten a mood or lift a troubled heart.

The authentic adolescent voice produces a uniquely powerful narrative. Some of the truest works of YA literature are almost unbearably painful to read, vividly recalling incidents of awkwardness and humiliation in the experience of most readers. It is precisely this heightened, overwrought atmosphere of tension and angst that also makes humorous fiction for young adults such an exciting reading experience. The genuine adolescent protagonist who is able to laugh a bit amidst his tears is as lively and appealing a narrator as can be found in literature.

Notes

1. *Merriam-Webster's Encyclopedia of Literature* (Springfield, Mass.: Merriam-Webster, 1995).

2. *Oxford English Dictionary Online* (New York: Oxford University Press, 2004), http://dictionary.oed.com/entrance.dtl (12 November 2004).

3. Jaclyn Moriarty, *Feeling Sorry for Celia* (New York: St. Martin's, 2001), 4.

4. Karen Cushman, *Catherine, Called Birdy* (New York: Clarion Books, 1994), 6.

5. Chris Lynch, *Extreme Elvin* (New York: HarperCollins, 1999), 230.

6. Janet Tashjian, *The Gospel According to Larry* (New York: Holt, 2001), 176.

7. In the sequel, *Vote for Larry* (New York: Holt, 2004), Larry is dragged out of hiding, but he remains equivocal about his identity.

8. Ned Vizzini, *Be More Chill* (New York: Hyperion, 2004), 38.

9. C. D. Payne, *Youth in Revolt: The Journals of Nick Twisp* (New York: Doubleday, 1995), 498.

10. Unsigned review of *Feed* by M. T. Anderson, *Kirkus Reviews* 70:17 (September 1, 2002).

11. M. T. Anderson, *Feed* (Cambridge, Mass.: Candlewick, 2002), 70.

12. Terry Davis, *If Rock and Roll Were a Machine* (New York: Delacorte, 1992), 165–66.

13. For those who like high school Dada clubs in their fiction, see also Daniel Pinkwater's *Young Adult Novel*, reprinted in Daniel Pinkwater, *5 Novels* (New York: Farrar, Straus & Giroux, 1997).

14. Rob Thomas, *Rats Saw God* (New York: Simon & Schuster, 1996), 164–65.

15. Joan Bauer, *Backwater* (New York: Putnam, 1999), 181.

16. Carolyn Mackler, *The Earth, My Butt, and Other Big Round Things* (Cambridge, Mass.: Candlewick, 2003), 177.

17. Nancy Werlin, "Get Rid of the Parents?" *Booklist* 95:21 (July 1999): 1934–5.

18. Randy Powell, *Tribute to Another Dead Rock Star* (New York: Farrar, Straus & Giroux, 1999), 67.

19. Arthur Slade, *Tribes* (New York: Wendy Lamb Books, 2002), 1.

20. Susan Heyboer O'Keefe, *My Life and Death, by Alexandra Canarsie* (Atlanta: Peachtree, 2002), 6.

21. Sharon Creech, *Absolutely Normal Chaos* (New York: HarperCollins, 1995), 1.

22. Ric Lyndman Hardman, *Sunshine Rider: The First Vegetarian Western* (New York: Delacorte, 1998), 39.

23. Alison Goodman, *Singing the Dogstar Blues* (New York: Viking, 2002), 228.

24. Kathleen Karr, *The Great Turkey Walk* (New York: Farrar, Straus & Giroux, 1998), 70.

25. Gail Carson Levine, *Ella Enchanted* (New York: HarperCollins, 1997), 229.

26. Patrice Kindl, *Goose Chase* (Boston: Houghton Mifflin, 2001), 202.

27. Louis Sachar, *Holes* (New York: Farrar, Straus & Giroux, 1998), 230.

28. Joel Shoemaker, "Hungry for M. T. Anderson: An Interview With M. T. Anderson," *Voice of Youth Advocates* 27:2 (June 2004): 100.

Bibliography

Humorous YA Literature

Alexander, Lloyd. *Gypsy Rizka*. New York: Dutton, 1999.

Anderson, Laurie Halse. "Passport." 128–39 in *Dirty Laundry: Stories about Family Secrets*, edited by Lisa Rowe Fraustino. New York: Viking, 1998.

Anderson, M. T. *Burger Wuss*. Cambridge, Mass.: Candlewick, 1999.

———. *Feed*. Cambridge, Mass.: Candlewick, 2002.

———. *Thirsty*. Cambridge, Mass.: Candlewick, 1997.

Bauer, Joan. *Backwater*. New York: Putnam, 1999.

———. *Hope Was Here*. New York: Putnam, 2000.

———. *Rules of the Road*. New York: Putnam, 1998.

———. *Squashed*. New York: Delacorte, 1992.

———. *Stand Tall*. New York: Putnam, 2002.

———. *Sticks*. New York: Delacorte, 1996.

———. *Thwonk!* New York: Delacorte, 1995.

Bauer, Marion Dane, ed. *Am I Blue?: Coming Out from the Silence*. New York: HarperCollins, 1994.

Beagle, Peter S. *Tamsin*. New York: ROC, 1999.

Block, Francesca Lia. *Weetzie Bat*. New York: HarperCollins, 1989.

———. *Witch Baby*. New York: HarperCollins, 1991.

Brooks, Bruce. *Dolores: Seven Stories about Her*. New York: HarperCollins, 2002.

Burgess, Melvin. *Lady: My Life as a Bitch*. New York: Henry Holt, 2002.

Cabot, Meg. *All-American Girl*. New York: HarperCollins, 2002.

———. *The Princess Diaries*. New York: Harper Avon, 2000.

———. *Princess in Love*. New York: HarperCollins, 2002.

Clark, Catherine. *Frozen Rodeo*. New York: HarperCollins, 2003.

———. *Truth or Dairy*. New York: HarperCollins, 2000.

———. *Wurst Case Scenario*. New York: HarperCollins, 2001.

Clarke, Judith. *The Heroic Life of Al Capsella*. New York: Holt, 1988.

Cohn, Rachel. *Gingerbread*. New York: Simon & Schuster, 2002.

———. *The Steps*. New York: Simon & Schuster, 2003.

Cole, Brock. *Celine*. New York: Farrar, Straus & Giroux, 1989.

Colfer, Eoin. *Artemis Fowl*. New York: Hyperion, 2001.

———. *Artemis Fowl: The Arctic Incident*. New York: Talk Miramax/Hyperion, 2002.

———. *Artemis Fowl: The Eternity Code*. New York : Miramax/Hyperion, 2003.

Conford, Ellen. *Dear Mom, Get Me Out of Here!* Boston: Little, Brown, 1992.

———. *If This Is Love, I'll Take Spaghetti*. New York: Scholastic, 1983.

———. *I Love You, I Hate You, Get Lost*. New York: Scholastic, 1994.

———. *A Royal Pain*. New York: Scholastic, 1986.

Coville, Bruce. "Am I Blue." 115–26 in Bruce Coville, *Odder Than Ever: Stories by Bruce Coville*. San Diego: Harcourt Brace, 1999.

———, ed. *Odder Than Ever: Stories by Bruce Coville*. San Diego: Harcourt Brace, 1999.

———. *Skull of Truth*. San Diego: Harcourt Brace, 1997.

Creech, Sharon. *Absolutely Normal Chaos*. New York: HarperCollins, 1995.

Crutcher, Chris. "A Brief Moment in the Life of Angus Bethune." 54–70 in *Connections: Short Stories by Outstanding Writers for Young Adults*, edited by Donald R. Gallo. New York: Delacorte, 1989.

———. *Staying Fat for Sarah Byrnes*. New York: Greenwillow. 1993.

Cushman, Karen. *Catherine, Called Birdy*. New York: Clarion Books, 1994.

Danziger, Paula. *Remember Me to Harold Square*. New York: Delacorte, 1987.

———. *This Place Has No Atmosphere*. New York: Delacorte, 1986.

Datlow, Ellen, and Terri Windling. *A Wolf at the Door and Other Retold Fairy Tales*. New York: Simon & Schuster, 2000.

Davis, Terry. *If Rock and Roll Were a Machine*. New York: Delacorte, 1992.

Dickinson, Peter. *Eva*. New York: Delacorte, 1989.

Duncan, Lois, ed. *On the Edge: Stories at the Brink*. New York: Simon & Schuster, 2000.

Eberhardt, Tom. *Rat Boys: A Dating Experiment*. New York: Hyperion, 2001.

Farmer, Nancy. *The Ear, the Eye, and the Arm*. New York: Orchard Books, 1994.

———. "Falada, the Goose Girl's Horse." 44–54 in *A Wolf at the Door and Other Retold Fairy Tales*, edited by Ellen Datlow and Terri Windling. New York: Simon & Schuster, 2000.

Ferris, Jean. *Love among the Walnuts*. San Diego: Harcourt Brace, 1998.

———. *Once upon a Marigold*. San Diego: Harcourt, 2002.

Fine, Anne. *Alias Madame Doubtfire*. Boston: Joy Street Books, 1988.

———. *My War with Goggle-Eyes*. Boston: Joy Street Books, 1989.

———. *The Tulip Touch*. Boston: Little, Brown, 1997.

Fleischman, Paul. *A Fate Totally Worse Than Death*. Cambridge, Mass.: Candlewick, 1995.

Frank, Lucy. *Just Ask Iris*. New York: Atheneum, 2001.

Fraustino, Lisa Rowe. *Ash*. New York: Orchard Books, 1995.

———, ed. *Dirty Laundry: Stories About Family Secrets*. New York: Viking, 1998.

Fredericks, Mariah. *The True Meaning of Cleavage*. New York: Atheneum, 2003.

Gallo, Donald R., ed. *Connections: Short Stories by Outstanding Writers for Young Adults*. New York: Delacorte, 1989.

———, ed. *Sixteen: Short Stories by Outstanding Young Adult Writers*. New York: Delacorte, 1984.

Gantos, Jack. *Joey Pigza Swallowed the Key*. New York: HarperCollins, 2000.

———. *What Would Joey Do?* New York: Farrar, Straus & Giroux, 2002.

Gauthier, Gail. *Saving the Planet & Stuff*. New York: Putnam, 2003.

Gilmore, Kate. *Enter Three Witches*. Boston: Houghton Mifflin, 1990.

Gliori, Deb. *Pure Dead Magic*. New York: Knopf, 2001.

———. *Pure Dead Wicked*. New York: Knopf, 2002.

Going, K. L. *Fat Kid Rules the World*. New York: Putnam, 2003.

Goldman, E. M. *Getting Lincoln's Goat: An Elliot Armbruster Mystery*. New York: Delacorte, 1995.

Goodman, Alison. *Singing the Dogstar Blues*. New York: Viking, 2002.

Hall, Lynn. *Dagmar Schultz and the Angel Edna*. New York: Scribner's, 1989.

———. *Dagmar Schultz and the Green-eyed Monster*. New York: Scribner, 1991.

———. *Dagmar Schultz and the Powers of Darkness*. New York: Scribner, 1989.

Handler, Daniel. *The Basic Eight*. New York: Thomas Dunne, 1989.

Hardman, Ric Lynden. *Sunshine Rider: The First Vegetarian Western*. New York: Delacorte, 1998.

Hartinger, Bret. *Geography Club*. New York: HarperTempest, 2003.

Hautman, Pete. "Hot Lava." 85–92 in *On the Edge: Stories at the Brink*, edited by Lois Duncan. New York: Simon & Schuster, 2000.

Hesse, Karen. *Letters from Rifka*. New York: Holt, 1992.

Hesser, Terry Spencer. *Kissing Doorknobs*. New York: Delacorte, 1998.

Hiaasen, Carl. *Hoot*. New York: Knopf, 2002.

Howe, James. *The Misfits*. New York: Atheneum, 2001.

Johnston, Julie. *In Spite of Killer Bees*. Toronto: Tundra, 2001.

Jones, Diana Wynne. *Castle in the Air*. New York: Greenwillow, 1991.

——. *Charmed Life*. New York: Greenwillow, 1997.

——. *Dark Lord of Derkholm*. New York: Greenwillow, 1998.

——. *Howl's Moving Castle*. New York: Greenwillow, 1986.

——. *The Lives of Christopher Chant*. New York: Greenwillow, 1988.

——. *The Magicians of Caprona*. New York: Greenwillow, 1980.

——. *The Tough Guide to Fantasyland*. London: Vista, 1996.

——. *Year of the Griffin*. New York: Greenwillow, 2000.

Juby, Susan. *Alice, I Think*. New York: HarperCollins, 2003.

Karr, Kathleen. *The Great Turkey Walk*. New York: Farrar, Straus & Giroux, 1998.

Keller, Beverly. *The Amazon Papers*. San Diego: Browndeer Press, 1996.

Kindl, Patrice. *Goose Chase*. Boston: Houghton Mifflin, 2001.

——. *Owl in Love*. Boston: Houghton Mifflin, 1993.

——. *Woman in the Wall*. Boston: Houghton Mifflin, 1997.

Klass, David. *You Don't Know Me*. New York: Frances Foster Books, 2001.

Koertge, Ron. *The Arizona Kid*. Boston: Joy Street Books, 1988.

——. *Boy in the Moon*. Boston: Joy Street Books, 1990.

——. *Confess-O-Rama*. New York: Orchard Books, 1996.

——. *The Harmony Arms*. Boston: Joy Street Books, 1992.

——. *Mariposa Blues*. Boston: Joy Street Books, 1991.

——. *Stoner & Spaz*. Boston: Candlewick, 2002.

——. *Tiger, Tiger, Burning Bright*. New York: Orchard Books, 1994.

——. *Where the Kissing Never Stops*. Boston: Atlantic Monthly, 1986.

Konigsberg, E. L. *The Outcasts of 19 Schuyler Place*. New York: Atheneum, 2004.

Korman, Gordon. *Don't Care High*. New York: Scholastic, 1985.

——. *Losing Joe's Place*. New York: Scholastic, 1990.

——. *No Coins, Please*. New York: Scholastic, 1984.

——. *No More Dead Dogs*. New York: Hyperion, 2000.

——. *A Semester in the Life of a Garbage Bag*. New York: Scholastic, 1987.

——. *Son of Interflux*. New York: Scholastic, 1986.

——. *Son of the Mob*. New York: Hyperion, 2002.

Levine, Gail Carson. *Ella Enchanted*. New York: HaperCollins, 1997.

——. *The Wish*. New York: HarperCollins, 1999.

Levithan, David. *Boy Meets Boy*. New York: Knopf, 2003.

Link, Kelly. "Swans." 74–92 in *A Wolf at the Door and Other Retold Fairy Tales*, edited by Ellen Datlow and Terri Windling. New York: Simon & Schuster, 2000.

Lubar, David. *Dunk*. New York: Clarion Books, 2002.

——. *Hidden Talents*. New York: Tom Doherty Associates, 1999.

Lynch, Chris. *Extreme Elvin*. New York: HarperCollins, 1999.

——. *Iceman*. New York: HarperCollins, 1994.

——. *Political Timber*. New York: HarperCollins, 1996.

——. *Slot Machine*. New York: HarperCollins, 1995.

Mackler, Carolyn. *The Earth, My Butt, and Other Big, Round Things*. Cambridge, Mass.: Candlewick, 2003.

McCafferty, Megan. *Sloppy Firsts*. New York: Crown, 2001.

McKay, Hilary. *The Exiles*. M. K. McElderry Books, 1992.

——. *The Exiles at Home*. New York: M. K. McElderry Books, 1994.

——. *The Exiles in Love*. New York: Margaret K. McElderry Books, 1998.

——. *Saffy's Angel*. New York: Margaret K. McElderry Books, 2002.

Moriarty, Jaclyn. *Feeling Sorry for Celia*. New York: St. Martin's, 2001.

Naylor, Phyllis Reynolds. *Achingly Alice*. New York: Atheneum, 1998.

——. *The Agony of Alice*. New York: Atheneum, 1985.

——. *The Grooming of Alice*. New York: Atheneum, 2000.

——. *Simply Alice*. New York: Atheneum, 2002.

——. *Starting with Alice*. New York: Atheneum, 2002.

Nodelman, Perry. *Behaving Bradley*. New York: Simon & Schuster, 1998.

Oates, Joyce Carol. *Big Mouth & Ugly Girl*. New York: HarperTempest, 2002.

O'Connell, Rebecca. *Myrtle of Willendorf*. Asheville, N.C.: Front Street, 2000.

O'Keefe, Susan Heyboer. *My Life and Death, by Alexandra Canarsie*. Atlanta: Peachtree, 2002.

Paulsen, Gary. *Harris and Me*. San Diego: Harcourt Brace, 1993.

——. *The Schernoff Discoveries*. New York: Delacorte, 1997.

Payne, C. D. *Youth in Revolt: The Journals of Nick Twisp*. New York: Doubleday, 1995.

Peck, Richard. *Bel-Air Bambi and the Mall Rats*. New York: Delacorte, 1993.

——. *Ghosts I Have Been*. New York: Viking, 1977.

——. *A Long Way from Chicago: A Novel in Stories*. New York: Dial, 1998.

——. *Past Perfect, Present Tense: New and Collected Stories*. New York: Dial, 2004.

——. "Priscilla and the Wimps." 42–46 in *Sixteen: Short Stories by Outstanding Young Adult Writers*, edited by Donald R. Gallo. New York: Delacorte, 1984.

——. *A Year Down Yonder*. New York: Dial, 2000.

Peck, Robert Newton. *Horse Thief*. New York: HarperCollins, 2002.

Pinkwater, Daniel. *5 Novels*. New York: Farrar, Straus & Giroux, 1997.

——. *Alan Mendelsohn, the Boy from Mars*. New York: Dutton, 1979.

——. *The Education of Robert Nifkin*. New York: Farrar, Straus & Giroux, 1998.

———. *Young Adult Novel.* New York: Crowell, 1982.

———. *Young Adults.* New York: TOR, 1991.

Plummer, Louise. *The Unlikely Romance of Kate Bjorkman.* New York: Bantam, 1995.

Powell, Randy. *Is Kissing a Girl Who Smokes Like Licking an Ashtray?* New York: Farrar, Straus & Giroux, 1992.

———. *Three Clams and an Oyster.* New York: Farrar, Straus & Giroux, 2002.

———. *Tribute to Another Dead Rock Star.* New York: Farrar, Straus & Giroux, 1999.

———. *The Whistling Toilets.* New York: Farrar, Straus & Giroux, 1996.

Pratchett, Terry. *The Amazing Maurice and His Educated Rodents.* New York: HarperCollins, 2001.

———. *Carpe Jugulum: A Novel of Discworld.* New York: HarperPrism, 1999.

———. *A Hat Full of Sky.* New York: HarperCollins, 2004.

———. *The Wee Free Men.* New York: HarperCollins, 2003.

Pullman, Philip. *Count Karlstein.* New York: Knopf, 1982.

Rennison, Louise. *Angus, Thongs and Full-frontal Snogging: Confessions of Georgia Nicolson.* New York: HarperCollins, 1999.

———. *Dancing in My Nuddy-Pants: Even Further Confessions of Georgia Nicolson.* New York: HarperTempest, 2003.

———. *On the Bright Side, I'm Now the Girlfriend of a Sex God: Further Confessions of Georgia Nicolson.* New York: HarperCollins, 2001.

Rochman, Hazel, and Darlene C. McCampbell, eds. *Who Do You Think You Are?: Stories of Friends and Enemies.* Boston: Little, Brown, 1993.

Rowling, J. K. *Harry Potter and the Chamber of Secrets.* New York: Arthur A. Levine Books, 1999.

———. *Harry Potter and the Goblet of Fire.* New York: Arthur A. Levine Books, 2000.

———. *Harry Potter and the Order of the Phoenix.* New York: Scholastic, 2003.

———. *Harry Potter and the Sorcerer's Stone.* New York: A. A. Levine Books, 1998.

Sachar, Louis. *Holes.* New York: Farrar, Straus & Giroux, 1998.

Salisbury, Graham. "Frankie Diamond Is Robbing Us Blind." 118–41 in *Island Boyz: Short Stories.* New York: Wendy Lamb Books, 2002.

Sheldon, Dyan. *Tall, Thin and Blonde.* Cambridge, Mass.: Candlewick, 1993.

Slade, Arthur, *Tribes.* New York: Wendy Lamb Books, 2002.

Sleator, William. *Interstellar Pig.* New York: Dutton, 1984.

———. *Parasite Pig.* New York: Dutton, 2002.

Snicket, Lemony. *The Austere Academy.* New York: HarperCollins, 2000.

———. *The Bad Beginning.* New York: HarperCollins, 1999.

———. *The Slippery Slope*. New York: HarperCollins, 2003.

Spinelli, Jerry. *Stargirl*. New York: Knopf, 2000.

———. *There's a Girl in My Hammerlock*. New York: Simon & Schuster, 1991.

———. *Who Put That Hair in My Toothbrush?* Boston: Little, Brown, 1984.

Strasser, Todd. *Girl Gives Birth to Own Prom Date*. New York: Simon & Schuster, 1996.

———. *How I Changed My Life*. New York: Simon & Schuster, 1995.

———. *How I Spent My Last Night on Earth*. New York: Simon & Schuster, 1998.

———. *A Very Touchy Subject*. New York: Delacorte, 1985.

Tashjian, Janet. *The Gospel According to Larry*. New York: Holt, 2001.

———. *Vote for Larry*. New York: Holt, 2004.

Thomas, Rob. *Rats Saw God*. New York: Simon & Schuster, 1996.

Tolan, Stephanie S. *Surviving the Applewhites*. New York: HarperCollins, 2002.

Townsend, Sue. *The Adrian Mole Diaries*. New York: Grove, 1986.

———. *The Secret Diary of Adrian Mole, Age 13 ¾*. New York: Avon, 1984.

Trembath, Don. *The Tuesday Café*. Victoria, B.C.: Orca, 1996.

Vande Velde, Vivian. "Boy Witch." 91–104 in *Curses, Inc.* San Diego: Harcourt Brace, 1997.

———. *Never Trust a Dead Man*. San Diego: Harcourt Brace, 1999.

———. *The Rumpelstiltskin Problem*. Boston: Houghton Mifflin, 2000.

Vizzini, Ned. *Be More Chill*. New York: Hyperion, 2004.

Wersba, Barbara. *Just Be Gorgeous*. New York: Harper & Row, 1988.

———. *Love Is the Crooked Thing*. New York: Harper & Row, 1987.

Whytock, Cherry. *My Cup Runneth Over: The Life of Angelica Cookson Potts*. New York: Simon & Schuster, 2003.

Wittlinger, Ellen. *Hard Love*. New York: Simon & Schuster, 1999.

Wrede, Patricia C. *Searching for Dragons: The Enchanted Forest Chronicles*. San Diego: Harcourt Brace, 1991.

———. "Utensile Strength." 204–223 in *Book of Enchantments*. San Diego: Harcourt Brace, 1996.

Wynne-Jones, Tim. "Ick." 45–68 in *Lord of the Fries*. New York: DK, 1999.

———. "Tashkent." 43–54 in *Some of the Kinder Planets*. New York: Orchard Books, 1995.

Yolen, Jane. "Cinder Elephant." 17–29 in *A Wolf at the Door and Other Retold Fairy Tales*, edited by Ellen Datlow and Terri Windling. New York: Simon & Schuster, 2000.

Other Works: Secondary Sources and Literary Works Other Than Humorous YA Literature

Adams, Richard. *Watership Down*. New York: Avon, 1975.

Beard, Henry N., and Douglas C. Kenney. *Bored of the Rings: A Parody of J. R. R. Tolkien's Lord of the Rings*. New York: New American Library, 1969.

Bergson, Henri. *Laughter: An Essay on the Meaning of the Comic*. Saint Paul, Minn.: Green Integer, 1999.

Butler, Charles, "Interview with Diana Wynne Jones." 163–72 in *Diana Wynne Jones: An Exciting and Exacting Wisdom*, edited by Teya Rosenberg et al. New York: Peter Lang, 2002.

Campbell, Patty. Review of *Boy Meets Boy* by David Levithan. http://www .amazon.com/exec/obidos/ASIN/0375824006/qid=1089481964/sr= 2-1/ref=sr_2_1/103-9719095-8568635 (30 March 2004).

———. "The Sand in the Oyster: Funny Girls." *Horn Book* 75:3 (May/June 1999): 359–63.

———. "Young Adult Perplex." *Wilson Library Bulletin* 56:7 (March 1982): 533.

Cart, Michael. Review of *Boy Meets Boy* by David Levithan. *Booklist* 99:22 (August 1, 2003): 1980.

———. *What's So Funny : Wit and Humor in American Children's Literature*. New York: HarperCollins, 1995.

Crutcher, Chris. *King of the Mild Frontier: An Ill-advised Autobiography*. New York: Greenwillow, 2003.

Davis, James E. *Presenting William Sleator*. New York: Twayne, 1992.

Davis, Joann. "Spring Is a Season of Plenty for Children's Author Daniel Pinkwater." *Publisher's Weekly* (May 7, 1982): 53–54.

Dickens, Charles. *The Life & Adventures of Nicholas Nickleby*. New York: Oxford University Press, 1966.

Fine, Anne. *Step by Wicked Step*. Boston: Little, Brown, 1996.

Fraser, George MacDonald. *Flashman: From the Flashman Papers, 1839–1842*. New York: Knopf, 1970.

Gallo, Donald R. *Presenting Richard Peck*. Boston: Twayne, 1989.

Gantos, Jack. *A Hole in My Life*. New York: Farrar, Strauss & Giroux 2002.

Heaven, Patrick C. L. *The Social Psychology of Adolescence*. New York: Palgrave, 2001.

Hill, Karina. "Dragons and Quantum Foam: Mythic Archetypes and Modern Physics in Selected Works by Diana Wynne Jones." 40–52 in *Diana Wynne Jones: An Exciting and Exacting Wisdom*, edited by Teya Rosenberg et al. New York: Peter Lang, 2002.

Hogan, Walter. *The Agony and the Eggplant: Daniel Pinkwater's Heroic Struggles in the Name of YA Literature*. Lanham, Md.: Scarecrow Press, 2001.

Homer. *The Odyssey of Homer*. Translated with an Introduction by Richard Lattimore. New York: Harper & Row, 1967.

Hughes, Thomas. *Tom Brown's School Days*. Cambridge: Macmillan, 1857.

"Humor in the United States." 478–82 in *HarperCollins Reader's Encyclopedia of American Literature*, edited by George Perkins et al. New York: Harper Resource, 2002.

Jones, Diana Wynne. *Dalemark Quartet*. (*Cart and Cwidder*, 1995; *Drowned Ammet*, 1995; *The Spellcoats*, 1995; *The Crown of Dalemark*, 1995) New York: Greenwillow.

———. *Fire and Hemlock*. New York: Greenwillow, 1985.

———. *The Homeward Bounders*. New York: Greenwillow, 1981.

———. *The Merlin Conspiracy*. New York: Greenwillow, 2003.

Klause, Annette Curtis. *Blood and Chocolate*. New York: Delacorte, 1997.

Lang, Andrew, ed. *Blue Fairy Book*. New York: Longmans, Green, 1948.

Lewis, Joanna. Review of *Boy Meets Boy*, by David Levithan. *School Library Journal* 49:9 (September 2003): 216–17.

L-Space Web: A Terry Pratchett/Discworld Web Site. www.ie.lspace.org/books /analysis/stacie-hanes-2.html (2 February 2004).

Merriam-Webster's Encyclopedia of Literature. Springfield, Mass.: Merriam-Webster, 1995.

Myers, Walter Dean. *Bad Boy: A Memoir*. New York: HarperCollins, 2001.

O'Brien, Robert C. *Mrs. Frisby and the Rats of Nimh*. New York: Atheneum, 1971.

Oxford English Dictionary Online. New York: Oxford University Press, 2004. http://dictionary.oed.com/entrance.dtl (12 November 2003).

Pratchett, Terry. "Terry Pratchett: 21 Years of Discworld." *Locus* (May 2004): 9, 58–59.

Roberts, Patricia L. *Taking Humor Seriously in Children's Literature: Literature-Based Mini-Units and Humorous Books for Children Ages 5–12*. Lanham, Md.: Scarecrow Press, 1997.

Rohrlick, Paula. Review of *Dark Lord of Derkholm* by Diana Wynne Jones. *KLIATT Review* 32:6 (November 1998).

———. Review of *Wee Free Men* by Terry Pratchett. *KLIATT Review* 37:3 (May 2003).

Rosenberg, Teya. "Introduction." 1–12 in *Diana Wynne Jones: An Exciting and Exacting Wisdom*, edited by Teya Rosenberg et al. New York: Peter Lang, 2002.

Salinger, J. D. *The Catcher in the Rye*. Boston: Little, Brown, 1951.

———. "For Esmé—with Love and Squalor. 131–72 in J. D. Salinger. *Nine Stories*. Boston: Little, Brown, 1953.

Shoemaker, Joel. "Hungry for M. T. Anderson: An Interview With M. T. Anderson." *Voice of Youth Advocates* 27:2 (June 2004): 98–102.

Silver, Steven H. "A Conversation With Terry Pratchett—Part I." April 2000. www.sfsite.com/04b/tp79.htm (11 December 2003).

Simon, Neil. *The Odd Couple.* New York: Random House, 1966.

Sleator, William. *Oddballs.* New York: Dutton, 1993.

Spinelli, Jerry. *Knots in My Yo-yo String.* New York: Knopf, 1998.

Sterne, Laurence. *Tristram Shandy.* Rutland, Vt.: C. E. Tuttle, 2000.

Stover, Lois T. *Presenting Phyllis Reynolds Naylor.* New York: Twayne, 1997.

Tolkien, J. R. R. *The Lord of the Rings.* Boston: Houghton Mifflin, 1993.

Tredell, Nicholas. "Terry Pratchett." 815–17 in *Contemporary Novelists.* Farmington, Mich.: St. James Press, 2001.

Unsigned review of *Feed* by M. T. Anderson. *Kirkus Reviews* 70:17 (September 1, 2002).

Unsigned review of *The Amazing Maurice and His Educated Rodents* by Terry Pratchett. *Kirkus Reviews* 69:20 (October 15, 2001).

Unsigned review of *The Rumplestiltskin Problem* by Vivian Vande Velde. *Kirkus Reviews* 68:19 (October 1, 2000).

Unsigned review of *Young Adult Novel* by Daniel Pinkwater. *Horn Book* 58 (June 1982): 301.

Unsworth, Robert. Review of *Young Adult Novel* by Daniel Pinkwater. *School Library Journal* 28 (May 1982): 74.

Voigt, Cynthia. *Homecoming.* New York: Fawcett Juniper, 1982.

Wallace, Nancy K. Review of *The Amazing Maurice and His Educated Rodents* by Terry Pratchett. *Voice of Youth Advocates* 24:6 (February 2002): 450.

Werlin, Nancy. "Get Rid of the Parents?" *Booklist* 95:21 (July 1995): 1934–35.

Zindel, Paul. *The Pigman and Me.* New York: HarperCollins, 1992.

Index

Absolutely Normal Chaos, 196–97
Achingly Alice, 24, 25
Adams, Richard, 168
The Adrian Mole Diaries, 57, 70
Adrian Mole Diaries (series), 4, 11
The Agony of Alice, 24, 25,
Al Capsella (trilogy), 95, 102,
    115–16
*Alan Mendelsohn, The Boy From
    Mars*, 75–76, 106, 107
Alexander, Lloyd, 134
Alias Madame Doubtfire, 2, 13–14
Alice, I Think, 61, 68, 75, 82–83, 130
Alice in Wonderland, 169
Alice (series), 2, 3, 24, 27, 120
All-American Girl, 179
"Am I Blue?" 53
*The Amazing Maurice and His
    Educated Rodents*, 167–71
The Amazon Papers, 101–2, 127–28
Anderson, Laurie Halse, 7

Anderson, M. T., 78, 109–12, 183,
    187–88, 201
*Angus, Thongs, and Full-Frontal
    Snogging*, 70
animals, 69, 84–85, 87, 89, 197; in
    fantasy, 17, 148, 150, 159,
    161–63, 165–69, 172, 175
The Arizona Kid, 30–31, 124, 138–39
Artemis Fowl (series), 147–49
Artemis Fowl: The Arctic Incident,
    147–48
Artemis Fowl: The Eternity Code,
    147–48
Ash, 2, 15
The Austere Academy, 90

Backwater, 9, 122, 191–92
The Basic Eight, 185–86
Bauer, Joan, xi, xii, xiii, xv, 2, 3, 9,
    19, 80, 81, 100, 109, 110, 113,
    119, 121–22, 135, 179, 191–92

Be More Chill, 133–34, 184–85
Beagle, Peter, 7
Beautiful Losers, 9, 98
Behaving Bradley, 39, 58–59, 109–10
Bel Air Bambi and the Mall Rats, 29n7
Big Mouth and Ugly Girl, 40, 103–4
black humor. *See* humor, black
Block, Francesca Lia, 6, 124, 139
Blood and Chocolate, 112
Blossom Culp (series), 120
Blue Fairy Book, 161
The Boy in the Moon, 20n5, 28, 29, 96, 124
Boy Meets Boy, 141–44
"Boy Witch," 164–65
"A Brief Moment in the Life of Angus Bethune," 52–53, 106
Brooks, Bruce, 55
Burger Wuss, 78–79, 109, 110, 183–85
Burgess, Melvin, 186

Cabot, Meg, xi, 179
Campbell, Patty, xii, xiv, 143, 156
Carpe Jugulum, 170
Carroll, Lewis, 169
Cart, Michael, 142–43
Castle in the Air, 120, 174
The Catcher in the Rye, 20n24, 105, 183
Catherine, Called Birdy, 181–82
Celine, 8
Charmed Life, 125, 171
Chrestomanci novels (series), 125, 171
"Cinder Elephant," 161, 165
Clark, Catherine, xi, 79
Clarke, Judith, 10, 95, 116
Cohn, Rachel, 6–7
Cole, Brock, 8

Colfer, Eoin, xi, 147–49, 166
comedy, romantic. *See* romantic situations
Confess-O-Rama, 29n7, 31–32, 96, 124, 129, 143
Conford, Ellen, 121, 179
conformity. *See* popularity and peer pressure
Count Karlstein, 91
Coville, Bruce, xvi
Creech, Sharon, 196–97
crime fiction *See* mystery and crime fiction
Crutcher, Chris, xv, 106
Cushman, Karen, xi, 181

"The Dada Boys in Collitch," 76
Dagmar Schultz and the Angel Edna, 120
Dagmar Schultz and the Green-Eyed Monster, 120
Dagmar Schultz and the Powers of Darkness, 120
Dagmar Schultz (series), 120
Dalemark Quartet (series), 171
Dancing in My Nuddy-Pants, 70–71
Danziger, Paula, 15–16
Dark Lord of Derkholm, 171–75
dating. *See* romantic situations
Datlow, Ellen and Terri Windling, 165
Davis, Terry, 188–90
"Dead End Dada," 76–77
Dear Mom, Get Me Out of Here!, 33–34
detective fiction *See* mystery and crime fiction
diary novels/epistolary fiction, 4–5, 11, 57, 104, 131–33, 180–82, 188–90

Dickinson, Peter, 186–87
Discworld (series), 167, 169–70
divorce. *See* parents, single, divorced, or absent
Dolores: Seven Stories About Her, 55
Don't Care High, 47, 121, 122
Dunk, 131

The Ear, the Eye and the Arm, 14, 91
The Earth, My Butt, and Other Big, Round Things, 98–99, 116, 192–93
Eberhardt, Thom, 120
The Education of Robert Nifkin, 10–11, 39, 71–72, 81–82, 106
Ella Enchanted, 120, 160–61, 199–200
embarrassment. *See* self-image
Enchanted Forest (series), 91–92, 160
Enter Three Witches, 4, 129–30
espionage. *See* mystery and crime fiction
Eva, 186–87
The Exiles, 125
The Exiles at Home, 125
The Exiles in Love, 125–26
Extreme Elvin, 12, 26–27, 106, 107, 182–83

fairy tales. *See* folk and fairy tales
"Falada, the Goose Girl's Horse," 162–63, 165
fantasy and romance, xiv–xv, 17, 32–33, 91–92, 112, 119–20, 125, 135–36, 147–53, 159–76, 200–201. *See also* folk and fairy tales
Farmer, Nancy, 14, 91, 162–63, 165
Fat, a Love Story, 9, 98

Fat Kid Rules the World, 107–8
A Fate Totally Worse Than Death, 153–56
Feed, 110, 187–88
Feeling Sorry for Celia, 104–5, 131–33, 180–81
feminism, 159–66, 199–200
Ferris, Jean, xi, xv, 119
Fine, Anne, xii
Fire and Hemlock, 171
Flashman (series), 32
Fleischman, Paul, 166, 171
folk and fairy tales, 124, 159–76, 199–200. *See also* fantasy and romance
food, 34, 56, 68–69, 76, 81, 92, 124, 144, 154, 160; appallingly bad, 10–11, 33–35, 39, 168; cannibalism, 159, 160; junk, 18, 78–79, 98–100; overeating, 98–100, 108, 161; vegetarianism, 128, 197
Frank, Lucy, 84–85
"Frankie Diamond Is Robbing Us Blind," 64–65
Fraser, George MacDonald, 32
Fraustino, Lisa Rowe, 2, 15
Fredericks, Mariah, 72–73
Frozen Rodeo, 35

Gallo, Donald, 1, 12
Gantos, Jack, xv
Gauthier, Gail, 80
Geography Club, 141–42
Georgia Nicolson (series), 5, 11, 57–58, 70
"Get Rid of the Parents," 13, 194
Getting Lincoln's Goat, 40
Ghosts I Have Been, 61–62
Gilmore, Kate, 4, 129–30

Gingerbread, 6–7
Gipsy Rizka, 134
Girl Gives Birth to Own Prom Date, 3, 123
Gliori, Deb, xi, 149, 166
Going, K. L., 107–8
Goldman, E. M., 40
Goodman, Alison, 197–99
Goose Chase, 17–18, 161–62, 200
The Gospel According to Larry, 133, 184
The Great Turkey Walk, 198–99
The Grooming of Alice, 24–25, 28
gross humor. *See* humor, gross

Hall, Lynn, 120
Handler, Daniel, 185–86
Hard Love, 137
Hardman, Ric Lynden, xi, 197
Hardy Boys (series), 24
The Harmony Arms, 29, 124
Harris and Me, 14
Harry Potter and the Chamber of Secrets, 89
Harry Potter and the Goblet of Fire, 90
Harry Potter and the Order of the Phoenix, 71
Harry Potter and the Sorcerer's Stone, 108
Harry Potter (series), 2, 24, 32, 89, 108–9, 112, 175
Hartinger, Bret, 141
A Hat Full of Sky, 167, 169–71
Hautman, Pete, 96
Heidi Rosenbloom (trilogy), 139
The Heroic Life of Al Capsella, 10, 95, 113–14
Hesse, Karen, 88
Hesser, Terry Spencer, 44, 73
Hiaasen, Carl, 37, 63, 87

Hidden Talents, 33, 45, 65
Holes, 91, 200–201
Homecoming, 13
Homer, 196–97
The Homeward Bounders, 171
homosexuality. *See* same-sex attraction
Hoot, 37, 63, 87
Hope Was Here, 81, 122
horror fiction, 150–59
Horse Thief, xi, 89
"Hot Lava," 96
How I Changed My Life, 4
How I Spent My Last Night on Earth, 123
Howe, James, 68–69, 106, 131, 140–41
Howl's Moving Castle, 174, 175
Hughes, Thomas, 32
humor: black, 7, 97, 107, 129, 151–59; gross, 65, 148–51, 159, 197

"Ick," 40
If Rock and Roll Were a Machine, 188–90
If This Is Love, I'll Take Spaghetti, 119
I Love You, I Hate You, Get Lost!, 121
In Spite of Killer Bees, 13, 194–95
Interstellar Pig, 157–59
irony, 48, 112, 133, 147–76, 194. *See also* satire and parody
Is Kissing a Girl Who Smokes Like Licking an Ashtray?, 123

Joey Pigza Swallowed the Key, 74
Johnston, Julie, 13, 194
Jones, Diana Wynne, xi, xii, xiv, xvi, 119, 125, 167, 171–75

Juby, Susan, 68, 75, 82, 130
Just Ask Iris, 84–85
Just Be Gorgeous, 139

Karr, Kathleen, 198
Keller, Beverly, 101, 127–28
Kindl, Patrice, 119, 120, 162
Kissing Doorknobs, 44, 73–74
Klass, David, 7, 38, 128–29
Klause, Annette Curtis, 112
Koertge, Ron, xi, xii, xv, 2, 3, 28, 29,
    96, 100, 110, 114, 119, 129, 138,
    139, 143, 179
Konigsberg, E. L., 12
Korman, Gordon, xi, xii, xvi, 3, 9,
    45–48, 69, 83, 103, 110, 115,
    121–22, 127, 134, 179

Lady: My Life as a Bitch, 186–87
Lang, Andrew, 161
Letters From Rifka, 88–89
Levine, Gail Carson, xi, 119
Levithan, David, 141–43
Lewis, C. S., 173
Link, Kelly, 165
The Lives of Christopher Chant, 125,
    175
A Long Way from Chicago, 89, 134
The Lord of the Rings, 173
Losing Joe's Place, 47, 83, 122
Love. *See* romantic situations
Love among the Walnuts, 91
Love Is the Crooked Thing, 9, 98
Lubar, David, xvi
Lynch, Chris, 110

Mackler, Carolyn, xi
The Magicians of Caprona, 134, 175
Mariposa Blues, 20n5, 28
McCafferty, Megan, 75, 105, 136, 183

McKay, Hilary, 10, 125
The Merlin Conspiracy, 171
The Misfits, 68–69, 106, 131, 140–41
Moriarty, Jaclyn, 104, 131, 180
Mrs. Doubtfire (film), 2
Mrs. Frisby and the Rats of Nimh, 169
My Cup Runneth Over, 102–3
*My Life and Death, by Alexandra
    Canarsie*, 12, 195–96
My War With Goggle-Eyes, 5–6, 16
Myers, Walter Dean, xv
Myrtle of Willendorf, 99–100, 104
mystery and crime fiction, 91,
    147–55, 165

Naylor, Phyllis Reynolds, xii, 120–21
Never Trust a Dead Man, 165
No Coins, Please, 121, 122
No More Dead Dogs, 3n6, 69–70,
    103, 122–23
Nodelman, Perry, 39, 58, 109

Oates, Joyce Carol, 40, 103
obesity. *See* weight problems
O'Connell, Rebecca, 99, 101, 103
The Odyssey, 196–97
O'Keefe, Susan Heyboer, 12, 195
*On the Bright Side, I'm Now the
    Girlfriend of a Sex God*, 5, 58
Once Upon a Marigold, 91, 120, 163
The Outcasts of 19 Schuyler Place, 12
Owl in Love, 120, 162

Parasite Pig, 157, 159
parents, single, divorced, or absent,
    2–18, 24, 29, 89–90, 97, 129,
    180–81, 193–99. *See also*
    stepparents and blended families
parody. *See* satire and parody
"Passport," 7–8

Paulsen, Gary, 14, 55
Payne, C. D., 2, 185–86
Peck, Richard, xii, xv, xvi, 63
Peck, Robert Newton, xi, 89
Pinkwater, Daniel, xi, xii, xv, xvi,
    156–57, 166, 171
Plummer, Louise, 144
Political Timber, 9–10
popularity and peer pressure, 26, 39,
    100–106, 113–16, 136, 140. See
    also self-image
Powell, Randy, 123, 179
Pratchett, Terry, xi, xiv, xvi, 167,
    169, 170–75
The Princess Diaries, 128
Princess in Love, 119
"Priscilla and the Wimps," 37, 62–63
Pullman, Philip, 91
puns and wordplay, 16, 99, 142,
    149–53, 160–65, 167–72
Pure Dead Magic, 14, 90–91, 149–51
Pure Dead Wicked, 149

Rat Boys: A Dating Experiment, 120
Rats Saw God, 115–16, 188–92
realistic fiction, 119–20, 122
regional flavor, xi, 15, 63–65, 79,
    87–89, 192, 196–97, 198–201. See
    also rural settings
Remember Me to Harold Square,
    15–16
Rennison, Louise, xi
Rita Formica (trilogy), 9, 98
rivalries, family and sibling, 13–18
romance. See fantasy and romance
romantic situations, 35–36, 45–47,
    64, 82, 119–44, 183, 192; in
    fantasy, 163–65, 200; parental, 3,
    4
Rowling, J. K., xiv

A Royal Pain, 121
Rules of the Road, xii, 80–81,
    100–101, 121
The Rumpelstiltskin Problem, 163–64
rural settings, 14–15, 30–31, 59–62.
    See also regional flavor

Sachar, Louis, 91, 200–201
Saffy's Angel, 10
Salinger, J. D., 152, 183
Salisbury, Graham, 64–65
same-sex attraction, 30, 52–53, 99,
    104, 131, 136–44
sarcasm, 105, 168, 183, 190–91
satire and parody, 32, 70, 76, 105,
    110, 147–76, 185–88. See also
    irony
Saving the Planet & Stuff, 80
The Schernoff Discoveries, 55–57
science fiction, xiv-xv, 16, 123,
    147–51, 157–59, 171–75, 184–88,
    197–98
Searching for Dragons, 91–92, 160
The Secret Diary of Adrian Mole,
    Aged 13 3/4, 4–5, 11
self-consciousness. See self-image
self-image, 5, 10, 24–27, 29, 32,
    95–116, 127, 129, 133, 135–36,
    192–93, 202. See also popularity
    and peer pressure; weight
    problems
A Semester in the Life of a Garbage
    Bag, 9, 46, 122
series, novels in, 23–24, 120,
    147–53, 167–71, 174–75
A Series of Unfortunate Events, 2,
    14, 90, 151–53
sex, 4–5, 24–25, 27–31, 40–41, 76–77,
    112, 123–24, 184, 186–87, 190
Sheldon, Dyan, 136

short stories, 23, 51–57, 62–63, 121
Simply Alice, 24
Singing the Dogstar Blues, 197–99
single parents. *See* parents, single,
    divorced, or absent
Slade, Arthur, 74, 77, 112, 195
Sleator, William, xii, xv, xvi, 157,
    159
The Slippery Slope, 151–53
Sloppy Firsts, 75, 105, 136–37, 183
Slot Machine, 12, 26, 72, 73, 106, 110
Snicket, Lemony, xi, 151, 153, 167,
    175
Son of Interflux, 46–47, 122
Son of the Mob, 45–46, 115, 121,
    127–28, 134–35
Spinelli, Jerry, xii, xv
sports, 4, 36–37, 38, 52, 56, 71–74,
    104–6, 108–9
Squashed, 100, 121–22
Stand Tall, 109, 121
Stargirl, 136
Staying Fat for Sarah Byrnes, 97, 100,
    106
Starting with Alice, 24
Step By Wicked Step, 20n27
stepparents and blended families,
    3–8, 161, 165–66, 194. *See also*
    parents, single, divorced, or
    absent
The Steps, 7
Sterne, Laurence, 151
Stoner and Spaz, 28, 96–97, 100, 124
Strasser, Todd, 123
*Sunshine Rider: The First Vegetarian
    Western*, xi, 197, 198
supernatural fiction, xiv, 4, 45, 120,
    129–30
Surviving the Applewhites, 180
"Swans," 165–66

*Taking Humor Seriously in Children's
    Literature*, xii
Tall, Thin, and Blonde, 136
Tamsin, 7
Tashjian, Janet, 133, 184
"Tashkent," 54–55
There's a Girl in My Hammerlock, 9
Thirsty, 111–12, 187
This Place Has No Atmosphere, 15–16
Thomas, Rob, 115, 188–90
Three Clams and an Oyster, 36–37,
    123
Thwonk!, 121, 135–36
Tiger, Tiger, Burning Bright, 28
"To Esmé, With Love and Squalor,"
    152
Tolan, Stephanie, 180
Tolkien, J. R. R., 170, 171, 173,
    175
Tom Brown's School Days, 32
The Tough Guide to Fantasyland,
    173–74
Townsend, Sue, 4, 57, 70
Trembath, Don, 85
Tribes, 74, 77–78, 112–13, 195
Tribute to Another Dead Rock Star,
    123, 194
Tristram Shandy, 151
The True Meaning of Cleavage, 73
Truth or Dairy, 35–36, 79
The Tuesday Café, 85–87
The Tulip Touch, 41–42

*The Unlikely Romance of Kate
    Bjorkman*, 144
urban settings, 6, 15–16, 83
"Utensile Strength," 92, 176n13

Vande Velde, Vivian, 163–65
A Very Touchy Subject, 40–41

villains, 7, 71–72, 84–85, 87, 89,
    128–29, 149–53, 198–99; in
    fantasy, 14, 15, 71, 89–92, 162, 165
Vizzini, Ned, 133, 184–85
Voigt, Cynthia, 13
Vote for Larry, 203n7

Watership Down, 168
The Wee Free Men, 167
Weetzie Bat, 124, 139
Weetzie Bat (series), 6
weight problems, 26, 52–53, 97–103,
    106–9, 140, 192–93. See also self-
    image
Werlin, Nancy, 13, 194
Wersba, Barbara, 9, 97, 139
What Would Joey Do?, 42–44
What's So Funny?, xii
Where the Kissing Never Stops,
    114–15, 123–24
The Whistling Toilets, 123
Who Put That Hair in My Toothbrush,
    9, 18
Whytock, Cherry, 102

The Wish, 136
wit, xi, xvi, 71, 96, 100, 105, 106,
    109, 110, 112, 124, 142, 147–76,
    183, 190–91
Witch Baby, 139–40
Wittlinger, Ellen, 137
A Wolf at the Door, 165
Woman in the Wall, 6, 16–17,
    162
wordplay. See puns and wordplay
Wrede, Patricia, 91, 160
Wurst Case Scenario, 34–36, 79
Wynne-Jones, Tim, 54

A Year Down Yonder, 59–61, 134
Year of the Griffin, 32–33, 171–75
Yolen, Jane, 161, 165
You Don't Know Me, 7, 38–39,
    128–29
Young Adult Novel, 76, 156–57
Youth in Revolt: The Journals of Nick
    Twisp, 2, 185–86

Zindel, Paul, xv

About the Author

Walter Hogan is a librarian and an associate professor at Eastern Michigan University. He is a reviewer for *Voice of Youth Advocates* and *Choice* and has published articles on a variety of topics. His previous book, *The Agony and the Eggplant: Daniel Pinkwater's Heroic Struggles in the Name of YA Literature*, was also published by Scarecrow Press.